The Poetry Center *of* Chicago
Language Where it Lives

Published by The Poetry Center, Chicago, Illinois, 60603

Copyright © 2006 by The Poetry Center
All Rights Reserved
Printed in the United States of America, May 2006
ISBN 0-972-0751-6-X

Book Cover Design: Guy Villa. **Cover image:** "Blurry Lights No.3," Guy Villa
Design Consultant: Ohn Ho

Edited by Lisa Buscani, Sarah Schroeder & Michelle Taransky

The Poetry Center was founded in 1973 by a team of influential Chicago poets. The organization's charter established three guiding principles: to promote and develop the public's interest in poetry, stimulate and encourage young poets, and advance the careers of poets by offering them professional opportunities.

The Poetry Center of Chicago has six branches of programming which include: 1) The 33- year-old Reading Series, which brings nationally renowned poets to Chicago audiences; 2) The *Hands on Stanzas* literacy-through-poetry program in public schools; 3) master poetry workshops and community poetry writing workshops; 4) Multi-disciplinary projects, such as The Poetry Center Broadsides Series of limited-edition fine art prints and The Public Art Billboard Project, which places poetry on Chicago billboards and EL station platforms; 5)The Lip reading series, which features emerging poets; 6) Merit Prizes, which honor poetry teachers, performers and writers.

Table of Contents

Foreword

And the words kept coming. Idea after idea after idea.

When we first began to edit the 2005-2006 *Hands on Stanzas* Anthology, we knew we'd see great work. The buzz from our poets in residence was exciting; they'd told us they'd seen terrific poetry coming from their students.

But we just didn't expect the emotion, the detailed pictures of life as kids live it. We didn't expect the humor and the anger and the pain, expressed in the simplest, most eloquent language they had. In short, it was exhilarating.

This year, 6,600 students in 63 residencies at 51 Chicago Public schools began their journey into the world of words. The results were stronger writing, reading and public speaking skills, more classroom engagement, and strengthened self-esteem. It was a journey that was worth the trip.

We'd like to thank all Chicago Public school administrators and teachers involved with the program for their time, attention and support. We'd also like to thank our donors and sponsors for the financial backing that makes *Hands on Stanzas* possible. And of course, we'd like to thank our poets in residence. Every voyage needs a guide; thanks for leading us.

We hope you enjoy this year's anthology.

Lisa Buscani
Executive Director

HANDS ON STANZAS

2005-2006 Anthology of Poetry

Addams Elementary School

Garrett J. Brown, Poet in Residence
Principal: Noemi Esquivel
Program Coordinator: Margaret Slamkowski
Teachers: Ms. Campbell, 5th; Ms. DiFillipo, 5th; Ms. Knight, 4th

Tiger
Juanita C.

It walks real slow along the way.
Hunting, looking for his prey.
He sniffs and smells something good today.

He pushes his way through the trees
Running away from all the bees
There is an animal on his elbows and knees.

There he goes to attack.
The animal is on his back.
The tiger is ready for a snack.

Video Games
Vicente C.

When I play
a game I
get into
it. When I
lose I feel
sad, mad,
depressed, and
angry. I
keep on
trying
trying
trying.
Then
I win.
The remote
is like a TV
remote.
The remote
controls
everything.

Outer Dream
Juan C.

You are sleeping. Then,
you're in a place. It's dark,
has no gravity. There're little
white marks on the black sky.
Nothing but rocks. You see other
circles and one with a hula-hoop
on it. Open your eyes and
then it's light.

Hush Hush Little Puppy
Susanna A.

Hush, hush, little puppy.
What did you say? You swallowed
my guppies? No it's not time to play!
No! No! Don't go that way.
I won't read you a story.
No, you were mean to your friend,
Ed Muffey. Please dog, hush,
hush. Yes, brush, brush. Okay.

Dreaming I'm a Baseball
Robert G.

When I see someone
hit me I hit the grass
and dirt. I bang the floor
and eat. I get hit very
hard and I sometimes eat
the bat. My eyeballs roll
when I hit the ground.
When I crack I'm a dead
man. I romp with joy on
the bookish ground.

Went and Back
Adrian B.

I went acting bad.
I came back acting good.
I went to practice playing bad.
I came back playing good.
Went to lunch hungry.
Came back from lunch full.
Went to the bank really poor.
Came back really rich.
Went to the dentist with yellow teeth.
Came back with white teeth.

A Black Day
Kevin R.

It's raining outside. It's a
thunderstorm too. I can't go outside
and the power is out. I feel
like a turtle trapped in its shell.
I want to go outside. I am very
sad. It is a black day today but it
might not be one tomorrow.

Rain
Melissa B.

Rain is cold. Rain is water. Rain is shining.
Rain is water you can drink.

A Weird Dream
Alejandra S.

You are walking and eating a sandwich.

You didn't know that the sandwich
had an ant in it.

The ant says, "It's my sandwich!"
You and the ant are fighting
over the sandwich.

Until the sandwich transforms into a monster.

You and the ant are running
from the monster, only a block away,
until you and the ant come to the desert
and the monster gets away.

My Identity
Armando G.

I am a drawer, I draw.
I didn't want to let people know.
Until the truth came out, it happened when
I was cleaning out my desk.
They found the truth.

Flowers
Beatriz G.

Oh, flowers so beautiful,
so bright! We are like sisters.
One day you will find a mister.

When I am in a flower
field I feel so suitable.
One more day
in the field I want to
stay and play. The flowers
will say, "Thank you! You're
my best friend 'till the end!"

Music
Fabian M.

When you get
lost in music
it's like being lost
in a forest. It's like
being lost in a maze.
It's like being lost in a
puzzle when you can't
find the piece that goes
with the little
piece.

This is Just to Say
Christina G.

I am sorry
what I did
to you I
hope that

you can
forgive me
soon.

I am sorry
for the things
I do, like put
an ice cube in
your shoe.

Birthday
Oscar P.

Waiting for my birthday is like waiting for a
person to get dressed.

Waiting is so difficult.
I want it now.
I'll get it in November.

Cloud
Dalia O.

The cloud comes by.
When the baby cries.
It looks at the street go by.
It never stops when it disappears.
It never looks at itself in the mirror.
It just goes on and on and on.

There are gray clouds coming by.
I think it comes to say hi.
When a cloud is full of tears it cries.
There are tears of God to say goodbye.

Reading
Kevin E.

Enter another world.
Visit me today.
Or go to be
in another world. We
go, we're here.
Humans can release
a 2-D world
or another place
where you're
meant to be.
An alternate
reality.

Another one
for violence
and another
for peace.

Bad Kitty
Chase F.

My little cat is furry.
We got her from Missouri.
Whenever she runs, you hear a bell.

Sometimes I get tired of it. I want to put her in a cell.

Bird
Lindsey L.

My bird scares me, I don't know why.
He looks at me strange.
It feels like I'm going to die,
even though he is in his cage.
When he looks he doesn't blink.
He gives me fear.
I wonder what he thinks.
For some reason, it makes me miss my dog, Bear.

Shy Girl
Yazmin P.

I am sometimes a shy girl
in this big world.
I am tall as my aunt,
I do not like cats.

I am caring to dogs.
I can see them through the fogs,
the puppies are so cute
I would even let them bite my boots.

Louisa May Alcott Elementary
Paige Warren, Poet in Residence
Principal: David Joseph Domovic
Program Coordinator: Elena Turczeniuk
Teachers: Mr. Benyo, 3rd; Ms. Vincent, 6th; Ms. Wynn-Buckner, 7th/8th

Amir B.

I wish my hamster was
a super hero.

I wish I met Elvis

I wish I had a
super power and I could
run really fast and
they would call me the
blur

I wish the Burger King man was my enemy
All super heroes have a have a villain

I wish I had a pet mouse

Brandon S.

Why do you fishes float to the top of the tank when you die?

Dogs what is it about your tail you have to chase it?

Dogs why is it when people fall down you run and lick us?

Pigs where do you put your babies when they're first born?

Wolves who in the family search for food?

Sharks when do you fall asleep?

Roaches how do you squeeze in tiny places?

Andrei B.

First I started out in a bus with vampires
I got out from the bus I went somewhere
I could see the moon it exploded. Then I
started

Charles G.

A boy with a mask
and his shoes un tied.

Brittany H.

The young African-American boy in
The class was filled with laughter
and joy. When he smiles his
face lights up the room, his
hair as soft as a baby's
bottom, his skin as smooth
as sheets. He's short and
cute, so adorable to many.
He loves the game of basketball
which he excels well. He's
quiet but talks a lot as well.
Such a joy to have as
a friend as well as a class
mate. His personality is great.
Who is this person I speak
on: Derrick the little
boy with a smiley face
on.

Red
Christopher S.

When I see red I see a cat
Walking across the sunset waiting to
Pounce on the sun, quickly trying to
turn everything to night. As you
see the sun set you can feel
the red wind swaying across your
face almost as if it was a part
of you. As the sun goes down
slowly you can almost see the
red stars as if you had put them in
place. Eventually the cat wins the red sun
has lost, but there is always another day
another loss or a victory for the red,
red sun, but only time can tell.

Dominique P.

When my sister is sleep she is sucking
her thumb or slobbering
When my sister is sleep she is very
quiet (except for the moans)
When my sister is sleep she
smells like bad breath

When my sister is sleep she is very
soft

Eileen S.

My country pooed on me
Right near the pigeon tree
Of thee I say poetry. O please
don't go on a pigeon tree.

Keontre M.

When tears fall,
Players drop the ball.
So now that man with all the ladies is alone,
Then he reminisces on what used to go on.
Tears fall as they are sweat from a
broken heart.
The taste of a sweet life
suddenly becomes tart.
He wishes the popularity will go away,
but that unlucky boy told them that he
was blessed with a gift everyday.
Tears come ruthlessly with no warning,
Birds don't sing a love song in the morning.
She was crying when her life crumbled,
Her voice of love became mumbled.
They say tears are good,
Make you think if only I would…
Why did you let my grandma and my uncles die?
Oh no here it goes please God don't cry.
Men cry in the dark, boyz cry in the
light,
Let the tears rain, forget about the
fight.
Women cry from the heart, girls
cry from the mind,
Let the tears come over, it won't
make you blind.
So next time that tear falls don't ask why,
it's your, his, hers tears fall when there
is and isn't a need to cry.

Kyana M.

Blue is cool.
Pink is light.
Purple is dark.
Black is dark too.
Green is kind of dark.
White is color you can't see.

I Love Colors
Manhoor S.

Red is nice.
Blue is cool.
Purple is dark.
Green is trees.
Pink is light.
Violet is flowers.

Be Yourself
Sharleen U.

I shall dream my own dreams.
You shall dream your own.

I shall pick my own flower.
You shall pick your own.

Don't follow me,
Be a leader.

I have my own thoughts,
You have your own.

If you follow me
Others will too.

William T.

Once I saw a king who lived
in the castle of the island of
far, far away. And the king threw
his ring and he liked to sing.
Then he started to sing sing
sing out. I threw my ring ring ring.
That was the last of that king.

Qonain B.

I'm walking through the streets of
Chicago
I hear jackhammers, people rushing
home from work, and something else.
Zzzzzzz.
What is that? I walk towards
the noise and I see a man on
a bench.
He was lying on the bench in
such a deep sleep that if a car
hit him, I wouldn't think he'd
awake.

Snoring away from his mouth, that's
surrounded by a forest of hair.
His hair, stuck up, going in
every direction possible.
His clothes ripped up, as if he
just found them in the street.
Holes in his shoes like black
holes that I wish sucked up the smell.
This just the outside, but don't
judge him, til you know the
inside.

Rey M.

I wish the sun will never die.
I wish the world will be a better
place.
I wish the world will be only
good people.
I wish the world will never die.
I wish no body can every die.

Tatiana T.

There once was a man
who was really confused…
he called home, they hung up.
"Excuse me," said the man the next
day he found out he was dead.
The end.

Tatiana T.

Once there was a dog
and a man the dog followed
the lady soon the lady died
No blood or anything just dog fur.

**I Remember
Group Poem
Mr. Benyo's Class**

I remember when my hand got burnt up.

I remember when I played 7Up thumbs up, heads down.

I remember when I first drove a car, I ran into the back of another car.

I remember when I moved away at the age of 11, when I came back I was going on 13. I told my grandma you can't whoop me no more I'm grown.

I remember when I saw my friend who has the same stuff and name as me.

I remember sharing money with my friends.

I remember when I liked a boy.

I remember my first dollar.

I remember my first try.

I remember being 50.

I remember when I danced.

I remember 50 mice and my dog.

I remember you were my friend.

I Remember
Group Poem
Ms. Wynn-Buckner's Class

I remember going to Florida and losing my older brother.

I remember playing in my room when tons of socks were poured on me.

I remember singing to myself when all hope was lost.

I remember when I saw a cow; it was missing its right eye.

I remember drinking hot sauce thinking it was Kool-Aid.

I remember asking "What's for dinner?" and being told "Don't worry about it, just eat it."

I remember when I used to play Mr. Freeze, Whooping Mama, 7Up and Red Light, Green Light.

I remember when I thought red was just a Kool-Aid flavor.

I remember when my Uncle Larry used to sing the blues.

I remember when my mom used to put the fan in the window.

I remember the first time jumping off a garage.

I remember when I threw a dictionary at a boy for looking down my shirt this summer.

I remember the first Christmas without my grandma.

I remember being at home and waking up during the afternoon during winter vacation.

I remember putting a lot of hairspray in my head so my hair would be nice for a party.

I remember being put in the corner for the first time in the third grade. (Thanks to Keturah.)

I remember when the class gave Mrs. Wynn-Buckner her Christmas gift. She cried.

I remember seeing a rat pass the alley when my sister and I were driving through it. It was so quick and chubby.

I remember the time when I bought 2 Lunchables, 2 juices and 2 sandwiches for my field trip, and I ate them all.

I remember my first baseball swing, someone yelled behind me "Strike three!"

I remember when gaining weight was easy and losing the weight was hard.

I remember the first time I lost my wallet that had $78.00 in it.

I remember the first wedding I went to. My feet were so numb.

I remember the first time I heard hip-hop music that made you bob your head.

I remember when my cousin was shot in the leg.

I Remember
Group Poem
Miss Vincent's Class

I remember when my sister found a drunk old man in the basement where she slept. He came out of the shadow and the dog was licking his hand. She started screaming and my mother, who had been sleeping on
the couch, ran and tripped. She broke her arm that night.

I remember a dream that me and my family were in a video.

I remember when a horse bit me in the head when I was next to a moped.

I remember when I had my first sleep. (It was peaceful – the only child.)

I remember when I tripped my brother and fell in the laundry basket.

I remember when a wolf attacked me and tried to steal my money.

I remember going home in a taxi and some stickers were peeling off the back of the seat.

I remember going to the movies with my cousins. We sat all the way in the front row. My neck hurt for two days.

I remember my older sister dressing me up when I was three. She burned my forehead with the curling iron once. Then she started laughing and told me not to tell my mom. I did.

I remember my sister's baby shower. She was mad; it was a surprise so she came in her pajamas and her hair was all frizzy and messed up.

Joan F. Arai Middle School
Meg Barboza, Poet in Residence
Principal: Barbara Hayes
Program Coordinator: Ms. Abdul-Malik
Teachers: Ms. Gunn, Ms. Mann, Ms. Mallet, 8th

How Can They?
Natasha S.

I stand up for myself
Because no one else will
So that I may be seen
I will do whatever I have to
Even be mean
I'm not a drama queen
But because you won't hear
I'm forced to be queer
But if you listen
I'll be sincere
But I can't
Because you don't see me
Because I won't be
What you want me to be
Forced to wear a mask
Invisible yet it lasts
I manage to rip it off
How can the world want me to change
When they're the ones that stay the same.

What I Stand Up For
Glynnika D.

I stand up for my sister.
I stand up for me.
Like Maya Angelou,
A Phenomenal Woman
Is what I'll be.
I stand up for my rights
I stand up for my life.
Anyone can come close
But they'll never be me.
I'll stand up for you
Will you stand up for me?

Lanadia M.

Wet with dirt: a late basketball day.

My Dream Deferred
Richie S.

I will tell you what happened to my dream deferred….nothing. It just shallowed away like a stray dog that broke its chains and moved from place to place looking for a home in someone's head. If it's fed it will stay, if not it will move, people say, like a dog, but I say a bird…if not treated right, they fly away and are never seen again.

Windy Weather
Donny P.

It is so windy
It sounds like a whistle,
It makes the cold weather,
It blows the curtains,
It blows my paper off my table:
The paper sounds like flapping wings.

The Crimes Of An Apple
Valisha W.

What can an apple really do
But change its disguise from color to color,
And its taste from crunchy to mushy.
An apple also involved in a crime scene
Adam and Eve in the Garden of Eden.

Can an apple really be a crime?
Yes, no, maybe so
I don't know.
You tell me, the people
Of my society

You, young man can an apple be
Commented of a crime…

Poetry
Devin N.

The rubber band: it
Expands and I expand.
You expand, but I bet you
Can't expand like me.

What I Stand Up For
April J.

I saw you running.
I see this everyday
On your way from school.
Why can't you just play?
I take a stand

From this day on
No one will pick on you
Not no more.

I take a stand
For me and you.
We were best friends
But not we're just cool.
Whatever happened to me and you?
I take a stand
Cause this was not true.

What I Stand Up For
Justin L.

I stand up for animal rights
Because animals deserve equal
Treatment just like any living
Thing. Animals should not be
Treated with less respect than anyone.
I feel that animals should
Not be treated different
Because they are creatures.

What I Remember
Sarah P.

I remember being when my
Ancestors was slaves, slaves that
Worked to sun to sun down. Now
It's changed, blacks can read and write
Blacks can stay out all night. We
Can go to school without being
Treated differently.

The Game
Jimall M.

The game we lost, uniforms that were red,
white; people were locking off. Even
though we lost the game, I had no shame
because I played my game the same. I blame
the team because we couldn't do our thing.
We usually rise above but we lost our
Will to win. We could have won. But there are no
could've, would've, should've or
didn't. I love the competition but in addition
to losing.

Ghost
Damian P.

Clear, shiny, see-through
Diamonds;
Which looks like a
Giant earring.

My Dream Deferred
Lakesha M.

I will tell you what happened
To my dream deferred.

Does it fade away like god?

Or like rainy clouds?

Do it fade away like jeans when you wash them?

Or like the love between you and your ex-loved one?

I See
Wilver B.

I see many things
Some are red, some are green
Some are flat, some are
Like a rocketship
And many people in red t-shirts
Move around the classroom
Like walking red birds.

My Dream
Travis M.

In my dream
I run like a
Toon. My dream
Crumble and stumble
And I like to rumble
Like a
          Lion in a jungle
But if you take away
My dream I won't
Be able to be seen.

On The Phone
Demilla P.

I talk all the time when I'm with
Antwone. I love him because
He's so fine. We do many things together
And best of all he's mine.

George Armstrong International Studies Elementary

Manda Aufochs Gillespie, Poet in Residence
Principal: Arline K. Hersh
Teacher: Ms. Karim, 6th

The Word
Kaleb W.

This stupid word
Stuck in my mind, wasting my time
Trouble seeked and trouble seen
Things I do, things I say.
Sorry Sorry Sorry, is all I hear
Acting out in every way
Can I break this trance
Is it possible do I have a chance
Should I go crazy or scream in fear.
I don't want it to happen
I'm afraid it's near, too late it's here
Forced to happen and the word was the end.

Blizzard
Wale B., Erick H., Gabriel Q., and Kaleb W.

Thunder is similar to the blizzard
It is the smell of the world
Tiny little lines falling on beasts
The snow in the winter
7-Eleven slushy in my mouth.

Dark Chocolate
Terrence E.

Dark chocolate is as dark as my skin.
People say I am dark. I don't care because
Black is beautiful. Dark chocolate is so good
When I eat it, it just melts in my mouth.
I love dark chocolate. I could eat 100 pieces of
Dark chocolate. It is so good I love it.

The Good Choice
Oscar H.

There's one God
There's one mom
The most important one is God and mom.

My Shadow
Raven B.

Each time I see myself
I see my dark side of me.
I don't know why, maybe it's
Because of all the madness
That comes to me.

All About Parim
Parim L.

Parim Lutolli is a legend. Parim Lutolli is great
He is a light, he flickers on and off
People and I, we can't live without him
We will. Maybe he is work
Maybe he will be bright as the sun
Maybe he will never die
He might only be good
Possibly he should be turned off forever
He will never be forgotten
Next year, he will give more light
But in life people say: if he dies
It will be dark forever.
This is just to say he is history.

How is the World Different
Wale B.

Is the way they talk
Or the way they walk
Can you understand animals
It is your destiny.

Ocean life is different
Than what you can feel
You breath over water
They breath under water
You choose your destiny

Why aren't I living in an aquatic life
Everything will always be nothing
And nothing will always be everything
You see what you can see
Faith does nothing when you have no destiny

Light does nothing, darkness does nothing
You find your life, the way of your heart
An aquatic life you can live, just believe
And that is how the world is different.

Night
Ricardo E., Beatris M., Eugenie N., Alexali S., and Shabrea W.

Night sounds of wings moving searching for kids
to put to sleep. The world sounds of killing other animals.
The smell is cold wind going against your face
Like being a friend of the dark
Air going through your head, rough fur
It taste like rotten nightmares.

Lightening
Michelle H., Claudia O., and Diana R.

It is silent you don't know when it will come, you see it
You are terrified. It took you by surprise.
It hurt with the force of a shark
It smells like a dead person, dirty, mud
It looks bright, you get to know it
You get terrified by its sharp teeth
You can't touch it will attack you will regret it will kill you
It tastes salty with poison coming down your throat
Burning inside out, a bloody feeling.

Thunderstorm
Shavonta B., Catherine E., Deni H., Angie L., Queen R., and Shannon R.

It is a whole group of people: commotion, yelling, screaming
They smell of fear, a little kid is in his first storm
Waves crash to the ocean shore
Soft and silky, yet hard and dark
It tastes like power, power of a king in control

The Chocolate is a Dark and Evil Presence in my Mouth
Syed H.

1. Evil
The chocolate is cold
So dark and creamy
As if it was the dark side of a heart

The evil comes
To take you away
You should run, but you can't hide

You can't escape
You just can't
Yet the voice says escape… escape… escape…

I want to hide
But I just can't
The evil comes to kill.

2. Darkness
It will
Come
You can't
Escape
Go away
Before it
Happens.

The Chocolate is Like a Rock.
Yanet M.

It taste like heaven when
It's in my mouth but like
The hate of my enemy when it
Goes down my throat.

History
Scorpio B.

Scorpio Browley is an animal who explores like a roaring lion.
He storms through the night, he sneaks up to find his prey.
People and I, we think of him as a dark night devouring everything in his path.
We try to stop him, maybe he is a god punishing us for our ways.
Maybe he is thunder roaring through the night causing fear upon us.
Maybe he is wind throwing our scent where he pleases.
He might stalk us during our every step
Possible he should be defeated for his wicked ways.
He should be jailed never to be seen again.
But in my words I would say: "he has perished for eternity."
This is a new beginning, he will not cause no more trouble,
For all of his wicked day are history.

Within Me There Lay an Invisible Summer
Susely H.

In the depths of winter, I
Finally learned that within me
There lay an invisible summer.
A summer of happiness and
Wonder. A summer I am
Happy to see in this cold
Sad winter. A summer that
I would like to share with
The world. But can not because
The invisible summer is only seen
By the ones that wish for it.

The Beast
Tevin C.

This guy is hungry, he's been wanting to feast and his whole village wants to eat. So he goes into the village and finds this beast, he tells all the villagers and they're wanting to get a taste of this beast. He looks, he sees, he can't find this beast. He says I have to eat eat eat. Where is the beast. He looks in the cave, he looks under a tree. Where is this beast. Nowhere in sight. He sees the beast's footprints he follows through the snow it leads to this cave this dark dark cave. He sees a shadow this deadly beast. He takes out his sword and kills this beast. Now at last his family may feast.

History of Jake's Dreams
Jake S.

Jake is a pirate, Jake is a bird.
He will find treasure, he goes to sea. People and
I, we are pirates in his crew. We play.
Maybe he is weak.
Maybe he is a bird.
He might only be a kid.
Possibly he should be a fish.
Next year, he will save the world.
But in Chicago people say: he cannot.
This is sad, he cannot be a pirate, a bird, a dog,
A kid. That's wrong and this is history.

Love
Donjeta A.

Love
Life
A Wish
Is a lie
Sweet but
Still broken.

Choco hate
Sheel S.

The wrapper is a thunder
Which opened
The chocolate velvet,
Red ocean,
Or a rose,
Crinkling out to the open.

Fairy Tales
Catherine E.

The chocolate is a fairytale
With a miracle bringing a princess through the night.
Clouds spreading the darkness away
And bringing out the great taste of love.

History
**Gamachu A., Wale B., Raven B., Jonathan D., Terrence E., Anthony F., Erick
H., Oscar H., Vanessa L., Javier L., Parim L., Nathaniel M., Jaime P., Gabriel Q.,
Daisy R., Mabinty S., Rachel T., Jennifer T., and Kaleb W.**

50 cent is half of a dollar,
50 cent is the king of the underground.
He's a buck-toothed nerd, he's a chimp.
People and I, we cry for him

History
**Zain A., Joana A., Scorpio B., Celina C., Christina C., Ricardo E., Justin G.,
Syed H., Michelle H., Rina K., Anna M., Beatris M., Yanet M., Brian M., Tyrone
M., Kevin M., Rashidah M., Kathy M., Joseline M., Eugenie N., Claudia O., Diana
R., Alejandra R., Eduardo R., Alexali S., Aaliyah S., Darryl T., Shabrea W., and
Luis Z.**

Chris Brown is an angel.
Chris Brown is a nightmare.
He swims through fire.
People and I, we look at him with disgust.
Possibly he should be turned into a frog
And tortured between glass.
This is Chris Brown he's singing
But his career is history.

History
**Donjeta A., Alex A., Vanessa A., Shavonta B., Maurishia B., Tevin C., Leon C.,
Minela D., Catherine E., Jarigsa F., Juan G., Deni H., Adrianna H., Mohsin H.,
Jasmine H., Jorge J., Susely H., Erick J., Sam K., Alia K, Angie L, Maurice M,
Eduardo M, Diana O, Bryanna P., Queen R., Shannon R., Hesham R., Jacob S.,
Sheel S., Daisy S., Ana T., and Jawuanza W.**

George Bush is a nightmare
George Bush is a monster.
He destroys the world, he kills.
People and I, we give him our death-stare
Whenever we look at him.
Maybe he's an asteroid from Mars.
This is the U.S., he continues the war.
And this is history.

Luis G.

The classroom. I am bored. I spot
A National Geographic Magazine so I grab it and look through the pages.
Something catches my attention.
A disturbing image, a man. He is very skinny.
His eyes are sad. He has a smile. His is horrified.
He has his head covered with a cloth.
The air smells sour. It is very hot and humid.
The man looks like he's working.
He has no shirt and clothes are wrapped
From his waist like a skirt.
I feel very sad and annoyed.
Then I hear someone crying silently.
I realize its me!
I am back in the classroom.

Hiram H. Belding School
Cecilia Pinto, Poet in Residence
Principal: Carol J. Habel
Program Coordinator: Lindsay Thornton
Teachers: Ms. Daniels, 5th; Mr. Elliot, 6th-8th; Ms. Washburn, 5th

Aztec Haiku
Ena M.

Aztec sacrifice
The Aztec rip out the heart
But souls always live on.

Moon
Savannah Q.

Like the clouds crossing over the moon.
The animals cease to talk.
A whistle is the wind.
Rustle the leaves.
Complete and total silence.
Sun comes up and there they are.
The animals wake up and find it to be dawn.
The dawn has come the night has left.
Now they come and go doing their own thing.

The sparkles and the sheet of black.
The night.
The heat the waves
The color orange. The dawn.

Amy G.

Come back along the trail
to our house where
you will see
prickly pears, and
play pokta-pok
with us.
See our temples,
the beauty and
preciousness of
them, climb the stairs
to the top
Where you will see, and
learn the game pokta-pok,
The lovely ladies' skirts,
made out of the
Quetzal bird. The most

honored bird of them all.
We will not kill them
but pluck the feathers
which do not hurt.

Haikus of a Dog
Monica K.

My friend has a dog.
The dog is weak, old too.
It won't do one trick.

The dog is stubborn.
The dog will not sit or speak.
He was just too sick.

Now I have a dog.
He is brown, like a tree trunk.
He loves to play catch.

On My Way to School
Edira S.

This morning on my way to school
I saw two squirrels beside a tree.
I am scared of squirrels so I had a fit
when they ran up to me.
They wanted nuts but I had none.
They scratched my feet
I got scared.
I wanted to scream
when one almost climbed my feet
But they got scared
and climbed up a tree
when a black cat
ran down the street.

Majestic Sea
Heather C.

The waves are very calm.
  The sea has a beautiful blue color.
The water in the sea is deep.
  Majestic sea

The sea lions frolicked by the shore.
  The sea shells were pretty colors.
The bright orange sun's rays glistened
  on the beautiful sea.
Majestic sea

The sailboats glide over the water
  so swiftly and gracefully.
The shiny silver fish swim
  casually in the depths of the sea.
The seagulls land on the
  beach and look for food in the sand.
Majestic sea

BrookLynne G-S.

Beneath my bed covers
and pillow
someone woke me
up. I looked out my
bedroom window.
The sky was
dark gray.
My sister was playing
with the
dog.
He was attempting
to nip her nose. His
black face looking playful
while he whined
for a pat on the head.

Dead Dog
Anthony T.

I thought I saw a
dead person on my front lawn
but it was my dog.

Oussama D.

The happiness of angels is in me.
        In my soul.
The fierceness of burglars is in me.
        In my mind.
The smartness of Isaac Newton is in me.
        In my mind.
The sadness of dead people is in me.
        In my heart.
The mournfulness of victims is in me.
        In my heart.
The rapidness of a cheetah is in me.
        In my legs.
The strength of the elephant is in me.
        In my body.
        This is me!

Me, the Apple Tree
Sonia I.

The rain cares for me so I
will grow to a lovely apple tree
to stretch my arms and branches
out in the sky to get some water
so I don't die and when the rain is gone
the sun comes out so you
can see me, the lovely tree.

James S.

The eyes of the owls yellow in the branches
I see the leaves dancing as they fall
The midnight air is crisp
I was aghast to see the face in the moon,
Where I was I, I don't know but I was happy.

I saw a deer in the depth of the dark night.
The moon was smiling,
It was like a lantern.
I like this day,
I like this night,
I like it.
I see the trees.
The night.
A deer.
A face…who was that?

I'm Alone
Jeff A.

I'm alone in the woods
on the left and right side
of me
trees dead on the ground.

I'm alone in the woods
on the left and right side
of me
with the deadness of trees
that they have lost their lives
to the fire.

I'm alone in the woods
on the left and right
the alone woods
always deserted trails.

Rain Fall
Michael S.

as the drips of rain
drops fell to the ground
I stared with a sloppy
gloomy face

watch as the yellow and
red leaves on the trees
get drenched

Blue into Black
Kevin G.

Black as the ocean
Black as the sky
Black as the lakes
Black as the rivers
Black as the color of the veins in your body
Black as the color of the blood in your body.

Jacob Beidler Elementary

Nannette Banks, Poet in Residence
Principal: Dr. Shirley Ewing
Program Coordinator: Sheila Keeley
Teachers: Ms. Peterson, 6th; Ms. Stevens, 8th; Ms. Breland, 6th

Making the Goal
Ravon W.

Did you hear about the football that ran for the goal?
Avoiding people that wanted to tackle it, it fell on the way to the goal
got picked up and ran some more.

Weather the Storm
Adonis J.

Did you hear about the bird that could fly through any storm?
It has been through rough times and good but continues to soar.

The Door
Marcus D.

I open the door
I see darkness, failure, and people looking sad
I open the door and see that is not me

Listen to Hear
Chastity W.

The sounds of nature is what I hear
birds, laughter of young children who like to hide, the rustling of dried leaves,
the moving of tall dark branches the evergreen trees, I never hear the horrible
beatings and bruises I always listen to music.

Power
Anthony A.

The power of control to stop the violence
The power of love so no one is lonely

Reflection
Mona M.

Did you hear about the mirrors reflection? Just an ordinary picture with no connection
a little girl with nothing on her mind, not knowing that a secret lay behind, no one
stopped to look
because they did not care about her and she didn't care about the reflection in the
mirror.

New Beginning
Angel C.

The door to a new beginning
God telling me the right thing to do
I see what's in store for me
I am working on that

Power
Lamar T.

The power of persuasiveness to change worldly ways
The power of invincibility to extend my days
The power of speed to run in the fields
The power of leadership to lead soldiers in the battlefield

The Mask
Dymond B.

We wear the mask to cover up who we really are shy, outgoing or mean
to cover our beliefs in God and his power, in education and its power, both are the
key

Boat Haiku
Cornelius T.

The boat set at night
Riders rowed it with power and
Still as the moonlight

For My People
Kiwanis V.

For my people who must always stay strong for the storm that is to come, wipe your
eyes
For my people remember that God is always near, never ever should you fear
anything
And just like a bird hold on to your wings…

For My People
Evelyn B.

For my people who struggled to get an education because they ended up pregnant
For my people who hung out with the wrong crowd and ended up on the streets
thinking of what you want to be
For my people with their life trying to make their children live without the violence of
the world
For my people getting shot on the street just like those two little girls
For my people fighting for peace and nonviolence so that the kids after us can live a
better life
Keep believing in God so your light can shine

Haiku of Lies
Vaneice W.

To lie is so wrong
it keeps growing bigger and
can hurt many friends

Trees
Ieshia C.

Trees and breezy winds
I swift through and turn heads – cold
winds blow I'm winter

Football Haiku
Jeremy W.

I saw a football
I wanted to play with it
I love the football

Growing Haiku
Jabria W.

The grass grows alone
It rains; it grows on its own
The grass shines brightly

Love Haiku
Nicholas J.

Love is when I love
Hurt is when I hurt inside
cry is when I cry

Sunny Haiku
Miasa H.

The sun warms the day
The moon sleeps while the sun warms
The sun warms creatures

Feathery Haiku
Bria R.

The feather tickles
The feather fell from the sky
The feathers are white

Morning Haiku
Nikki F.

The morning sunrise
it fills up the morning skies
with morning glory

Disappearing Haiku
Johnneisha F.

A red octopus
We're supposed to see had wings
And it disappeared

Mean Haiku
Eric P.

A lady was mean
to her children as they danced
she was really mean

No Mask
Cheyenne W.

I don't wear the mask; I am not ashamed of anything
I let out all my feelings, I hold nothing back, I do not wear the mask

Animal Haiku
Dangelo T.

They are orange and black
They live in the big forest
They are big felines

Rainy Haiku
Maggen J.

I cry out rain drops
Because I want to cry loud
I am sad, rain falls

The Power
Shavonna B.

The power of kids to learn
The power of people to stand together
The power of a kiss from mom and dad to make you feel great

Barking Haiku
Theo D.

Puppies are little
Their bark is annoying
But I like big dogs

For My Friends
Kiarra S.

For my friends who chose to make good decisions
For my friends who are always there to see me through
For my friends nothing will come between our…we will never be alone

Luther Burbank School

Daniel Godston, Poet in Residence
Principal: Dr. Hiram Broyls
Program Coordinator: Dewain Thames
Teachers: Ms. Arce, 6th; Ms Rivera, 5th; Mr. Stasiak, 6th

The Leader of the Tarantulas
David H.

A tarantula I am. I climb into stuff.
I have a strong web. I make trap holes.
I have a painful bite. I protect my kind,
so stay away from me.

Fall
Elisa C.

Fall is something tasty, pumpkin pie or hot chocolate.
Fall is feeling wind and rain. Fall is sounds like water
and leaves. Fall is having fun in the leaves.
Fall is smelling leaves and grass. Fall is last year's
memories, like going to a pumpkin patch on a farm.

Leaves Fall
Mathy D.

Leaves fall and a ball does too.
I love to drink chocolate milk
and eat apple pie in the fall.
When I go out I see leaves falling
from the trees and people having fun.
The season fall is cold, and you can
feel the wind. Old, old mare.
I used to play with my sister
in the fall leaves.

Fall
Sharitzi D.

Leaves are falling.
Kids are jumping.
Grandpa is eating pie,
While we are out in the breeze.
As soon as fall's gone, we
Have great memories of the smell
of turkeys, pies, and grass.

Fall
Yesenia P.

The breezes taste of apple peels.
The air is full of smells,
to feel ripe fruit, old footballs,
burning brush, new books, erasers, chalk.
And drinking hot chocolate.

When Water Falls
Pedro S.

The water falls just like leaves.
The spring is green just like leaves
and grass. I feel the wind that reminds me
of the water when it falls.
When water falls it smells like the river.

The Ringling Brothers Circus
Eric A.

            Rhinos are
            In the
            Net—they will
            Get us, we are
            Lunch—run for your
      l**I**fe—**I** do
            Not want to be lunch.
    They're **G**etting closer

      I've **B**een to lunch already so
         Run for it.
         Oh no, they are getting near.
         The net, where's
        t**H**e net?
      w**E** need it so we should
  capture the **R**hinos. I got
    the rhino**S**, so we're safe. Now let's go

    see the **C**lowns.
        I laugh at them.
      They'**R**e very funny.
        Clowns have big red noses.
    They j**U**mp very far with
  those big **S**hoes.

How Can I Get Out of a Blank Piece of Paper?
Constance B.

I was playing the game "Blank Paper"
and I got stuck in the middle of the game.
Then there were people popping up
out of the paper and I was very scared.
But then I went around all the pop ups
and then I got out of the game. I won.

El Museo Field
Afmari M.

Cuando yo Estaba en
      La otra escuela

Y fui a un Museo
      qUe hay en Chicago
y bi muchaS cosas en el
      musEo unas cosas
      comO flechas

      al Fonbras, Cuadros y muchas
cosas dIferentes
      Ellos nos llevaron
desde eL primer piso
      Del museo asta el ultimo

Escuela Burbank
Edgardo O.

Entre a la
eScuela ayer
Casi me caigo
cUando mire
El trabajo de
eL grado que estaban
hAciendo los ninos

mire la Basura
      qUe estaba en el piso y la
      Recoji y puse la
      Basura.
      Adentro de la aula
      No habia nadie ahi solo
      Kevin

The Auto Show
Enrique R.

          At the
        a**U**to show
         i**T** was so
        co**O**l

      becau**S**e there was a
          Honda, and it had
         c**O**ol rims and when we
  were done **W**e went home.

The Queen of Komodo Dragons
Jacqueline F.

Every day I stalk my prey.
I fill my drool with deadly venom.
I corner my prey. I go for the neck.
But I fall and miss. He tries to escape,
but I bite his leg, injecting my venomous drool.
In just a few seconds his leg is paralyzed.
It rises to move. Ripping off pieces of flesh,
the air fills up with the scent of blood.
Another komodo is nearby. He smells the blood.
He follows the smell. When he finds
The carcass I hiss at him. He is in my territory.
I show off my teeth and it works for a little.
The younger komodo comes back and we fight
for territory. I extend my three-inch claws.
I scare him away, and that's why
they call me the Queen of the Komodo Dragons.

The King of Elephants
Gabriel G.

Each day I wake up, I'm always glad
to see elephants following my rules.
These rules aren't like Fidel Castro's
or Saddam Hussein's rules that the fleas
on my back tell me. These rules are fun.
The only rule you have to listen to
is to watch out for tigers, cheetahs,
leopards, and lions. But beyond that,
everything goes fine.

Chess Poem
Charlotte M.

In the beginning of the game
it'll never be the same.
Then I got stuck in the game,

the Queen tried to kill me.
so I got the Queen and every single army
until I got the King.
I won the game, I was so relieved,
until something happened.
I was finally out of the game.
I kind of miss being on the chessboard.

Stuck in Narnia
Gianfranco O.

I was playing Narnia until I got stuck in the game
but it was different, Narnia was on fire.
Then a Huge Explosion! Christian came fighting
the White Witch and Nicholas was fighting
on top of water. I saw Tywane down.
I grabbed his sword and fought. Then 2,000,000 Orcs
and Cyclops came. So then archers came and scored 5.
I found out how to get out. I had to kill the White Witch.

The Queen of the Clownfish
Liliana O.

I am the Queen of the Clownfish.
I tell the other fish what to do, and when.
I am the color white and orange. I live in clear water
where I can always see everything and everyone.
I wonder how it would be not being Queen.

All I like doing is swimming and swimming.
If a shark comes nearby we trick him,
and he will never come back. So that is me,
The Queen of the Clownfish. Beware of me!

Halloween
David S.

Two years ago I went to trick or treat candy
from house to house. I saw a mouse in the house,
And a cat smacked the mouse on the couch.
The cat ate the mouse and sat on the couch.

In the next house I saw a dog playing with a fog maker.
The fog maker was small and the dog ate the fog maker.
Fog was coming out of the dog's mouth. The dog
was not happy about this. He sat on the porch.

Emperor of Jaguars
Jesus S.

I am the Emperor of Jaguars.
We live separately. We hunt for our food.
We give our leftover food to the jaguars at home.
We blend into the night with our short tawny
golden fur with black spots. We hunt
in the southwestern United States, Mexico,
and Central and South America.
Being the Emperor of Jaguars is a hard job.

Head Coach of Hyena
Erick S.

I am the head coach of hyenas
And I have a difficult life
Because hyenas usually just teach
Each other how to kill other animals.
We are wolflike animals. We are
Native to Africa and Asia. We have strong
jaws and our forelegs are longer
than our hind legs. Other animals
know if we are near by our laughs.
Beware of us.

Late at Night
Ruben H.

I got up late at night,
and I got scared with a real fright.
I did not know what it was
but deep in the corner I heard a small buzz.
I saw something lurking in the shadows.
Could it be a cat or could it be a dog,
or worst could it be a ghost?
I tried to wake up my big brother
but he didn't wake up so I
went to sleep with my mother.

John C. Burroughs School

Tracy Zeman, Poet in Residence
Principal: D. Richard Morris
Teachers: Mr. Gonzalez, 6th; Ms. Springer, 7th; Ms. Vale, 8th

Fall
Joseph E.

Fall is like jumping in leafs.
Fall is like raking leafs. Fall is
like getting punched in the
face. Fall is like seeing a blind
bee who can't speak. Fall is like
falling off a tree. Fall is like
an old man and an old lady
chasing me with a broom. Fall
is like seeing some fleas fighting
for freedom. Fall is like deers
running and hitting a tree. Fall
is like watching football and
someone gets hit in the stomach
with a major league
baseball. This is what is like.

Juan M.

I would describe myself as winter.
I would be cold and windy.
There will be much snow and frostbites.
I would be cold as a block of ice.
I would be as white as ice cream.

Autumn
Leticia D.

Autumn is like the dark.
The days of summer are happy and full of sunshine
and autumn comes and the days are shorter.
It gets colder and darker.
I am like Autumn because sometimes I am happy and
sometimes I am angry.
Like the colors that describe the seasons.
Autumn has the colors that describe me.
Some are bright and some are dreary.

Betty M.

I'm like winter and summer.
I know this sounds weird because winter
and summer are totally different. I'm like
winter because I'm sad part of the time,
and like summer because when something nice or cool passes
I feel really excited and happy like summer
and I could be a good person.

Alfonzo W.

Winter is like ice filling the air.
I am like winter because when people see me,
they just freeze up, with a pale face of astonishment.

5 Ways to Look at a Bamboo Plant
Araceli H.

Out of a million
Bamboo is the prettiest

Look at them like tall
trees on the ground

Green like grapes

Lucky like a horse
shoe when it's given
to you.

Beautiful like
a spring day.

Fours Ways to Look at a Flower
Melissa P.

Some flowers are feelings
Some flowers are tears
Some flowers are nasty
Displays of our fears

Some flowers could kill you
Some others give birth
The last ones will follow
By you in a turf

Some flowers, they favor
you with perfect smiles
Some flowers, they turn
All the eyes to your style

Some flowers are gorgeous
Expressions of love
They are gift of a Nature
But do we Deserve?

3 Ways to Look at an Onion
Pablo A.

An onion looks
like a baseball,
however is not,
and if you hit an
onion with a bat, and
then you opened,

the onion is going
to get angry and
make you cry.

If you see an onion
from two yards away
you are going to think
that is a green apple
and if you don't see the
difference you might bite it.

If you open an onion
you can see that it looks
like the solar system because
it has oval, and circle lines that
look like orbits.

Cape Cod Sunset
Benjamin Z.

The sun shining on the house
moving its shadow every time.
It's almost sunset.
The white house's shadow
its white paint peeling off.
The people in there waiting…
It's night now.

3 Ways of Looking at a "Window"
Johnny B.

1
The window reflects
when the sun shines.

2
The window
scatters with pain when it breaks.

3
But when you replace a window
it's like a new beginning.

The Peace Window
Margarita R.

Everybody at peace.
Happy faces peacefully,
watching everything that
you do. No chaos in
this artwork.
Blue the color of
peace. People very quietly staring.
Everybody is relaxed no
confusion in the act.
And if you see very close
you'll see a donkey's nose.

Cape Cod Sunset
Benjamin Z.

The sun shining on the house
moving its shadow every time.
It's almost sunset.
The white house's shadow
its white paint peeling off.
The people in there waiting…
It's night now.

Dear Future Rocio,
Rocio O.

What will change about me
When I grow old
Will I do what I am told
How will I change
Will I be smarter or
slower
What will I be
Will I still be me
When it's the future
you can never expect
what to see.

Yours truly, past Rocio

Church Bells
Cristal M.

Church bells are ringing
people are singing
Mary Ann is wearing a dress
gave to her from Aunt Bess
with a pretty white gown
walking with a frown
wanting to run away
wanting to avoid today
walking down the aisle
falling for a while
she wouldn't wake up
her heart wouldn't pump
her body was cold
church bells are ringing
people are dressed in black and white
and nobody knows why she died
that lovely night
rising to the sky
never seen again
because she's dead.

Life
Vincent L.

Life begins with the birth of a child
What is really life
Life is the beginning of a beautiful thing
As a baby no one knows what life will hold
Will the baby be an Astronaut
Will the baby be a doctor
Will the baby be a lawyer
Will the baby be a teacher
or will the baby just be a regular person
The baby will grow old
The baby will have good things happening and
bad things happening, some day the baby
will grow very old and one day will
have to die just like everyone else.

Sonnet
Laura R.

Shall I compare you to the sun?
You shine like the sun with
happiness you get us contagious
with your smile, your eyes
shine; your smile sparkles;
you are friendly and cool.
I see you everywhere I
go and it feels shined with
your rays and I feel
happy. You don't hide I
always see shining
and being very brilliant.
You shine and
illuminate the world.

Love Music
Amparito M.

What is love music?
Is it painful and harsh
Or is it caring and kind
Is it the beat of your heart
Is it like a flower blooming
Or is it a dead flower
Is love music the way you dance
Dancing and dancing like your heart tells you
I think love music as the sun
The sun rises and rises like the beat of your heart
I think love music as chocolate
Love music is sweet and dark
But people do not care what I say
That is the way I say it today.

Flowers and Trees
Alma C.

Shall I compare a flower to a tree?
They both make oxygen for you and me
one grows small
and the other one tall
they are both green
and they like to be seen
one has a stem
but not both of them
they both have a root
and one produces fruit
they both live
and they are a nice thing to give
we will admire them
as long as they live.

Demetrio S.

Calm land
green plains
old plants
wind blowing
leaves coming

calm water
soft grass
deer hunting
lives living
waiting to be
dead.

Ocean
Willie R.

Calm waters splashing around,
hearing the waves hit each other,
when it calms down
everything goes silent,
the water stops
clouds darken.
Lighting strikes,
water begins to go everywhere,
I begin to hear thunder.
Everything begins to look horrible,
but then it ends,
because it was all a dream.

Rosario Castellanos School

Joris Soeding, Poet in Residence
Principal: Myriam M. Romero
Program Coordinator: D. Guerrero
Teachers: Mr. Lukas, 8th; Ms. Mendez, 4th; Ms. Voynovich, 7th

Juan M.

My life I've been through a lot I've been jumped on my way home, got in trouble in school and at home. My dad loses his job he sends the pain below and wastes his pay in the bar. My mom came to my school at the end she was very disappointed. On the other hand my brother has gone in and out of juvenile now he's changed. He's in night school now. My family's life changed my dad found a job he's sober my brother turned his life around I'm trying to do better in school everything has changed I wouldn't switch places with anyone else.

Tereza V.

My only daughter suffers
a silent disease
in which others can catch from it
she's dying more and more
each day with no money for medicine
while she's at home
resting with her love not beside her
in Africa
I work the cold nights
trying to get money for her
in the United States.

If only I could trade places with her
I want to suffer her pain
I want to watch her from above
my only daughter
my only family
suffers a silent disease.

I am a poet
Jonathan G.

I am a poet
I write about what I feel and see.
I like to make words rhyme together.
Most of them are about me.
People like to hear them
and some like to write one.
That is why
I am a poet.

Ode to Tweety
Sonia A.

Tweety is so fine
He loves me the most
All the O'z are always hating cuz
I'm always with him
n talking to him on the phone
all the other O'z think they're the best
but they're not the best if Tweety
don't like them!

Love that Mother
Diana T.

Love that mother
like to be called
in the morning
and say I
love you mother
when I see
you in the
night and I
still say
love you
mother
and like
to smell
your
food
in the
morning.

Natividad V.

As I was one time in Mexico
I remember about my flag I left
at my old house. The flag was the best
flag I ever had, I want to have the
flag with me. I miss my house I had
in Mexico.

I loved that house it had nice
things I liked. The house was a very
special house I had in Mexico. The house
I miss and the one I left will be my
house forever.

I left my favorite friends in
Mexico they were my best friends I have
ever had in Mexico. My friends sometimes they
slept over at my house we were having
fun. My friends always played with me. I
miss them a lot.

Karen U.

People always say to me
questions like "what I want
to be when I grow up?"
And I say "why,
I think I'd like to be
the house or a mouse
or a sauce. Or maybe
the biggest car. Or
something boring, ugly
and nice, or maybe I
will like to keep
like that."

Berenice S.

People always say to me
questions like is she mean or he?
or where is the sky?
or why is it up high?
or why are you nice?
or are you a mice?
or why do you have dishes?
or will this poem finish?

Marco M.

Under a maple tree
the dog lies down,
lolls his limp
tongue, yawns,
rests his long chin
carefully between
front paws;
looks up, learns;
chops, with heavy
jaws, at a slow fly,
blinks, rolls
on his side,
sighs, closes
his eyes: sleeps
all afternoon
in his loose skin.

We real…
Joel R.

We real G's
who wear nothing but white tees.
We real boys
and there's nothing we can't control.
We real cool
except when you catch us in a bad mood.
We real smart
and we know everything by heart.
We chill at the crib.
We real straight
and when we go to the parties,
we make sure we get cake.

I Wish
Esmeralda C.

      I wish that I could stop time. I wish I could know why in every beginning
of May 3rd of my life, tell god on my hands and knees to never let me forget all my
special memories! See I'm only promised today. And if you smile time to go. I don't
want my love of my life to ever fade away. So one last time let me open my eyes and
see what my life used to be like! Ohh god! let me go back in the past and change my
life cause I done dumb, stupid things with my life so let me go back and try making
life better with progress and success.

Magali D.

You're my little angel.
Just having you close fills me
with love & hope.
Nothing is impossible with
you by my side.
I want to make you happy
because your smile
brings joy to my heart.

Thalia S.

Tacos is good
food. Tacos go to my stomach
Tacos. Go to the store and
buy tacos. To eat at my
house. They are good. For me.
And they are good to eat.
And we eat me and my
sister. Love to eat Tacos.
And we love to eat a lot.

Maura P.

When you're happy when
you're sad when you're
pretty when you're mad
when you're popular
when you're blue the
reason I love you
is because you're you!

Just Be You
Sandy P.

You are not ugly, you're beautiful
the only thing that's wrong with you
is that you used too much makeup and
that doesn't look like you. Something
that I don't like about you is that
you like to put on all the makeup you have.
You're not ugly just be you.

Kay P.

Mami, Papi, Mayra, Ugo and I and 5
of our family so long ago, one summer
long ago I saw a boy running by
an old tree. And I look and then
all alone I took pictures and it was a
very good memory to me.

There were beautiful colors and I
touch back around pictures of the
tree. I touch the tree and it smells
so beautiful air. And now they are in Arizona.

They are great friends and they
seem so nice and one day it was
frozen all along and I had seen Mercury
on the top of the moon.

Chef
Elisa C.

First of all, I would be great
In that job because I know how to cook
very delicious. And I would be the most
famous chef if I try hard. Secondly, I
would make a lot of money because a lot of
people would order my delicious food.
And finally, I would like to take that
job because I like to do a lot of
exercise while I'm cooking. I would be
the famous best chef if I practice
and try hard.

Beautician
Rogelio R.

A beautician can make a lot of money
by selling famous people's hair
in different places and make millions
and millions of dollars. You can be a great
beautician because you could be
a good hair cutter.

Edgar D.

Everyday I go to play soccer
Demonstrating how good I am
Giving my best shot at being goalie
And getting trophies for being goalie of the year
Reminding me how good I was when I was little

Eugenio R.

Exciting at the beginning
Unfortunate in life
Genius in inventions
Enroll in drawing
Now my dream is to build a house
Imagination in stories of magic
Out of life, but will happen in my life?

Grandmother
Lorena R.

My grandmother was 63 years old she always cared about me.
One day she came and said to me "I want to be a singer"
I told her O.K. she started to sing. Then she started saying a poem.
She starts saying "love is like my heart I open my heart to everyone."
Love don't cost nothing. My heart is to love you. And to care about you.
I start crying my drops were ugly but I said my heart is love my mom and my dad
I remember that day what my grandmother said love don't cost a thing.

Julissa C.

Flying in the air where clouds show
I have a diamond ring that glows
fireflies are flying all around me
I feel I'm in the ocean that I can't believe.
Sometimes I fall asleep I can't even see
I have flowers and a gown and that is my dream.

Fireflies in the Sky
Erika A.

Sometimes it seems like all the stars
have fallen from the skies when
I see they are like bees
flying in the sky and have
light and I know they are fireflies
in all the sky flickering fireflies I see
you in the sky.

Beveto B.

Dear Monkey
I love your brown
hair. One year I
have not seen
you and you sure
have more hair.

Monkey how
old are you?

Love Beveto

P.S. I hope you
come back.

Renato S.

They boycotted the buses
and they changed people's lives
they fought against racism
and they changed people's lives

Everybody mourns for Coretta Scott King
Oprah and Bush show their respect
she can finally see her husband
but she can't see everybody cry
Coretta and Martin side by side
both changed the world and our lives.

Death Is a Relief
Saira G.

death is a relief
no sadness
no awkwardness
          just an out of breath relief
          in which
          no laughs
          no smiles
          only
          crying
          screaming
          shouting
          stop
     no more crying
     death is a relief.

Looking Upon
Martiese C.

Bright light comes, speeding lights
fainting voice yelling those words
It's not that time to come.

The White Owl
Benny M.

So much depends
upon a white owl
glazed with the
night in the woods
with the branches.

Cesar E. Chavez Multicultural Academic Center

David Rosenstock, Poet in Residence
Principal: Sandy Trabak
Program Coordinator: Stacy Ambler
Teacher: Ms. Rantisi, 7th

My Own Life
Ana A.

here what happened? it was in Mexico when I have six years old, I live with my family, my mom, my father, and two brothers. we live in a house of wood everything was great but when my father started to leave the house, and we stayed in home alone, that thing happened in the past that we share things, work hard to help each other, but he started to drink, take drugs, and all love that we have go down, my father go and we ask what happened and he said, don't talk to me or I'll kill you, and then we see what happened with him, he leave, and leave, and one day my life and my heart broke down. we are waiting for dad but we receive a call that my father killed a person and he go to jail. all go to the police station and first I see my father, he was crying, and I said why, and he tell me that he don't want that I know that, so, he asked if I stopped loving him, so I said not no more what happened will he be my father of all day and my life. now my heart is not complicated because my heart complicated are my mom and father but now I have only my mother and father not, and not one would take the place of my father of my heart. Nightmare what happened always I love and remember my father.

My *Papá*
Manuel M.

To me *tobaco* is evil
It kills lots of people
Even my own

It killed my *Papá*
I didn't think that would happen
I'm lonely now

He left me *El Malibu*
You know what else
Lots of payments

La Revolucion changed my life
I live in an apartment
On my own
Waiting for someone to jump
Into my life

I work as a matador
For little pay

And also work at *El Mercado*
To afford *El Malibu*
I just wish for my *Papá* back

Bottle
Evelyn Q.

I am a bottle
I'm used to being kicked around on the street
Nobody notices but I'm still full
Of soda until one day a boy
Kicked me too much and I
Burst all over him

A Rope
Vicente M.

I am a rope
attached to an oak.
The oak is old.
It's been there longer
than the beach.
The beach is not dust
like the sun.

My Mom
Gaby M.

My mom is getting as short as me
or shorter.

My mom is sleepy
because she works at a laundry till
midnight.

She cleans the washing machines
where the people put the soap.

She cleans it with water and
vinegar.

She sweeps the floor.

She mops the floor.

She counts all the money
she made in her list.

Till midnight she waits
and then she leaves.

My Dad
Marie B.

He puts down carpet in
different houses
like small ones, fat ones,
ugly ones, and fancy ones.
He works as hard as it is to
get through snow in the winter
when the snow is piled up to your knees.
He comes home looking
like a homeless man
with holes in his pants,
glue and cuts on his hands.
Then he cleans himself up
and just lays down on the couch,
the TV control in his hand,
one shoe on and the other
half off. He eats and sleeps.
Then the glue on his hands,
the holes in his pants,
and the cuts on his hands
all come back again.

My Dad
Ruben C.

thousand   My dad works at a_____. He
games   works with his boss and my_____.
two   He gets paid every_____weeks. He
pawn shop gets paid almost_____dollars. He
guitars   works near_____. A few blocks
stereos   away from the_____. He
jewelry   sells video_____and
downtown   _____and_____.
Sears Tower

Fisherman
Josefine A.

Being a fisherman is no pickle...sometimes we don't get fish at all...it smells
horrible...sometimes I can't get the smell out of my head...others I get nightmares...
but...a job's a job...I feel awful seeing all those innocent animals die...their eyes are
open...and they look at you...like they will...come back....

Machine Girl
Tamara M.

My job is difficult...but fun. I love cars. I loved 'em ever since I was a girl. The sound
of drills and hammers knockin' stays in my head when I get home...you know what I'm
saying. I like being rough. Seeing feminine girls around isn't my thing. Cars are. My
job is to build cars after they design 'em. I'm different. What else can I say?

Dark Matter
Bryant H.

Dark matter fills my life
like the deep, deep outerspace.
I don't know who I can trust anymore.
Besides family I don't have any friends
only acquaintances. They say ordinary people
ignore the weird and unusual,
however, I'm weird and unusual.

Racism
Shatrice M.

I hate racism! And I think
I know who is racist. His name is the president!
I know that he don't like black people.
Every time I see his squirmy face
I think of the atoms
where you put two magnets together
and they fight against each other.
Why Mr. Sir why?
If you want your responsibility,
you can't hate!

Money
Eduardo M.

I hate money, which makes them rich,
thinking they're high class. They're as
sensible as a glass. They spend their dollars
so much but when the dollars are down who is
high class now. They think money is everything,
stealing it, living to get it, even selling drugs,
but who is the one at night sleeping.
Us not having to fear of getting shot or
killed or sentenced to jail.

Ouija #3
Blanca C.

600 zombies all over the cemetery
Yes, they're hungry and restless
30 have no arms or legs
80 are looking for their eyeballs
No, they can't find
children to eat

Dear Prisoner
Roberto R.

Of culture.   The fear   of not being
loved. People   fearing your   own
culture.   Being   mixed cultures
isn't always fun.   Being Mexican-Indian
people calling   you   Pocahantas.

Ghost
Claudia R.

I am a creepy, pretty white ghost
I spin and spin to play
but no one plays because of my
pointy tail. I feel so sad
my eyes grow watery.

Oscar
Jennifer R.

Shot on your own Birthday
Died too young
For being in a gang
You were like an older brother
You would help
With my problems,
My schoolwork.
You could've done a lot more
With your life
But you took the easy way out

Chicago, Chicanos, and Chicanas
Erika L.

Ridin en el barrio
Going to the suburbs
Smellin those dirty streets
Seeing the Latinos
At those malls
Different gangs
Ridin around los barrios
People dying
People be having beef
With other people
Fightin in the streets
Police arresting them
Taking them to Juvenile
Familes crying for
Their gang members
Their sons and daughters

Instructions on How to Kill a Rat
Ricardo S.

First you put a hot tortilla with grease under a car in your yard. You can hear the rat smelling the hot tortilla. Then the rat comes close to the tortilla. You stay in your hiding spot. Then when the rat starts biting the tortilla you shoot the rat with a slingshot. But the hardest part is to hit the rat on the nose.

This is Your Life
Melissa R.

Yesterday is a wrinkle on your forehead.
Yesterday is a promise
You have broken.
Don't close your eyes to this life.
And today is all you got now.
And today is all you'll ever have.
Don't close your eyes to this life.
Yesterday is a kid on the corner,
Yesterday is dead and over.

Some Children
Beatriz R.

Many children have a Papa and a Mom. Some children
don't have parents.
Some children lost their parents
because they smoked tobacco
and got cancer.

Many children go to the market with their
aunts and uncles because they lost
their parents.

Some children used to go for rides in their Parents'
Malibu, and some didn't.

Many parents died doing many things
like the revolution of their land or
in a car accident.

Some children wish they had parents, but some
feel bad for other children. Like I do.

Chicago
Serita L.

I live in a place called Chicago
where everything goes wrong.
I just want to go to my regular home.
Shots every night.
I just want to catch that next flight to Elgin.

I'm failin'.
I miss my father though.
He's gone
so I'm going to end this poem without
my father cuz I live in a place
called Chicago.

Chicago
Gaby P.

I'm dyin' just tryin'
to think of a rhyme
my mind goes blank and
I go blind.
It's so cold in Chicago
I don't know how I live
and then there's poor people
who say please just give.
It's a beautiful place, but
not everyone is loved
by color or race.

People
Blanca T.

The people are good
With the people can do activity
And if there are not people we can live
The people can show the art

With the people can do activity
The children can play to do the people happy
The people can show the art
If there are not people there are not houses

The children can play to do the people hurry
There are neat love the people
If there are not people there are not houses

A Four-Finger Hand
Fernando L.

I am a four-finger hand.
I am always alone with no way
to attach to an arm. Lying in a
dusty bed, I have goose bumps still
waiting for my other finger to
grow. But I guess it won't,
since I've been waiting almost a year.

Henry Clay
Elementary School
Matthias Regan, Poet in Residence
Principal: Joseph Potocki
Program Coordinators: Vivian Gryzb, Lesley Weems-Hannah
Teachers: Ms. Barrett, 7th; Mr. Berdusis, 8th;
Mr. Laurincik, 8th; Ms. Preston, 7th

Unreachable
Kristal G.

In the far
corner of
the roof

where no one
can reach
unless they

jump out the
window lies
an empty

brown crate
turned upside
down.

Motion of Plug
Corey K.

two eyes one mouth
    power to give
    motion
school
    don't notice
it is in use but not
all
    a plug of life
can give you
    the
        power of the motion
        like the emotion
    losing a loved one
an outlet

Poem
Kacie M.

making yourself into
the hands of
a clock

wearing giant glasses
when you want
to read

talking to dolls
pretending their
real

chasing the dust
bunnies under the
couch

using spaces under
pillows and
cushions

to store all
the things you
use everyday

Latina
Denise P.

Soy Latino,
Hablo dos idiomás
Inglés y español. Soy
Latina y orgullosa de corazón!

Mi mamá de un rancho,
Mi papá de un pueblo,
Mi hermana y yo de la ciudad,
Mi mamá nos dice: ustedes
Son de Estados Unidos, tienen
Que ádáptance a la sociedad.

Soy Latina,
Hablo dos idiomás, y
Ahún que hable más
Español que inglés, voy
A bilingüe para aprender.

Adaptarce A estados Unidos
Es un poco complicado, pero
Mi orgullo de ser Lation
Me da la energia para
Seguir luchhando.

Soy Latina!!!

Photograph
Thomas S.

I miss that town
I miss their faces

You can't erase
You can't replace it

I miss it now
I can't believe it

So hard to stay
Too hard to leave it

Faces
Cynthia A.

The shiny front windows
of the

hospital where I
see people happy

and sad, in which
shine the broken

pieces of their sad
faces.

She
Lizzy A.

positioned at an angle
the sunlight attempts to gleam off
dirty, doesn't work
blurry
face saddens
wanting, needing attention

glass is wiped
frame straightened
girl smiles
back to good

Two Schools
Jesse M.

Walking on steps
white and black class uniforms
waiting before wooden doors
real wooden floors

Now
blue and gold uniforms
running up the black stairs
tile floors

My Mind Like A School
Anthony D.

my mind thinks like a
school it does math it
thinks of how to do
stuff like in school

when you have to talk
to teachers its like
talking to your mom
and you friends are
like talking to your
brothers

all the colorful things
in school just like
my rooms and the rest of
my house

when you get in trouble
at school it is just like
getting in trouble at home

Recess
David C.

Time off during school
children running and playing.
Many children like this
but apparently not adults.

Joy for some
headaches for others.
Children swinging back and forth
some hanging upside down.

The Discipline Office
Jamie W.

four walls around
three chairs, three chairs empty
no one's around

no one is sitting there
I'm all alone in there

Room 302a
Holly D.

Never notice
this room

small and empty
nobody usually in it

always there
nobody notices

Book bag
Daniel C.

I see my book bag every day I use it
except on weekends
Always with me but
I never think about it

My book bag
so supportive
every day the same

My supplies in it:
books, paper, pens
I see many more at school

Book bag on the highway
run over by a car
turns over on the road
ripped

Like a bum--raggedy
on the side of the road

C/o '06
Jacenta M.

On the date of
06/12/06
they will need preparation . . .
. . . time

we will be acknowledged
for the eleven years
past.--do you believe?

There are diplomas to be passed
a stage to be swept
the curtain call practice
microphone check
student count
and in the end . . .
       . . . tears of happiness
         smell of pine-sol

A Movie Scene
Jameea B.

Freezing, probably gonna die soon
looking at each other, cold.
People groan and moan helplessly—
Help, save us they cry.
The great ship has sunk.

I love you
Rose says scared.
Don't say that
Jack says firmly.

You're gonna die old, not here
Jack says looking at her, please.
An hour later a boat arrives.
Rose kisses Jack's hand saying bye.
I will never, ever let go.

Poem
Janet F.

Everything comes to life.
Desks stand as if water
had suddenly turned
into a full land
of hard, cold ice.

Images of life appear
but hidden under the desk
a telephone hangs mysteriously

Mi Recamara
Leticia R.

En mi recamara
hoy muchas cosas estranas y,
encuentras coasa incomunes.

Hay muchos libros y fotos
las fotos son de animales,
munias, y Egypto.

Entras a un lugar de antiquedades,
encuentras libros de historia y
cosas muy valiosas y misteriosas.

La Lúz
Lucia S.

En la lúz los niños
no temen, los flores se
ven, el cìelo es azúl
y los pajarillos cantan.

Pero en la oscuridad . . .
todo es negro
nada es azúl y
los niños temen.

Entonses la lúz es vida
y la oscuridad el terror.

Jose De Diego Community Academy

K. Bradford, Poet in Residence

Principal: Alice Vera

Program Coordinator: Michale Nuccio

Teachers: Ms. Baez, Ms. Jindrich, Ms. Pietrucha, 4th

The Fire that Burns
Govanni R.

Fire burning deep inside it feels like I'm
gonna die. It's burning so much I feel like
I can touch so much fire I feel I'll
flare up. I'm on fire yes I am. But
I don't give a blam! I feel so much
fire inside of me. It's burning deep down
so much fire yesiree. I'm done with
fire I've had my share I wouldn't
dare to have more how about you
share yours.

Burning Fire
Dyamond J.

The fire burning in my house.
It was so dark under that thunderstorm.
The electricity went out
Fire was the only thing in reach
The fire didn't just brighten my house up.
The fire burning deep inside was
much, much worse.
I think of that day when it was dark.
I was mad.
The smell was boiling bad.
I was mad, the smell had gone up my
nose to my lungs.
That is what fire was like burning
in my house.
It reminded me of the past, now
electricity.

Is That Light I See
George C.

Is that light I see what
is it so bright bright as the sun it's
in the sky I know what is the
light should I walk closer it
has a very weird shape what
can it be is it a star no, an airplane

no, a helicopter no, the sun no,
what is it this light what is that
No it can't be how can't I not know
his I'm an idiot it's the moon!

Big Explosions That Sparkles the Sky
Jonathan I.

Boom, bash fire works fly
big explosion sparks the sky
making a big light so bright
that can keep you awake all night
some make light bright and some
make colored light like red, green
and blue too the bright light
can be brighter than a flashlight
and can block out the stars all night
but not in the day when it's bright.
Boom Bash Bash Boom Bash Bash Boom

Fireworks
Joshua J.

Fireworks, fireworks, fireworks I see you
glistening every 4th of July I see you
sounding with sonic boom Some of your
sounds even sound like a car going
room! room! room! Fireworks, fireworks,
fireworks that's all I have to
say now so it's been nice hearing
Your pitter-patter in the sky.

Stars At Night
Savannah C.

Some stars I see are bright.
They look so bright at night.
They are so big I feel like I
can touch the sky. They are so
close to the ground, sometimes
they look so round. But most of
all I like stars because
they are so bright, they can
light up the whole sky at
night! I hope the stars come out
tonight.

Flashlight
Jafet N.

One time I was lost at night.
Lucky I had a flashlight.
I could see very bright.
I hold it tight.
I saw a cat.
Then a hat.
I saw a mouse.
Finally, I saw my house.

Sunlight
Nathan V.

Sunlight sunlight is a light
that shines on us it's a light
that's bright and out of sight
it's good and tight and bright with
a night light. It's a bright
light.

Sunlight sunlight so so bright

Sunlight sunlight always
bright never go dark shine on
the floor and the door all
the way to the whole world
you think you're blind but
you're not it could be
behind look so pretty
Outer space.

Sunlight sunlight so so bright

Sunlight is so bright
it shows in every sight
in my eye it will never
die glow and show the
bright light it's height
is like a kite going
up to the sky like it's
gonna fly sunlight will
never move in sight
when it's gonna be night.

Bursting Light
Jonae M.

Red light, green light
show me the light
I see you lighting
up the sky. I see you bursting
I see you crackly
and falling with fire.
You're round. You make
different noise and
blow on the 4th of July.
Your light it's bursting
in steam. I see
you flying in different
colors oh I see one
red, green and write

I see you lighting
up the sky with
joy, of people or kids.

Sunlight
Oscar L.

God's golden chain is the light for
The world. His chain is so
Bright it is the sun he is in
Heaven watching his chain is
Shining he is watching us.

My Sunlight
Maxine T.

My sunlight a bright and powerful
sun it is. You will need sunglasses to
see it. If you go to it you might melt
A hot firey ball that makes day.
IT'S OUR SUN!!!

Fire
Ermilio M.

Red & orange light so bright
I can see you every night.
Sometimes I need you some
times I do not but I need
you as my night light. My
Mom said that you see the
fire bright so light.

Dewitt Clinton
Elementary School

Paige Warren, Poet in Residence
Principal: Teresa Moy
Teachers: Ms. Chikko, 6th; Ms. Katsafaros, 7th; Ms. Logothetis, 8th

Amelia S.

White foam,
Sea of the blue,
Fish of rainbow,
Whale of the mile,
Shark of the knife,
Live in the same home.
Rocks of the reef,
Weeds of the feet,
All in collaboration,
All love each other.
Old sunken ships,
House of the needy,
Of the sea.

Bibiana P.

Winnie to Jessie

Oh! Jesse my love with sweet ocean eyes
that bring harmony to my heart. With a voice
of a warrior and a heart of a rose
so selfless as anyone can be who could be
more perfect than you with sweet ocean
eyes.

Jessie to Winnie

Love of my heart girl of my dreams
why is it that every moment every
instant I think of you and why do you
bring my attention with no doubt at all
why does your face look like an angel
right from the sky I love you so please
be my love for life.

Seven Ways to Look at Shoes
Kyle B.

I. Shoes pattering on the hard ground clap, clap clap
II. Long heels, short heels, flat heels, shoes with soles without soles
III. Fabric stitched, bound together, rubber soles, rubber toe

IV. Running with no shoes on a road of thorns
V. Fallen down can't get up no shoes to help me stand
take one step, converse chucks turn red all except the
tread sole
VII. Now I walk with broken ease, my shoes all torn
fabric broken, boots are worn words are spoken.

Poem
Kyle B.

6 people on squiggly hearts
and mad puzzles guarding
entrance to the inner end.
Turnover and I see
a two trying to avoid a
diamond cutter. Four sharp
blades, cutting into the cover
of the two. There are two diamonds
in the center of the card waiting
for the two to become weak
so that they can attack the
two's that are corned by
the little friends of the
diamond cutters. I can see
a brutal scene of bloody
murder in which the people
were trying to turn me about.
I turn the card once more
and see a scene of peace.
The people are calm. They
tell a tale of a happy story.
six angels with wings in a happy
scene of blue.

Confused Spring
Martine L.

I smell the taste of hearing spring.
The bird's flying chirps filled the air.
My wet porch from the storm
rains through my mind of
thirsty flowers.

My day is longer then
winter days which are past days
now is spring.
Clear as mud with glass in-between.

Colored Life
Matt S.

Colored leaves that fall
will always paint a picture
in the eyes of God.

Philip G.

Next door to get some sugar from the old lady.

Don't go she's a mean witch!

She's not.

(A few seconds later)

Do you agree she's a witch now?

Ribbit!

Prasanth B.

1.   I am in the amusement park. Riding up and down
in a Ferris wheel. Singing and dancing with
crazy people. Losing my money every time I lose
a game. Hitting the target with my water gun.
Winning this game. Listening to the music and
singing with it.

2.   I am playing my violin with both my
hands. The music is very soft like a lullaby. Everyone
is listening without making a sound. They
are being calm and peaceful. The music ends
suddenly. Everyone stands up with clapping their
hands in a rhythm. I stand up along with my
friends and bow down, smiling.

Thunder and Lightning
Saad S.

Always in the air,
Giving children quite the scare.
Always making thunderous sounds,
Always hearing the guard hounds.

Made of lightning and causes fire,
Always at Zeus' desire.
It is scary but do not fear,
When it's over, you will cheer.

One Way to Capture the Sun
Saad S.

As I slid on the snow
ice clogging my senses
I could feel the rumbling as the snow melted underneath me.
I reached for it
Seems I grabbed a handful
of yellow snow - no wait it was
warm and comforting.
Seemed as if solar power was
cultivating in my hands
As I harnessed that energy
I reached for the darkened sky
to put back the missing
chunk of a broken sun.

I Remember
Group Poem
Ms. Chikko's Class

I remember the markings on books my sister
wrote on all the books with pens, just scribbling,
red, blue, black, now markers, pink, black, all colors.

I remember how my sister and I would watch
everything my great-grandparents did, wash
clothes, hang up the preserved meat, in the backyard
my great-grandfather cooking.

I remember how I would wake up, all alone
in the darkness of my bedroom and my sister already
awoken, watching T.V.

I remember how my aunts would gather at my
grandparent's house, making cheesecake and milk with ginger
juice and talk all night.

I remember my dad comforting me after I scraped my knee.

I remember reading a good book filled with
sadness that made me cry for hours.

I remember gunshots being heard in the
park after I just got away from "them".
I remember when I fell and scabbed my feet trying to
ride a two-wheeler.

I remember the time when my brother got burned by
tea.

I remember seeing my major obsession, my
first crush a hottie lifeguard at the pool.

I Remember
Group Poem
Ms. Katsafaros' Class

I remember when I first met my real mother, but I wanted to be
with my other.

I remember being sick in the winter.

I remember the tie when the only thing I
could turn to was my dad and a basketball
with a hoop.

I remember the time I felt like giving up
but I didn't.

I remember being alone, waiting everyday at the
door for my dad to come back until I saw him
running to me and I realized I was in his hands.

I remember scraping off my big toenails with
the metal door downstairs.

I remember the time of 9/11 when I
was so scared.

I remember the time when I crushed
one of my fingers while closing the
door.

I remember getting my freedom. The
freedom of looking at the green
paper. The freedom of touching and
smelling and using it.

I remember the time when I let my
voice go on its own. I heard
the beautiful sounds I've never
known. I was singing on the
stage. I was in the limelight.
How frightening it was to see
all those million eyes!

I remember going to a pool. I was
in funny outerwear and covered
with lotion. The water first seemed

cold, but later on I was used
to it. Splish and splash was what

I heard the most.
I remember the dark bruise I got for being
disobedient.

I remember the continuous miracle of waves by
the lake.
I remember the long hours at the mall just choosing
what scent of body wash/perfume I liked.

I Remember
Group Poem
Ms. Logothetis' Class

I remember going really fast on my bike and
crashing into the wall.

I remember looking at a lion from only 5 feet away.

I remember reading books as fast as I can and getting
a severe headache.

I remember trying to fall asleep with my eyes shut tightly
but couldn't even get close to falling asleep.

I remember the thick cheeseburger I ate last week.

I remember trying on these
jeans I really wanted at the
mall.

I remember the first time I
made cookies and burned
them.

I remember drinking through a bottle until I was 5.

I remember tucking in my shirt everyday before I went to school.

I remember playing tag with my cousins late at night while my aunt and
mom sat on the front porch.

I remember going to store to take a family portrait and I
was so embarrassed because my whole family looked so funny.

I remember letting my friend borrow a game but he moved before
he returned it to me.

I remember running to the post office in order to win a
contest and to beat a deadline.

I remember having some sort of crush on a girl in third grade. She was wearing a scarlet turtleneck shirt, black jeans, and was very pretty. I have never seen her since.

I remember having a pet goldfish, golden yellow and orange. It went through the drain and was gone forever.

I remember the fright of the closet a long time ago.

I remember when I nearly
made a man blind by throwing
a big branch at his face.

I remember when my friend
Anthony got hit by a van
because a white woman didn't like
blacks.

I remember the first time I saw my mom cry.

I remember when I didn't know what
the word "naked" meant until
2nd grade when my best friend told me.

I remember getting away with
everything because I was an only
child and getting whatever I wanted.

I remember the scuff mark on my dress
shoes.

I remember my dad's blue tie for his
job interview.

I remember how much I wished for
a baby brother, but I ended up with a sister.

I remember waking up early to
watch Saturday morning cartoons,
eating bacon bits straight out of the canister.

I remember having a pet frog,
rabbit, snake, bird, dog, cat,
lizard, fish, turtle and accidentally
drowning my rabbit while taking
a bubble bath with it.

I remember the group of older kids
I played with and being
the only one who wasn't black.

I remember seeing a dumpster

in my alley lit on fire, a
kid from my building get arrested
and his mother crying.

I remember the huge New Years'
party my mom threw when
I was 4 and the drunk people squeezing my cheeks.

I remember the owner
knocking on our door asking
for money and no one
answered the door.

I remember my first pair of
Air Force One's and trying so
hard to keep them clean.

John B. Drake
Elementary School

Tracy Zeman, Poet in Residence
Principal: Yvonna Jones
Program Coordinator: Donna Bronson
Teachers: Mr. Faber, 8th; Ms. O'Daniel, 7th; Ms. Russel, 6th

Iyani H.

I wish I could go back in time and change everything that already went by.
Cause sometimes I'm sad or even mad.
If I could go back in time would I be glad?
I think I would know I should go back in time.
To change everything that's not right
or what happens in the middle of the night 1:00, 2:00, 3:00, 4:00
it doesn't matter the world should have a stopwatch
because everything you do wrong you can stop it just like a song.
Go back in time, go back in time, the world shouldn't have any timer.
You should be free and independent. Not have to stop and watch the time.

Cartier B.

If I were a season I would be summer because of the girls,
playing basketball, eating ice cream, a chocolate swirl,
I wouldn't want to be in the house playing the game all day,
sitting in the house, with lames all day.
I would want to be outside with all of my guys,
we would be talking about girls, telling some lies,
shoot a three in his face, swish, if I could dunk I'll fly,
I really do wish it was summer right now,
if I could wish upon a star, I would wish it was then take a bow.

Tiffany F.

I can be like the four seasons on a Thanksgiving Dinner.
I can be as cold to people just as cold as they can be to me like winter.
I can shine like a light bulb in a crowd like summer.
I can be as warm and nice like spring.
I can be as cool and fun just like jumping in leaves like fall.
I can be like all four seasons.

Jervontae R.

I am like the freezing point of water.
I am the snow that I have packed up with my bare hand.
I am like a $50,000 chain that gave somebody chill bumps.
I am like a fan in the window in the fall.
I am like a person without a home
without a blanket.
I am just the coldest thing on the planet.

4 Ways to a Good Personality
Demarco B.

First you will need 3 cups of respect.
Second you will need 4 cups of a good attitude.
Third you will need 5 teaspoons of a good friendly person.
Fourth you will need 6 pots of trust.

My Neighborhood
Jasmine N.

In my neighborhood, you see
plenty of houses and
big, tall trees.

In my neighborhood,
you see elderly people
as well as youngsters.

In my neighborhood,
you may see drug dealers,
but they hustle out at night.

You may even see poor people
sitting on a milk carton
by a burning garbage can,
in order to stay warm.

They may even ask for
transfers. Or beg for 10 cents
to hustle up enough to
buy some McDonalds.

Our neighborhood is not
the best. But it is where
I live. So this is what
I have to deal with.

DecQuortney M.

Kiwi oh kiwi thank you for picking me.
Kiwis are so tasty that how could I have forsake thee.
If you look over there it's kiwis everywhere.
Kiwis floating in a moat.
I'm sorry for the kiwis that went down my throat.
But that's okay cause there are more
and there are even some within my drawer.

Kassia B.

R&B, Hip Hop, Rap, Jazz…the rhythmical sounds of a quiet mind.
Cool, relaxed free to speak of what's on one's mind.
As time passes I feel a new life has just begun.
New generations of people. My type of people.
Walking down 47th street with the bright quiet street lights.
Walking down the street I see only nothing but a door
so I open the door and everything disappears
and I see a bright light then I'm gone. Do you really exist?
Do we really exist? Am I real?

Marque C.

When I am behind my camera lens
I can make people stand closer, wrap their arms around each other,
even get them to smile. When I am behind my camera lens
I see things others don't. I can record a single moment.
That distorts or tells the truth.
When I am behind my camera lens I can see everything
except my own self, hiding behind my camera.

My Life
Ashley W.

I am a generous mother of two.
When I came to Chicago I let everyone in my family stay with me
and I found out from my son at 82 that his son had a child named Ashley.
I was so happy and filled with glee
and a month later when I woke up my arm was blue and purple,
because I didn't know how to drive I asked my son
to take me to the hospital. My arm was cut off because of no blood circulation.
I had a lovely life and loving family and at age 99 I died.
I left sweet memories of me and hearts broken.

City
Nikko S.

People, dancing in the streets
jumping, playing crazy beats
walking, shopping conducting music
applauding for the crowd of all
giving money to the players
collecting it back from the mayor
at the end it's time to go
even if they song is medium slow

Sonnet
Lorenzo S.

What is the difference between
tall and short?
Tall is able to ride the roller coasters.
Short is able to move quick, tall is
able to reach tall spots, short
is able to jump high. Tall can
swim over 5ft of water. Short
has to stay in the kiddie
pool. Tall buys clothes from the
adult section. Short gets something
from the kid department.
In the barbershop tall does not
need any support, short needs a
booster chair.

Dear Fish,
Tamara A.

How is it under the sea? Did you get eaten by a shark?
I swam by yesterday and you weren't in your coral.
I thought you went out to eat but I guess you got eaten.
If you get this letter swim by and we can eat shrimp and a seaweed platter, your
favorite.

Your fish friend,
Underwater

The Fear
Patrice G.

I'm scared.
I'm so cold I can see My Breath in
front of me. My Blood Chills, my hands
shake, I know I must encounter
the Fear!
        The Fear belongs to me.
No one else can face it.
Everyone who has breaks under
Pressure. The Pressure to be brave,
the Pressure to stay strong and hold
on. I know it's hard, I've seen
it before women running out crying
and crushed. I'll go, I won't fear.
I won't fear to hear the Doctor
say this is your last day here.

Dear Mom,
Amerie S.

All of the things you do I can
never repay you I can't imagine life without
you my mama my raw dog. I remember back in the
day when we couldn't get much, tv wasn't
color and the floor was tore up now you
juggled 3 jobs just to take care of
me your baby girl late night shifts
day time til the a.m. coming home late
then was my best friend my soul mate
yes my big brother the one who tucked
me in put me under the cover when I had
nightmares you came right away read
me bedtime stories to chase them away
my beautiful black queen my everything
the one who keeps this heart pumping every
day I'm a young woman now but my
plan is to show you that I really
understand mama, I love you.

Poem
Renald W.

This is dedicated to my mom
who has kept me calm
and when I was a shortie
she held me in her arms.
She's been there for the longest
been through a lot of stuff with us
that's why she's the strongest.
She never drank or smoked
and has always been there for a cold.
She's got gray hairs now
but when she gave birth to me
she said it was something about
me that would make her proud.
She's raised a star
so hold on longer because living
in apartments and riding hoopties
will be very far.
From my first walk
to my first talk
I knew I was going to be famous
my name all around the world
from Jupiter to Uranus.

Sonnet
Sidney T.

Shall I compare spring to summer?
Spring is when the flowers are blooming.
Summer is when you get to go to water parks.
Spring is different because it is kind of cold and we still have school.
Summer is when you can have parties outside because it is hot.
Spring is when bees come for honey.
When it's summer you can go swimming.
Spring is when the grass starts to grow.
Summer is when it dries up.
Spring is when the leaves change colors.
Spring is when I go to my friend's house.
Summer is when I go bowling.
Spring is when I help people out.
Summer is when I barbeque.

Mercedes B.

I'm like summer because I'm as hot as the sun
as hot as the water that comes out of your sink
as hot as the flaming hots that you eat.
Last but not least I'm as hot as rice coming out of the oven.

Sonnet
Sherri J.

Is Valentine's day what it used to be?
With all the flowers, hearts, and chocolate bunnies.
There are many teddy bears.
On Valentine's day people care.
Is Valentine's day what it used to be?
We'll just have to wait and see.
So much, marriage, marriage, marriage rings
blue birds sing, sing, sing, sing.
Is Valentine's day what it used to be?
Your heart will fly
fly up high
you know yeah yeah
just wait and see.
Is valentine's day how it used to be?

Marcus W.

Spring is like a star burning bright in the sky.
Spring is like the wind that blows the corner of your eyes.
Spring is like the rain when somebody cries.
Spring is like the freshness of a homemade pie.
Spring is like the cover-up you make when you lie.
Spring is like what happens when you chill outside
Spring is like everything or what you choose to do every single day.

Winter
McCoy C.

Winter is like an Alaskan trip. It
makes me happy like a sea of clouds
floating. Full of Ice as I am some days.
Alone like first snowfall to the day it
melts. Cold and unforgiving like my
plans and pranks. Soft like a snowy
happy attitude.

Traveling Through the Hood
Chiffon M.

As I walk I see bad and good things.
I see a family barbequing chicken wings.
I see a bunch of kids hitting each other.
I see arguing from sisters and brothers.
I hear gun shots flying in the air.
I see girls fighting and pulling hair.
Homeless people ask me for change.
Some kids didn't go to school
and don't know how to spell their name.
That is what it is like traveling through the hood.

Amelia Earhart School

Felicia Madlock, Poet in Residence
Principal: Patricia Walsh
Program Coordinator: Caryn Wasniak
Teachers: Ms. Bangston, 6th; Ms. Cosley, 8th; Ms. Shipp, 3rd

Our Funny-It Don't Make Sense Poem
Group Poem
Ms. Shipp's Class

My desk went flying out of the door and started shaking
A kangaroo came into our class and said "Hip Hop Heeezy to the Bang, Bang"
A dog ran after me
While a blackboard crashed on my paper
My aunt was excited, she said "boom shocka locka shocka locka"
My teacher's shoes went to the board and wrote "I love disco"
A lot of books were break dancing in the middle of the classroom
A mouse flew out of the desk singing 50 cent's song "If I was your best friend"
The books jumped and danced
 I woke up and went to school, but no one was there except Ms. Shipp
My toes tickled
The class was strange, running and eating chocolate
Friends told bad jokes and nearly had a stroke
Friends with names beginning with C, R, and Y
The windows in the classroom ran away because of a spider
Students' heads were hit by flying gorillas
A spider monkey stole my gold
He was blue and silver
The school's silly chair was laughing
The class flew out of the window
As the chalkboard started to sing Elvis' songs
Funny huh
But doesn't make sense

Life Is
Group Poem
Ms. Cosley's Class

Life is hard and complicated
Life is challenging
Life is depressing
Life is boring and tedious
Life is delicate
Life is full of dreams
Life is magnificent
Life is worth living
Life is something individuals take for granted
Life is unfair and stressful
Life is suspicious
Life is Love
Life is wonderful

Summer
Tyree H.

Summer is my favorite season
Just remember it's only for one reason.
We are out of school
There are no more rules
I am so happy
You might want to clap and tap for me
The only problem I have
Is that summer must end
I have so much to do
It will make my head spend
Summer is so much fun
I want to share this poem with everyone
This is not the right season
Writing poetry is the reason.

What is Christmas all about?
Jazmine H.

What is Christmas all about?
Is it about gifts?
Is it about lights?
Is it even about the Christmas tree?
None of these things are special.
The only thing that matters is your family
And the love that you have for one another.
This is what Christmas is all about.

The Poetry of My Name
Dominique

D stands for the destiny I have in me
O stands for the opportunist I am
M stands for misjudge
I stands for intelligence
N stands for nice
I stands for interesting
Q stands for quiet
U stands for unique
E stands for excitement

Looking Glass
Lauren W.

Look in the mirror
Ask me what I see
All of the things that I could be
I see an inner portal of myself
I see a million things I am
A young woman, a black child
A winner, best friend, a grand child
A daughter, sister, poet, dancer, singer
I am all of this and MORE!

No Father
Cia F.

I did not have a father
To teach me how to ride a bike
Or give me a birthday card
On all of my 12 birthdays
When I got hurt
I did not have a father to kiss my wounds
I only had a mother
I did not have a father
When I had nightmares
He was not there on my first day of school
He did not tell me which shoe was left
But I'm not on the streets selling drugs or doing wrong things
I did not have a dad to guide me
But I'm still me

Arisse S.

You said we were cool
That was a lie
You were my friend
Until you made me cry
Again and Again I thought
Why is this happening to me?
I stored anger quietly
Nothing has ever happened like this
We had happiness and comedy
And sheer bliss.
I guess that time is over now,
But I have a question
Why and How?

You see what this world has done to me
Jonathan J.

Do you see what this world has done to me?
Sex, lies, and drugs are wiping out the community
Making it hard for me to see parts of the world that has beauty
Gangs and poverty is not good for the young children to see
Do you see what this world has done to me?
Stealing and killing
I can't stand to watch our soldiers overseas
That's how strong it is affecting me
You know what would satisfy me
If they came home to be with their families
One day this world will come to an end
And you might not be around your friends
You will not have all of your inns and your fancy benz
They would be blowin in the wind
This world has done a lot to me
It has nearly drowned me like the deep blue sea
If we can all clear our minds and be free
This is what the world had done to me.

I Cry
Tyla M.

You'll wondering why I cry
I cry because so many people are dying
Why do we always have to be lying
I turn on the TV and see black on black crime
When will it be the time?
The time for us to join together
The word hate will be lost forever

Aunt Mille
Symone S.

I remember like it was yesterday
When I saw you go away
But this memory in me won't fade away
I saw you laugh, cry, and have fun
But I didn't see this day coming to an end
Now, I won't see you ever again
Until the next time I'll see you
Always remember
That Ms. Symone loves you

Camille B.

School is the best
Yes, we try to impress
Come to Earhart, and you'll learn the rest.

Mathew R.

The rain is blue
The sun is red
The trees are brown.

Ode to Rosa Parks
Tierra S.

I thank you for setting us free
I thank you for standing by our side
I thank you for speaking your warm loving words
I thank you for standing up for what you believed in
R.I.P. Rosa Parks

John F. Eberhart
Elementary

Naima Dawson, Poet in Residence
Principal: Joyce Jager
Program Coordinator: Assistant Principal Jacqueline Johnson
Teachers: Ms. Gill, Ms. Place, Ms. Snulligan, 6th

I Remember
Miranda D.

I remember I was 2
I remember that was the year I got adopted
I remember that was the year my other sister who was 3 at the time got adopted too.
I remember the nice people who adopted me
I remember it was August 11th the day after my sister's birthday
I remember going to court
I remember going to the house
I remember unpacking my clothes
I remember saying bye to my birth parents
I remember my adoptive mom telling me that they were using drugs
I remember being sad
I remember being glad at the same time
I remember my other sisters not being with me
I remember being sad
I remember today not remembering what they looked like
I remember, I remember, I remember

Broken
Miguel M.

I've lost my chain
Losing my chain broke me
Sorrow losing it
God telling me it's ok
Me not understanding
Just wanting the chain
It's been with me since I was 7
Losing it destroyed me

Without a Mother
Alexander S.

So there she stood
Looking at her deceased mother
In her mind everything seemed dark
Miserable she had to live without her
From time to time she visited the grave
For a 9 year old it must have been hard

Prison
John Z.

A prison is a horrible place
The tall and wide bars of cells
The foul smell of cigarettes
And sounds of mice nibbling at the wall
The cracked ceilings and floors
Cell doors opening and closing as guards chain inmates
The rusted handles of the cat walk
Torn and worn out beds of the same color.

"Rancho"
Aracel S.

"El Rancho" A beautiful picture comes to mind when that word is said. The freshness of the air, the beautifulness of the animals. "Pero" screams my grandfather as stray dogs came in begging for food. "Ninos" says my grandmother begging to get the kids to eat. Family always around you, helping you, nudging you, listening to you. But when it's time to go I cry until the next time a year later, until I visit "El Rancho."

The Cold Attic
Melissa P.

In the attic where the roof used to leak.
It's so cold.

You could feel the windows shaking with fear.
Where spiders might make you shiver when you are asleep.

See the view of the roof tops of every house in the neighborhood.
Once it is night go on roof top and see the stars shine.

Should I?
Monica A.

What should I do when a bad problem comes through?
What should I do if I have no answers?
What should I do if I am the center of attention, but really I don't want to be?

What should I do?

Should I walk away in silence?
Should I cry until they leave?
Should I just sit there and watch them watch me?

Christian Ebinger School
Cassie Sparkman, Poet in Residence
Principal: Marilyn LeBoy
Program Coordinator: Assistant Principal Janice Stein
Teachers: Ms. Dao, 3rd; Ms. Hartzell, 6th; Ms. Keany, 1st;
Mrs. McGowan, 3rd; Mrs. Murphy, 3rd; Ms. Patel, 2nd

Proud
Stephany B.

Proud is a girl. Her favorite color is green. She makes happy sounds when she enters a room. She acts like a wild dog riding in the wind. She smells like baseball fields in the middle of the Atlantic Ocean. She runs all around just to pitch for the Cubs Team. Proud will be in a parade and give everyone new proud thoughts. She runs fast, so fast that she has speedy power. Her favorite food is Salisbury Steak. She loves it when it is 70 degrees.

Anger
Doug C.

Anger is a boy that wears a black shirt every day. He sounds like the roar from a Tyrannosaurus Rex when he talks. He lives in every dark corner of your room. When he comes out, a breeze comes by. He would work at a barber shop disguised as a person. He would have a pet dog that is vicious. He would bring a fire ant everywhere. His superpower would be super speed so no one sees him when he moves.

Depression
Evan A.

Depression is a gloomy purple.
He can't think of anything joyful.
He finds himself alone so he will find
You and weigh your spirit too.
He moves slowly so
You can get
The better of him.
Where ever Depression goes, a
Storm cloud goes with him. It
Follows him like a
Magnet to metal.
Depression sometimes tags along with fear
So be careful!

Ode to an Orange
Cassidy M.

Orange, you are so beautiful.
You are a sun and your peels
Are beams of light.
You warm me with your vibrant color.

Ode to a Goldfish
Annie B.

O beautiful fish,
You are an orange swimming by a tree.
You are a slippery dragon.
You are a butterfly flying in water.

Ode to a Dragon Vase
Aaron P.

O dragon vase, you are pretty with flowers.
You are a pink dragon on a Japanese parade.
O you are as beautiful as a pink rose that just sprouted.
Your pinkness has blinded me with love.
I put you on the table and I can't stop looking at you.
You make an old rusty house look wonderful.

Ode to a Goldfish
Kendra B.

O beautiful goldfish,
You remind me of a huge lion.
Your gills are like big waves in the water.
You feel like plastic rubber.

Ode to Books
Emily E.

I love your gold stripes,
and your beautiful pages
filled with words and chapters!
I love your way of making me comfy
before I go to bed.
Brother of paintings,
son of boxed cards,
grandson of words,
you are better than anything.

Ode to Stars
Group Poem
Ms. Keany's Class

O stars, you are so beautiful. You are like the moon. You are like flowers. You are like a shiny spoon. You are a bright sun. You are light bulbs in space. You are like shiny lemons. You are diamonds. You are like rainbow bubbles popping, so beautiful.

I Wish I Were a Dog King
Drake L.

I wish I were the King of Dogs, controlling every dog alive,
Telling them all to listen to their owners or guard the house.
I wish I were the best skater alive, grinding and doing tricks
Everywhere I can, the skate park, the school, and the driveway.
I wish I were a horned toad scaring old women and little kids
Who play with me, poking them with my spines.
I wish I were a teacher, teaching young kids how to skateboard
And read, write, do math, and learn about our country.
I wish I were an African villager protecting my tribe
From lions, hyenas, black mombas, and crocodiles.
I wish I could drive a Lamborghini Diablo in a race
On the Indianapolis Motor Speedway going 200 mph.
I wish I were a volcano exploding my top, causing
Destruction and mayhem over the towns around me.

Serena T.

I wish when I clapped my hands
Seven times I would be where ever
I'm thinking of. I wish Christmas
Was every first day in a month so I
Could have presents early.
I wish I had a driver's
License so I could run over
My 12-year-old brother Stevie.
I wish I had all the books
In the world so I didn't have
To go the book store.

Daniel C.

I wish I were a peregrine falcon so
I'd swoop down at 150 miles per hour.
I wish I had invisible powers to
Disappear with a stick in my hand.
I wish I were flying on a shooting star
So I'd see the whole universe.
I wish there were no parents, we
Would rock down the house.
I wish I had too much family so

I'd get to sleep easier.
I wish I were a candy bar so I could
Get eaten before the earth loses gravity.
I wish I had a humongous brain so
I won't have to go to school because
I'm too smart already.

Bobby G.

I am sorry
I mowed the
lawn and left
one strip
to make it
look like
it had a mohawk.
It looked very
funny but then
you could not
start the lawn
mower again and
you could not
fix the lawn.
I think this
made you embarrassed
and I am
sorry because you
only told me
to get gas
for the mower
about 100 times.

Confession
Hannah R.

I went to Happy
Foods with my baby
sitter and when she
turned around to get
milk I took a
piece of candy with
out her noticing or
the store I confess
it. At my nap
I would eat it.
It tasted so good
that I did it
every time if I
had pockets so I
am sorry but I
was only 3 and
I didn't know what
stealing means.

How to Stay Home from School
Arica H.

Soak your forehead in warm water. Put black circles under your eyes with your Mom's makeup. Put butter on your tongue. Don't take a bath for 4 days. Sleep extra late and say "I'm so tired". When you stand up, fall on the ground. Let your little brother annoy you so it looks like you are too sick to care. Mix salt with tuna and coco puffs cereal together and say you threw up. Say you can't see and trip on your cat. Somehow forget the way to school.

Rachel B.

I remember in second grade my pants fell down and I screamed and cried really loud and boys were looking! I remember when I got my cat I thought it was a robot toy! I remember when my dog and cat died and my dad burst into tears. I remember when my dog pooped on the carpet but my dad caught it into his hands just in time. I remember my first day at Ebinger -- I was scared to death. I remember when I fell off the slide and broke my back at Ebinger. They rushed me to the hospital and gave me a neck brace and I got knocked out. I remember when I met my best friend. I remember when I dreamed I had died!

Azalia R.

I remember when I was little, my dad gave me a bath.
I remember I wanted a bike with pink bells on it.
I remember my brother got sick and puked, and then I puked too at a party.
I remember when me and my cousin Alexis were fighting. She punched me in the stomach. She was younger than me and stronger. She still is.
I remember Miss T. from kindergarten. Her real name was Miss Tambokas. She has blonde hair with highlights. She has brown eyes.

Sofia P.

In Egypt, I was at the airport. It didn't look like one. It had a big window of fish in the air with no water. And the roof had trees hanging upside down. It looked like a circus! I thought I was seeing things but I was not. Then I met a creature who had the body of a lion and the head of a man who talked like he was on Broadway and singing. All he could talk about was apples. Apple pie, apple juice, apple cobbler, and apple ice cream. Then he was gone, and I was back in Chicago.

Megan W.

I was in my bed. When I woke up my room was like a rain forest. I went to my rat's cage deep at the end of the jungle. I opened it up, but I found a hungry cheetah. I went to see my brother Connor's room. It was like space. Connor was sitting on a star. I picked him up and carried him out. I told him to stay. I went to the kitchen and I found roosters running everywhere. One said, "Why are you here?" I said, "I live here." I shouted out loud. I took him outside and told him to change the house back. When I looked down the block, all, I repeat, ALL of the houses were made of candy. The rooster said, "Are you sure?" I said, "Never mind!"

Kellan M.

I draw an ice-cream cone. I draw a boy running to it. That is my picture of tasting. I draw a dog taking the ice-cream cone. That's my picture of stealing. I change the boy to a girl. That's my picture of happiness. I draw a cat chasing the dog. That's my picture of fear.

Andres L.

I draw a man with a green camouflage suit and a green hard hat and a gun. This is my picture of sadness. But if I erase the soldier and draw two Generals with pistols in their pistol holders, now this is my picture of decision. If I erase the two Generals then draw a soldier's family praying, it is now a picture of hope. If I draw a soldier with his family and they are smiling, it is a picture of happiness. If I draw two soldiers hugging it is a picture of friendship. If I draw a soldier and his wife hugging it is a picture of love. But if I draw a picture of a lot of soldiers than I draw a picture of WAR.

Lucas D.

I draw a man of flame dancing and he is so ruby red.
That's my picture of fire dancing.
I also draw a man with a bucket of water
and that's my picture of putting out the fire.

In Your School Dream
Group Poem
Ms. Keany's Class

You are at your desk. Suddenly, your teacher jumps out the window. A sumo wrestler jumps INTO the room. You wrestle with him. An elephant enters the room. You are surprised. The pencils come alive. You scream and run.

In Your School Robot Dream
Tyler G.

You are playing on the playground. The whole playground changes into a robot. You talk to the robot. You say, "Can I ride in you?" The robot changes back into the playground you were at. School is over now. You go home, frightened.

Kathleen B.

You are sitting in the park
next to a fountain
watching a big bald eagle flying in the distance.
The sun is shining
and not a single cloud in the sky.
All of a sudden you feel the air get damp,
and in the distance you see a giant whale
flopping towards you

at least 60 feet long and very big.
It starts moving faster and faster towards you.
He looks hungry, and says he wants to eat you.
You run across the town, but then you are trapped.
Behind you is a building
lit up with flames.
You have no choice but to go in the building.
Then the eagle picks you up.
He flies you to the top of the building.
The whale comes closer.
You are not high up enough.
He is just about to eat you
when he starts to get scared.
He flops away faster and faster.
You look behind you, and see a giant wave.
It's so big that it fills the ground up
to the building and even higher.
You find yourself on top of the Eiffel Tower.
You get pushed down into the water where
a shark is waiting to eat you,
then you land on your bed
and it is raining outside.

The Wild Hockey Dream
Haley S.

You are a famous hockey player shooting a puck at the goalie. All of a sudden you blink and your agent is a giraffe. The giraffe says "Bring it" and you say "You're on." You play. Then you get a goal and suddenly you are in La La Land, but you blink and you are on the hockey channel! You get dizzy from moving to different places. You get hit with a puck, and you are put on the bench.

Anna W.

Once you dreamed about a crow changing into a devil and you dreamed that the devil was chasing you. You had to find a door that led you to math. You had to solve problems that were hard for you. You were scared to death and fell. The devil tied you up and tucked you away.

Brandon A.

I am a football player running faster than lightening.
I am a chicken wing, so much chicken on me to eat.
I am Elvis hair, so cool and so much style.
I am a Hummer, as tall as my garage.
I am Crash Bandicoot, as fast as John.
I am the Beatles, so much rock in the song.
I am an xBox 360 that can play any game I want.

Brianna W.

I am a shining star so bright I make the lights flicker near telephone poles.
I am Blaze, my dog stretching and squirming trying to get out of the house.
I am a fluffy white cotton pillow with rips and patches trying to fill in the missing spaces.
I am my old pink teddy bear wearing a football jersey named after Walter Peyton.
I am Mrs. Murphy, so sweet and so loveable.
I am shattered glass being swept up by a broom and flying into the garbage.
I am the baby sitter of doom watching my littler sister be a screaming cry-baby.
I am a tornado with a lot strength ripping up the biggest towns!
I am Brianna, a brown-eyed girl with attitude. I love that song!

Nadia J.

In the darkness
of the deep blue
I found a hotel,
In the hotel I
got a room.
I opened the
door and found an
alligator drinking lemonade
on my bed.
I got scared.
I screamed
and shut the door.
I swam out of the hotel.
I found a seamonkey. I asked
"Why are you purple
in this big blue?"
He looked at me, confused
"Why are you so small?"
I asked again.
Then he said, "You that ask
so many questions
turn around." "That's not
an answer," I said. He pushed my
head. I spun around and found
behind me nothing but grass lands
shining in the darkness.
I was no longer under water.
I stared straight ahead
in the dark of the quiet air.

Emma B.

I meet Cocopoodledoo
in the state of Alaska.
He looks like a rooster
and a poodle. I run away
in the steamy air. He

follows me and says, "do you
like my pink tail?"
Then, I disappear into the air.

Barbie the Cat
Ariel P.

Barbie the cat, why do you like it when I sing?
Most people do not like my voice.
It sounds like it feels when you get a bee sting, Barbie the cat.

You follow me around the house, meowing loudly.
How I wish I could understand you,
my little cat, Miss Meowy.

What do you do when I'm gone?
Do you play with the other cats?
Do you turn on my radio? Sometimes I find it on,
Barbie the Cat

Stephanos T.

I chased a frog into the bog and beside me I had my dog. It hopped real fast and
was hard to see. I could barely see in front of me but I want to catch it really bad
so as you thought, I didn't give up, we kept on sprinting through the bog and I was
panting like a hog but then the frog hopped straight into an old mud filled log. I took
a stone out from the weeds and hit the log consistently and when the log broke the
frog shot out like a bullet, my dog ran second and I ran last and both of us were
really fast but then I couldn't stop. They passed a log, shot out of the bog, my dog
got real close to the frog and then out of nowhere they stopped -- hmmm, I never
knew how much dogs like to eat frogs!

Ode to a Teddy Bear
Michael L.

O teddy bear, you are a cheetah.
You are very good at catching bad guys.
You feel like cut up pieces of yarn one centimeter long.

Sarah E.

I have put
all sorts of bugs
in my brother's
underwear.
When he put
his underwear
on he
screamed his head
off.
Forgive me
brother I

could not help
it. The bugs were
so slimy and squishy.

Reasons to be Afraid of the Dark
Patricia Z.

I am scared of the dark because:
the floor feels like it is about to crack,
the branches of the trees feel like they are opening a door and taking me away,
the snoring feels like devils chanting, laughing, and walking in the town,
the spiders feel like they are going to bite me and
the coldness in my bed feels like I'm sleeping in the snow.

People and Things I Know Nothing About
Jordan R.

Girls
My parents when they were kids
What happens around the world
Books
What happens after school
Elevators
Stairs
What happens at home when I'm at school
The president and his wife when they are sleeping

Ode to a Wooden Spoon
Andrew S.

O beautiful wooden spoon,
You are a sword for a fight.
You are a Storm Trooper hitting a Jedi.
O beautiful wooden spoon,
You are hot chocolate, hot pudding
In my cool room.
O beautiful wooden spoon,
You are a rocket blasting off into space.
O beautiful wooden spoon,
You are Darth Vader.

Ode to an Apple
Davin C.

O apple, you are a Tennessee ball in my mouth
Bouncing with pride. You are money in my house.
You are a dragon flying in the wind.

Michael Faraday
Elementary School

Pam Osbey, Poet in Residence
Principal: Dr. Shirley A. Scott
Program Coordinator: Sheila Keeley
Teachers: Ms. Dragos, 4th; Mr. Charlton, 5th/6th; Mr. Petties, 5th/6th

Voice
Barbara D.

A sound no squeaks.
I sound that way
because I am me.
Voice, I have no choice.
No one tells me, I'm on
my own.
Not trying to be grown.
I am me because of my
voice, I sing every where.
People hear.
I don't change to fear.
It's my voice.
Voice.

Children of the future
D. K., Glen C., and Onijhia J.

When I look into any room.
I see doctors, movie stars, lawyers, chefs
And the judges of the future.
A classroom of seeds.
Tall green pines, sweet maples,
Strongly stately oaks, dark beautiful
Ebonies.
Children of the future.
Everywhere, in parks, in schools, in the playgrounds.
On the buses, on porches, in the streets, and in the fields
Playing ball.
The children of the future, now will lead us to a new destiny.

Slow Moving
Exodus R.

Slow moving like a turtle
so slow moving.
or like a shell.
It's hard to ring the city bell.
Slow moving like a body of water.

Which body of water?
I don't know
I know these things are slow moving
slow moving...
slow moving...
slow moving...
Slow moving like a traffic jam people
late for work or a line trying to get somewhere
slow moving...
slow moving...

Invisible Fever
DeWayne B.

Gone.
Nobody see you.
Ignore like someone small.
Like an ant.
People don't see you.
Never seen.
Like a ghost that don't be seen anywhere.

Run around like somebody.
Trying to be seen running. Jumping.
Dancing and tapping people on the shoulder.
But still nobody see me.

I'll do anything to be seen.
In a world without people
seeing you.
Weird one.
I ask people for directions,
they will turn around.
Keep walking like
I am nobody.

Swimming Fever
Ronisa F.

Splashing.
Floating on your back.
With the cold blue water
Stinging your eyes.
Stroking on your back.
While the water is splashing you
In your face.
Diving in the cold water.
On a nice sunny day.

Unique
Unique N.

One of a kind.
Unique; bold, brave, beautiful.
Unique; out in the open.
Unique; like a bird in the sky.
Like the sun.
Unique; so sweet so full of full Unique.
Unforgettable, Unique, so...unafraid, unlike.
So sweet. So me.
I'm Unique.

The Path of My Feet
Nickole P.

It is appropriate that I sing the path of my feet.
I walk the trails of the world.
Going to Wisconsin.
Being the first in my family to meet Nikki Giovanni.
My feet shows the future of my abilities.
As I walk the path like Rosa Parks, not being afraid
of nobody.
My feet shows me who I am.
It is appropriate that I sing the path of my feet.

Poetry Is
Group Poem
Mr. Petties' Class

Poetry is a time when you brain's cooking and your pen
Brings fire to the paper.
Poetry is beautiful like my pink roses.
Poetry is.
Poetry is a feeling I want to unleash.
Why I write...to share my feelings
With others to tell my pain and to express
My love and to tell my story with my pen and to share
Feelings how I like beautiful feelings.
I love poetry.
The feeling overwhelms me.
A swelling of the heart.
Poetry takes my hand and leads me
By the heart over a beach of sand.

Poetry is bliss.
Poetry is a choir on a Sunday morning.
Poetry is a song like R&B on a Monday.
Poetry is yours and only your emotions.
It's what makes you diverse and unique
Like a sparkling diamond.
Poetry is like thoughts being let out that

You'll never say out loud.
Poetry is a beautiful butterfly on a sunny day.
Poetry is a wish to leave the country and go
To a far away place.
I write poetry because I can dream to fly in the wind.
Poetry is creativity.
Things that tells about the sun, moon, sky and solar system.
Let your pen do all the writing.
Praise your pen to writing.
Poetry is something that can make your mind feel good.

Poetry is a thing that could get you through life.
Poetry is part of writing that some people like writing.
Poetry is very beautiful like red roses and full of dreams
And hopes.
Poetry is beautiful and full of wishes.
Poetry is unique, it's one of a kind.
Poetry is a very joyful story that brighten my eyes.
Poetry is sadness like when the frustration comes your way and wipes
The smile right off your face.
Poetry is like catching a pail of water on Easter Sunday.
Poetry is an expression diary.
Poetry is.
Poetry is a feeling I want to unleash.

The Flow of Words
Group Poem
Mr. Charlton's Class

Poetry is water that flows like elegant
silk in a river of gold.
Poetry is the sound of thunderstorms on a cloudy day.
Poetry is love and joy like the beginning of summer.
Poetry is expression and reflection…
Poetry is loveable like gospel music on a Sunday morning
from the organist.
Poetry is the first sight of danger…it lets you know that
Danger is coming your way!
So I advise you to stay away from POETRY.

The flow of words.
Expressions flying through the air.
Jazzy words all around in the air.
Words are pouring down.
Poetry is a hot night outside looking
up at the amazing lights in the night sky.
Poetry is a way of my life.
It expresses my joyfulness when I get a good grade.
Poetry is a way to let my inner self from being shy.

The flow of words could be the talent of me.
The flow of love could be the happiness you see.

The flow of words could be leading me to the top.
My words could be the heavenly hill, the perfect movements.
My words.

Poetry is the first sight of love and gospel beat
That is making my head nod up and down.
My pencil tells stories of courage.
Tells stories of dreams.
I write because words are beautiful.
I use my pen, my lovely little pen, to express
All my unforgiving sins, that brought me pain,
hatred and shame.
I use my pen because I'm in pain.
I use my pen, my black ball of fire pen, because I'm happy.
I love poetry because it brings out my feelings.
I love poetry because it brings out my creativity when I write.
I love poetry.
The running poetry man …running on ice
To offer me a drink of ice…cold water…but
I don't accept it.

Poetry is like the smell of food in the morning.
Poetry is how I live.
My words flow through the sky.
Silkiness of poetry comes through my pen to the paper
And write the best poem we can write.

I love poetry because its the flow of words.
Expressions flowing through the air.

Words are pouring down.

Poetry Is Sweet As Sugar
Group Poem
Ms. Dragos' Class

Poetry is like cold ice cream
On a hot summer's day where
I'm at the park with my family.
Poetry is sweet as sugar when you
put it on the pancake.
Poetry is sweet just like when you
put sugar on cereal.
Poetry is like hot chicken wings
that are spicy.
Poetry is like melted cheese on top of a pizza.

Poetry lets out stress when you have
told your sins and they aren't forgiven yet.
Poetry lets out stress when
your temper is as hot as a heat wave.
Poetry is like chocolate ice cream on
a sugar cone melted in my mouth.

Poetry is like a redwood rose and rhythm
daisies in a poetry garden.

Roaring like tigers.
Poetry wants to die like stars in the sky.
Poetry is like a crashing car -- throwing a football
so far that I can make a touchdown, like a
basketball going round and round!
Poetry is like waking up on a bright
sunny day ready to go play football and
tackling someone so so hard.
Poetry ice cream takes so good.
It has rhythm nuts, rhyming nuts, raisin
nuts, sugar-coated with my strong voice.
Poetry ice cream makes me happy.

My ColorsToday
Tarina H.

Monday, I'm feeling moody and mad just like red and black.
Tuesday, I'm calm but bored like green.
Wednesday, I'm ready to have fun like yellow.
Thursday, I'm ready to get out of school like orange.
Friday, I'm ready for the weekend like purple.
Saturday, I'm ready to go shopping like pink.
Sunday, go to go to church.
Feel mad because I have to go back to school.
Now the colors will start over again.

Boycott
Louis M.

Rosa Parks showed us how to ignore the boycott
And ignore the name calling.
If it wasn't for Rosa Parks, there probably would still
Be boycott buses.
And it was good by standing up to the boycott.
There is good Dr. Martin Luther King, Jr. Rosa Parks
And Jesse Jackson and all other kind of American black
History save our lives and gave us freedom.

A Black Star
Melvin T., Darvonta W., and Tywon J.

A black star shine.
So bright at night.
At early time, sunshine.
Glow in dark like a black trap star.
We will go far.
A black star is me.
Like chasing a car but we will stay on top.
We won't stop, a black star.

Haiku
Donicha G.

Death burns into life.
You are born, then you will die.
Live life to the end.

Haiku
Whitney T.

When lightness comes up.
And the moon disappears I
See nothing but sun.

Gale Community Academy

Dana Vinger, Poet in Residence
Principal: Joseph Peila
Program Coordinator: Deena Lazar
Teachers: Ms. Hayes, Ms. Miller, Ms. Noble, 8th

I Am (a found poem)
Morgan S.

I am the dark-skinned child who
is as black as night from the scorching
of the African sun.

I am the mountain that stands out
from the rest.

I was born of the dirt and shall
return to give life to the ones
after me.

I speak to God with my body
as it sways left and right to
the beat of the drums in my soul.

African winds surround me so
that I may never forget my heritage.

I am the purple blossom
on the ancient tree.

I have been embroidered with jewels
and made with the finest silk because
God said I deserved it.

Born at the crossroads of lightness
and darkness.

We choose the path.

We are whole.

A Quiet Time
Gregory S.

A peaceful moment
To heal my soul
To steady the pounding

Within my chest

A quiet time
To make me whole

Let me rest

Angry Dog
Lawrence H.

An angry dog growls
Don't like to be messed with,   or
He'll bite your shoes.

Hoping
Marco A.

My family
Hoping for opportunity
So that I can grow

Grandmother
Bianca A.

Her smile was sweet

          like her rice pudding

She was strong

          like two bricks

She always shined

          like a star

She was beautiful

          like a pearl

And I

          her baby girl

Best Friend
Jaimee H.

She's the peanut butter, and I'm the jelly. We stick together.
She's an old treasure box where I hide my secret notes.
She's a warm blanket when I need comfort.
She's a soft pillow when I need rest.
She's a book that's full of thousands of stories.
She's expensive jewels that are hard to find.
She's a phone. We talk all day.

She's my best friend.

Five
Rashad W.

    Fine
    Important
  lo**V**e
for**E**ver

Boys
Mercedes A.

    Bums
  s**O** stupid
alwa**Y**s playin' games
    So immature

Adonis H.

A percentage of this, and
a percentage of that.

Roots are identified,
but I've never known.

Am I African-American?
Am I Puerto Rican?

I do know one thing,
I am what I am.

History made us,
history will destroy us.

A Response to Raymond Carver's *In the Lobby of the Hotel de Mayo*
Edith I.

His face and body is covered in blood.
Words don't want to come out.
He takes them to the harbor.

He is about to faint.

Words don't want to come out.
The ships are destroyed.
He is about to faint.
Blood everywhere.

The ships are destroyed.
They look at him.
Blood everywhere.
He drops dead.

They look at him.
Everything is dead.
He drops dead.
Not even the sun is alive.

Everything is dead.
He takes them to the harbor.
Not even the sun is alive.
His face and body is covered in blood.

A Response to Raymond Carver's *In the Lobby of the Hotel de Mayo*
Tykeiah H.

The girl closes the book.
The man puts away the broom.
The boy puts down his watering can.
The clerk gets up.
The woman puts down her letter.
The old man sits up.

The man running towards the hotel starts yelling.
Someone is chasing him.
That someone has a gun,
and is shooting at him.

The man running is dodging shots.
People on the streets run for safety.

The girl stands up.
The man...
The boy...
The clerk calls the police.
The woman stands up.
The old man asks,
"What's going on?"

Sirens.
Police.
The shooter runs,
but is trapped.

The ambulance takes the man to the hospital.
The shooter is put in jail.
All is the same again.

Another hot Sunday afternoon.

Success
Melissa A.

Soon the world will know me
Can you **U**nderstand how I feel
Can you handle my truth
Can you
Everyday brings me one step further
Shame is not me, not even close
Someday I will change the world forever

Kevin
Kevin V.

A **K**nife that cuts deep.
Evening rain that ruins your day.
Victory
something I can't achieve.
Inside purgatory.

Never to find out my fate.

Nathan
Nachelle B.

Nothing means more to him than his children.
All he wants is to provide for his kids.
To us, he is *Mighty Dad*.
He works for everything.
As Life moves on, his kids grow knowing that he risked it all.
Now he can rest.

Kaneesha H.

to imagine friendship
far, far away

Summer
Chiquita B.

beach, swim, food
swim, food, home
food, home, sleep
home, sleep, awake
sleep, awake, dinner

Tiffany B.

A rainbow
A red rose

           children playing

Relaxed
Hot summer

           Freedom

Spring Break
Latoi B.

eleven, awake, shower
awake, shower, clothes
shower, clothes, shoes,
shoes, outside, play
outside, play, fun
play, fun, flowers
fun, flowers, friends

Angela P.

Bright palm trees
Schools of fish
Sounds of adventure
Deep, pure water

Summer ahead

Amber B.

Ocean
Water

Sea creatures

The air
Of freedom

Basketball
Tyrell W.

    Baseline driving
    Assist
    Scooping through the lane
    Keeping high score
    Easy baskets
    Too many points
un**B**elievable dunks

All eyes on me
Leaving my defense
Listening closely to my coach

Grandmother
Peter M.

A young grandmother
calling my name.

I will always love her, and
she will always love me.

Karlita D.

Going to the movies
Popcorn and things
Cousins calling my name

Marlen M.

woods and trees
smells
birds singing
air on my skin
good food

Mexico

Chelsea W.

Beautiful palm trees
Freshly sliced oranges
Waves of the ocean
Sun beaming down
Freshly sliced oranges

Peace around me

Heaven
Phillip M.

Angels
Blossoms on trees
Peaches
Plums
A wonderful breeze

I'm in heaven.

Sister
Mercedes M.

Secrets I tell
I'll never tell anyone else
Sharing love stories
Till the end of the world
Even through thick and thin
Respecting, loving, admiring

Friendship
Bianca G.

Future
Remembrance
In sight
Evenings
No days
Due to the
Starting of
ex**H**austion
m**I**ssing your
Peace and love

Galileo Scholastic Academy

Eric Elstain, Poet in Residence
Principal: Alfonso R. Valtierra
Program Coordinator: John Beven
Teachers: Ms. Garay, Ms. Lewis, Ms. Otero, 4th

The Dinosaurs of Time
Carlos O.

A Dinosaur of time
A Rex of time
A Monster of time
That I ride on
it takes me to the time
of cavemen. It takes
me to a cave of time
when I say goodbye
I go into the cave
of time it takes
me back to the future
where cars are in the sky
and there are robots that
help. Then I find a
robot of time it takes
me back to when I rode
the Rex of time then
the robot of time goes
back to its home
then I go on a Triceratops
of time then it takes me
back to my town of people
and that's how I went
on the dinosaurs of time.

Creepy Sword
Ana C.

Sometimes weird things happen
Why? Creepy swords are in the sea
One fish might be scared of this
Rocks are where they hide
Dolphins are being eaten by this
Fish are getting wise
I think we should be wise, too
Sharks are worse to know what to do
How can the sea survive?

My Crazy Poem
Cynthia T.

Yellow
Tail lizards
Who poison
Rocks
The Declaration
of
Independence will
be signed in 2027
Buttersticks
lost
one whole hair
The world travels around the
Sun.
But outerspace
is made of a blue blanket and
little helicopters got stuck
in it.
The speck
went to college.
Write anything
you've
heard recently.
When I am alone I am not.

Gum
Jacinto P.

Columbus came to America
"Do your homework," he says.
I look at gum on my first
sunny day and when I am
alone I have parties and
that is why gravity helps you
stay on the ground.

The Following of the Moon
Majestic J.

The moon is bright and the cold is near.
The moon was half eaten by an alligator.
Lucy is on the moon right now.
I shot an arrow an arrow on the moon
and it shined so brightly.
Echoing on the moon.
On the moon people call me Do-Do head.
I will sing on the moon and float on the air.
But I will have a space dog.
My scientific is when you put ice cubes
in an ice tray they will freeze.

When I am alone no one would not
find some interesting things on the moon.
Astronauts go to the moon for the very
first time. And so to the moon it is.

Pink
Amber B.

Pink is the color of shyness
when you're really blue.

Pink is the color of loneliness
when you're in the zoo.
Pink is the color of caring
when you're in the moon.

Pink is the color you have
inside your heart.

Pink is the color of helping
when someone needs you.

Pink is the color of me
when I help someone in need

Pink is the color of sweetness
when you're so nice

If you were pink what
would you do?

The Color of Black
Maria G.

Death is the color of Black.
English is the color of Black.

Winter is the color of Black.
A water bottle is the color of Black.

A nail is a color of Black,
the color Black is the color of Heights.

A tie is a color of Black.
A pencil is a color of Black.

Homework is the color of Black.
Chalk is the color of the Black.

A jack is a color of Black.
A tick tock is a color of Black

hate is a color of Black.
Black is the color of under.

Black is the color of underwater soil.
Gorillas are a color of Black.

Death Dance
Salvador M.

I dreamed a dance
Dr. Pants.
You'll do the death dance!

Slither like snakes.
Just don't wheeze,
eat some cheese.

Mr. Lance,
hold your pants,
it's the death dance.

Jump like frogs.
Flying ghosts.
You guys really are hosts.

The death dance,
I'm begging please
I'm just right on my knees.

Now you look dead.

Flash
Kyra P.

Say
cheeze
oww my
eye like
1,2,3
wake
me up
no
wait I am
looking at
amazement
I
C
that love
is eternal
now wake
me up now it
is no good killing

wait I am not dreaming
I am crying
boo hoo
2 many flashes

Who Was It
Kiana S.

In my dream I
awoke in someone's silhouette

I wandered around and
came across a golf course

the size of a
football field

I looked up there
as someone was erasing the course

He had gray hairs and
bruises on his face

As I walked back to
my original spot

I wondered who that
was and why he put

me in a silhouette

According to The Palace at 4pm (based on a sculpture by Giacometti)
Gabriele E.

It looks to me like
a museum
*

An exhibit of an experiment
Made from toothpicks

Made from bones.

Can be a trap
Made out of a map

With some bones hanging

Opens at 4 a.m.

Closes at 4 p.m.

Better hurry before you get
locked inside.

And won't come out until
4 a.m.

Grim Reaper
Shalon C. and Jeremy J.

I'm thinking of a creature can you guess what it is?
It is a creature whose heart is as black as his soul.
He sucks blood of horses and bats and people.
I saw him once, he was lightning.
Once I saw him take the meat off of someone.
He digested the meat in a blink of an eye.
Once he was in someone's house.
Once one person was killed by touching his hand.
The blue and bluer seas swam with him in it
but was killed by a swarm of sharks.
His hearing is a spirit but be still walks the dead.
He has a new method of killing in sleep.
Once upon a time he was a kid just like
us but killed his family and was taken in by the
devil for his deeds so he is called
the Grim Reaper.

Making Cookies
Dakota O.

I would have known they were making
Cookies, so I was alone in the living room.

Tyler bent down so
He could pour the brown sugar.

I stirred the eggs,
And we were saying words, too.

No one was on the front porch because it was cold,
And the oven felt like torches to the cookies.

Looking
Vanette W.

Today I am on the ground
looking for my crown

Today I found it!
But when do I pound it

Today I'm on the ground
Looking for some one to pound

Today I found them
But how do I crown them

Dimarre W.

Snapping unwrapping
all these sounds
in one place
the sounds are
making me think
what is going
on skipping scouting
people walking
where are these
sounds coming from
they're coming from
the world

Robert L. Grimes Elementary

Ray Bianchi, Poet in Residence
Principal: David Dalton
Program Coordinator: Assistant Principal Judith Carlson
Teachers: Mrs. Achtenberg, 5th; Mrs. Conlon, 6th; Mrs. McCabe, 6th

Mexico
Abel M.

Coxmte
Xiomec
Comixe
Omix
Emo
Emix
Ime
Ocixem
Mo
Em
Om
Xi
Xie
Xem
Xemic
Xomie
Xiomec-xo
Comcer Xn
Xio Omix
Xem Xomie
Coxmie emo
Ocixem

Yeah

Antonia, Mi Abuela
Stephanie B.

She left without a word
we miss her

I can't wait until I see her no suffering, pain,

To see her beautiful smile
hear her laugh

I miss her so much. I can't Believe she is far away from me
but I know she is watching

Yesenia
Jennifer G.

She was so young
when something stopped her lungs

Her parents rose,
when they saw blood on her nose,

They got worried
so to the doctor they hurried
The doctor said she was in bad condition
and to save her was their mission

They couldn't save her so she died,
Her parents were sad and everyone cried,
At the funeral I saw her face
She looked so peaceful and full of grace

Ode to My PS 2
Andrew H.

My PS2 is awesome because
it is fun to play the games

I have fun when my cousin comes over to play my PS 2
My PS 2 is awesome because I
have games that are rated T-M I have 47 games

My PS 2 is like a virtual world of mayhem. I can blow up stuff like buildings, people
and cars

Why I Can't Write a Poem
Jacqueline E.

I can't write a poem because my stomach hurts
My pen ran out of ink
I do not have any paper
I am nervous
I cannot think
I do not know what to write about
I am scared
My sister's radio is too loud
The television is on
It is too noisy
My phone is ringing
My Mom is yelling
I cannot hear my thoughts
My cousin is crying
I have to do my chores
Someone is at the door
I have to help my mom

I cannot rhyme
I cannot concentrate
I have to make my bed
I am being bothered
I have to put my pajamas on
I have to wash my face and brush my hair
I have to brush my teeth
My Sister is calling my name
I have to take a shower
I forgot my poetry tools
My hand hurts
I have to wash dishes
I have to feed my cousin
I have to eat dinner
I have to clean off the table
My head hurts
I am not good at writing poems
I have homework to do
I have to study for a test
I have piano lessons
I cannot find my glasses
My throat is dry I need water
It is time to go to sleep
I can no longer think
I guess I will have to try and write my poem tomorrow
If I can…

Love is Stupid
Stephanie Z.

When I see the guy I love
I stare at him for a long time

        The first time I saw him
    I fell in love

        But I heard he liked my friend
I felt really sad
I cried cause she lied to me

She said she didn't like him
but she lied, I'll never forgive her

Cause she has the guy I love

Alone
Karen G.

I'm all alone
I'm alone in my room in
my house
I'm always alone

sometimes it's good to be
alone
sometimes it is not
sometimes it is so boring to
be alone
I don't like being alone

Bear
Ivan R.

Fluffy and Hairy
so cute the best dog
he is like little baby
the way he whines and cries,

White and black fur
Dumb and glum
Fast as a cheetah
They treat him like a baby.

The way they carry him,
Kiss him on he head
and let him sleep with
them all the time

When Christmas Morning Comes
Jacqueline G.

I feel so happy

When I come downstairs
It's a joyous time!

When it's time to open presents
the youngest child goes first

When I get a present I really want
I jump for joy!

It's time for giving and loving each other, so
Everyone should give to the poor.

When Christmas morning comes
You know God is with you!

Poetry-My Doggy
Zbigniew B.

In the living room,
underneath the ceiling
there is something
that I can see

I can see the bone
my doggy chewed on
in my mind
I can see the picture

in my special hiding place
I cried so much
he smelled
like he just got washed

he looked so white
with long ears
he was beautiful and small
with a big heart

I can see
playing ball with him
now you are dead
and I miss you so much

Winter
Manuel R.

Winter is great
winter is cold
when I see snow

I am happy.

When the snow falls it looks
wonderful and when it blows
on my face it feels
great

Winter comes and
just like every year and when It comes I am
always going to be happy

The Cat
Crystal R.

the cat is small
he's funny and sweet
sometimes during the day
he likes to sleep

His fur is grey
with black stripes
he's very playful and he
loves to hunt bugs

He loves to bite things
and tries to climb the tree
and sometimes he likes
to chase bees

When he's bored
he sleeps almost all
day but when he wakes up
its time to play

Aunt Lupe
Ivan R.

in the dark in my room
I see shadows, I
see faces, can't think
right, too hard to forget

Still see her smile in
her poem still all
stuff
mirror still has her face.

Alvaro Z.

as midnight comes on
a full moon under
the covers I hide there is
no one near me no
midnight comes you
hear howls in the
wind the moon shining
so bright it does not let me
sleep as
midnight comes scared
as I may be I know
I have to sleep
peacefully

John Hay
Community Academy
Aaron Plasek, Poet in Residence
Principal: Beryl D. Guy
Program Coordinator: Assistant Principal Patricia Smith
Teachers: Mr. Cobb, 6th; Ms. Henderson-Johnson, 4th;
Mr. Threewitt, 6th

Should I
Quinton H.

Knowing I want to
Is it the right thing to do?

What will happen if something goes wrong
I have been waiting to do it for so long.

NO! I shouldn't, I can't I won't
But what will happen if I don't

I may lose a friend forever.
It will not happen never.

I shall face my fears no matter
how scared I may be
Okay here I go, running as
fast as I can.

My decision
Marques H.

Today's decision is a big decision whether
I want to go to a wedding or a funeral. Both
of them are serious and real, but when I
try to pick one I get the chills. So I got
to vote and which ever one lose I'm just going
to have to write them a note. So I picked
the funeral because it's the last time I'm
going to see them.

Poem
Terron W.

I saw the frozen
river beneath the
ice.

They were tears frozen
with fear.

With all the

commotion I
heard a sound.

It was a whale
singing under the water's mound.

But even through
that I fell asleep
on the snowy ground.

Denise

I wake up I feel sad do I have to
go no! I will not go I'm sleepy I'm tired you go
you go bye bye leave I'm sleepy
don't come back until you're twenty then
I will be awake awake to hear to hear
you talk about your marriage to the prince.

Jasmine

The night snuck up on me.

**In School
Jermaine C.**

School is the place to learn things
that are important and not so easy
to work with it. the teacher
talks all day long, morning to
afternoon all, day long. When the
bell rings loud and clear to
go home.

**The Thinker
James P.**

There was a young fellow
who thought very little, but
thought it a lot. Then at Long
last he knew what he wanted
to do, but before he could
start, he forgot.

Timothy B.

Today I saw a car driving up the road
I heard the engine roar like a lion's
roar it bumps up and down like a grasshopper
jumping and turned a down right and
what a sight only it was a bore.

Big Sis
Denise B.

She sits in a chair but
feels like talking. She is confused.
This was about waiting for a chance
to say She loves her sister.
Nothings a blur. So simple, so obvious.
but what to say is confusion.
open your eyes and say those words
I love you little sister and it's not
a blur. A blur is opened not yet closed.
but still the sorrows hurt but the end
is here

Ramesha

We're born not knowing anything
and as we live we learn. We're taught
things don't come easy and what we
want we earn.

But lessons were taught in school
like share say please be nice is
all about the golden rule

We cannot foretell the future
though many wish they could we
also can't change the past if
so many would.

Try not to act in anger or vent
while your upset Things we say or
do we may later regret

Jermaine C.

the time is coming for winter
to be over and summer comes
and the hot dry wind blowing
past you and it starts to
rain like a giant crying
over us

Mother
Cherrell A.

The telephone is ringing
Is that my mother on the phone?
The telephone is ringing
That's my mother on the phone
The telephone is screaming

won't she leave me alone?
The telephone is ringing
Is that my mother on the phone?
Every women in my family
becomes my mother in the end.
Every women in my family that's around
me becomes my mother in the end.
I hear my mother calling me
But I don't need her as a friend.
Oh mother I love you please listen
and don't ignore me.
Oh mother please have mercy
let your daughter be.
I'm almost a teenager.
Oh mother let your daughter be free
but don't ignore me.

Poem
Antonio B.

You will look dumb for talking to a
pencil that don't talk back and it's
Just like you're talking to yourself.

Pencil
Quinton H.

The pencil wears green clothing, and
pink shoes with gold socks covering
them.
It stands taller than some at
a height of 7".
It writes a letter to who ever
it wants and always makes mistakes.
Although it writes it never says a word.
it is so quiet.
Standing on its head with its hair
at a point.
And in about a week it is gone
or lost or maybe on an adventure.

Dimitri M.

The ISAT makes me feel mad.

All the things I know will come from my
Head

It's not easy as cutting wood

I wish I could avoid it.

Ohh! I wish I could.

Practice, Practice, practice it's all
about practice now.

If it wasn't so long I wouldn't
have this frown.

Valentine Date, excerpt
Cherrell A.

He changed his clothes ten
times before he took her on a date.

He was in a cold sweat, he panicked
and it made him late.

he tried to call her up and explain
but it wasn't easy he had to strain.

he got the heebie jeebies before he
went reaching for the phone
he dialed the number ten times before
he chickened out and decided she was
not at home.

Road
Lauren R.

A dark road that keeps going on
Never know when it'll end
But one thing. I keep wondering
When will I ever know
Not able to read its mind
Only having one expression
at all times. I ask, why
and how can this be?
Thinking everything is perfect
Letting people walk and run all
over itself. This is
one of those unique one-of-a-kind
roads. It never twists and turns
just going straight ahead
Not changing for anybody.
Not caring what others think
of itself.

I Saw
Diamond S.

I saw a man
with an extra mouth
On the side of his face.

I saw a women
with one arm
And with five
Children with her
trying to cross the
Street with all of them.

I saw a little
Boy with a real
Clown nose.

I saw my Aunt
go into labor
And saw her
When she was
Having the baby.

I saw my life
Going into a
turn of life.

I saw Life.

Dreams floatin away
Kalin C.

Dreams are like balloons
filled with air they usually
float away as if you don't
care trying to find a dream
but as they fad away there's
less and less until there's nothing
left in the world for you
and if you don't take
your chance somebody else will

Department Store
Devante B.

This is a story and a poem
about a boy who went to the
Department Store. This boy is
named Nick. Nick was 12
years old the day he woke the
day it was cold. he went to the
store and all he saw was
bricks and stones.

Ray M.

I hate this time of year!
Sat down with my heart filled with fear!
At this time of year!
Teachers make you do extra work

Tied down and forced to do the test.
E I can't eat can't sleep!
Still too nervous to even beep.
T still tied down and forced to do the
Test.

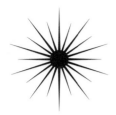

John Hay
Community Academy

Avery R. Young, Poet in Residence
Principal: Beryl D. Guy
Program Coordinator: Assistant Principal Patricia Smith
Teachers: Ms. Anderson, Ms. Cole, Ms. Whiting, 5ʰ

You Dried My tears
Sergio S.

You dried my tears
with your love
of sensible vanilla
skin.

You dried my tears
with your most wonderful
voice I ever heard,
better than the voice
of the beautiful bird.

You dried my tears
With your natural
smell of roses.

Tu Secus Mis Gotas de Agua
Sergio S.

Tu secus mis gotas de agua
con to amor te cuerpo de vanilla

Tu secus mis gotas de agua
con ta vose mas vonita mejor
que un bajaro

Tu secus mis gotas de agua
con perfume de roses natural.

Poem About Oscar Brown Jr.
Sernetra S.

Oscar Brown sing
classic jazz
love songs
slow, soft, deep
like Lake Michigan
bordering tall, wide
building holding people
who dance to "Work Song."

Billie Tyson Jr.
Denzel M.

Because he wouldn't teach
his son
to say NO,
his junior took to crack
like bees take to red shirt
and snowballs.

For Coretta Scott King
Mark C.

skin of sunset
hair of coal
smile of sunshine
eyes of gold

Shadow
Cyera B.

If I was your shadow
I would pursue you
Chase you
Go where you go

Stay where you
jump
run
spin and twirl

Unlike regular shadows
I would be with you
even in darkest
of times

Mr. Crow
Angel L.

because he wouldnt teach
black kids
to read
they didn't learn
Martin Luther King Jr.
helped blacks and whites
come together
and give young black
kids a place
in school

The Ballad Poem
Tyrie W.

If I was a ballad
I would sing u nothin
but my highs and lows.

maybe a little blues
sing with rhythm make
u feel emotion

girl. u are my emotion
I will be the potion
sing u songs of bitter
and sweet somethin
to make u laugh.

u are my energy
not my enemy
wont you be my baby?

if I were a ballad
I would sing you.

Theodore Herzl Elementary
Alison Gruber, Poet in Residence
Principal: Betty A. Green
Teachers: Ms. Adams, 4th; Ms. Gordon, 5th; Ms. Wilson, 3rd

About Me Poem
Bernard N.

        I am a funny kid
I hear the bell in the
morning I see insects
flying birds dying
I feel people
people then feel me
then I become happy
I wish that there was good
I cry when someone dies
I laugh when something's
funny. Don't try to
        act surprised.

Confused
Asia S.

I hear gunshots but there is nobody here.
You see people yelling but no sound comes out.
I hear thunder but the sky is clear.
What's going on? I don't know.
Next time I will not hit the floor.

Earthquake and Jaguar
Edward B.

An earthquake comes
it messes things up
it sounds like a jaguar's roar

It cracks really fast
like it is racing a jaguar
for fame and glory

For the earthquake is mean
it is powerful
like the bark of a jaguar.

It's scary, it's crazy
you don't want to be there
you're going to die hard.

By Myself
Aliyah D.

When I'm by myself
and I close my eyes
I'm a twin, I'm a dimple
in a chin, I'm a room
full of toys, I'm a squeaky
noise, I'm a leaf turning
red, I'm a loaf of brown
bread, I'm whatever I
want and when I open
my eyes what I care
to be is me.

Rain Falls
Antionette J.

When the rain falls down, it meets the ground.
When the wind blows, it makes a swirling sound.
As soon as the sun comes out, it makes
a bright glow. When the sun sets,
it sets from below.

Rain
Dijonnay D.

Rain is as important as
two diamond rings.
It comes from a sense
that smells like tangerines.
When rain falls it meets
someone sweet
When rain comes
tumbling down it makes
a great sound. She sparkles
like diamond rings. He
smells like tangerines.

I Am a Black Child
Kaniyja M.

I am a black child
so, you see, I am a black
child that will succeed.
I am a black child that's
proud of being me,
I am a black child that
you will always see.

No Judges
Quiana M.

No judges, please
I am unique I am black
I am proud, can't you see?
I can be kind or I can be mean
but please don't judge
me. Don't judge me by
the way I walk or the
way I talk just judge
me the way I would,
I sure hope you would.

A Sad Morning
Andrea M.

one morning I was
crying then a cold chill
went up my spine.
I started to think
about the rights and wrongs
then my grandmother died
because I made her cry
but I know one day
I can do better than cry
because things that should
be right are wrong.

All About Black
Ebony M.

Black is beauty.
Black is love. I can reach
the stars above. Black is nice
black in white. I just ate black
rice. Black is black. I got a black
hat that made me soaking wet.
Black is you, it's blacker than
my black shoe.

I'm Hurt
Brittany S.

I'm hurt
I got knocked out
I'm hurt
I got smacked down
I'm hurt
I got punched in the eye
I'm hurt
I got slapped in the face
I'm hurt
I got hit with a desk
I'm hurt
I got put out of school
I'm hurt
I got to say I'm sorry
I'm hurt
Somebody broke my leg
I'm hurt
I got kicked in the face
I'm hurt
That's the end of my poem
I'm hurt

Sadness
Jamilla S.

There is a sad woman
wandering in the park. She
doesn't know what to do
because she is so sad.
And when it rained
she was crying. Oh
sad woman. Oh sad
woman. Where would
she be? Sad woman!

Poem for Rent
Brianna J.

This poem is so bad it's
hard to sell.
This poem is so bad
it starts to smell.
This poem is so bad
it's so good.
This poem is so bad
it could break wood.
This poem is so bad
it scares babies.
This poem is
so bad it would trip a
grown lady.
This poem is
so bad it's all the rage.
This poem is
so bad it's falling

o
f
f

t
h
e

p
a
g
e

Life in Chicago
Lenora F.

Life in Chicago is
bad it makes my head
spin, putting black men
in the state pen. Makes
me wanna stop having
conversations, it's
humiliation. Then we have kids
twelve and thirteen prostitutes
and over nineteen baby daddies
and when they all get put under
D-C-7-5. What now?
They don't
know!

Edward N. Hurley Elementary

Nannette Banks, Poet in Residence
Principal: Ruby L. Coats
Teachers: Mr. Garner, Ms. Thomas, Ms. Wood, 6th

Wind
Sahar A.

I can go wherever I want to
I leave with the flow
I can run fast and slow
I play around
Go up and down
I blow things away
There is not much to say
When the day is done
No more fun
I sleep on the clouds.

No School
Charles S.

I cannot go to school today,
Because I have nothing to say,
But I can go out and play.

Yesterday
Oscar R.

I was so excited
I got good grades,
My parents were proud.
These next grades
I will remember…yesterday

Follow Your Heart
Jocelyn M.

One person can break your heart
saying "you can't do it," …you know you can,
if one person said it… does not mean it is so.
Think of something…you want to be
follow what your heart …tells you to do.

Not Today
Osartein O.

I cannot go to school today,
In my bed I really must stay,
I should just close my eyes and lay,
For hours and hours in my bed,
My mom came in and she said
"Are you feeling better yet?"

I Know
Manuel M.

It doesn't matter what they say
about me…That's what
they think, about me
But I know
what and who I am!

Lies
Roselia M.

Lies, all lies
Are they truth or lies?
People always lie, never the truth
Is it work or nothing or just lies that hurt?
They hurt me and my family also friends
Why lies, why not the truth
I only want the truth not lies

Don't Get Discouraged
Alex B.

If they say you're short
Don't Get Discouraged
If they say you're weird
Don't Get Discouraged
If they say you're not cool
Don't Get Discouraged

Going to College
Avery B.

You go to college, after that you get a job,
even own your own company.
hook line and sinker, an advance
to a better future, you got it on the hook now,
to catch it you must graduate.

Away from Home
David L.

I was born in Colombia,
Colombia is my home
I came on a plane, 3 hours to Miami
With 1 hour to rest…
then 3 more hours from Miami to my new home Chicago.
When I grow up I want to be a Pilot in the Navy.

Don't Give Up
Tracy R.

Don't give up,
Never give up,
Believe in yourself
If you try hard
Anything is possible
Don't give up!

I Love
Jacqueline A.

I love to write
I love to ride bikes
I love to chill, get fresh air.

Keep a-going
Rebecca D.

You can do anything if
You put your all into it…do it.

The Tooth Fairy
Viviana G.

My little Brother woke up, looked under his pillow, nothing was there; he went to my mom crying.
 "Oops," I forgot, I then put the money under his pillow and shouted, "The tooth fairy, the tooth fairy!"
 My brother came running, "Where is the tooth fairy?" "You missed her, but she left you a present!"

The Door
Shoney T.

When I open the door to freedom,
I see a better place
I see better people
a better world
better streets,
better jobs
I see open minds
I see different people.

Another door
Miguel G.

When I open the door I see
cotton falling from the sky
birds soaring and cutting through the air
a ball cutting through the wind
I open the door I see books which take me to another door.

Hurricane Katrina
Stephanie N.

Times when nobody can wake up with joy
Times when people need homes
Times when children get sick
Times when people need plenty of food
Treacherous floods that destroy many lives
Children need help with love
Please Katrina don't hurt our world…

The Door
Jesus G.

When I open the door I see
water coming out of peoples' eyes.
When I open the door I see
nothing but pure darkness.

Her Eyes
José Z.

When I opened the door
I felt a soft floor,
it was the ocean shore
I looked into her eyes
she froze me into really thick ice.

Where I'm From
Terriana N.

I am from hot combs
and sweet potato pies.
I am from broke elevators
and gangster rats and roaches
I am from broke teenagers
also known as Edwina and Deaque.
From *that's my baby daddy* and
no I ain't .
From *I brought you into this world*
and I can take you out.
From *I think I'm this and'*
I think I'm that
with attitude.

Love is a Curse and a Gift
Karen M.

Love should give you a kiss when you hurt
and love should hug you when you're sad.
Love should give a gift every week to
know he or she cares.
Love should buy what you need.
Love should protect you from sadness
and love should be your family or a friend.

Rock Music Should
Farzana O.

ride a skateboard down a steep hill
taking dares that will knock your socks off
Rock should dress like a punk rocker
with silver chains, a spiky necklace
black Converse
and spiky maroon and black hair
Rock should eat sub sandwiches
and watch music videos all day long
Rock music should go to loud concerts
and rock n' roll for hours
Rock music should play an electric guitar
and be in a rock band
Rock music should rock your socks
Rock your life,
And Rock your world.

Bull's-Eye
Richard G.

What you see
small and short
but you are wrong with your bull's-eyes
and I am
Superman
in only my own mind
because it's invisible to humans, why
it's like hot sauce dipped eyes,
blind eyes in the sky
unable to see what I can be if I really tried.

Where I'm From
Maya B.

I am from cookies and sweet potato pie
and sharing a room with my brother and sister.
I am from getting down doing the cha cha
and music and dancing.
I am from an imaginary world with books and
peace. I am from watching BET.
I am from athletics and totally fit
and getting in trouble when I stay outside too long.
I am from brown eyes and permed hair and
old family baby pictures my mom shows all her friends.
I am from a heart murmurer and a girl
the color of milk chocolate which is my favorite flavor.
I am from a brother that gets on my nerves.
I am from slavery and the ghetto talking
bay bay kids running around the house.
I am from people back then who didn't get treated
right back then by other races.
I am my own past, present and future.

Villanelle
Elisha M.

Do not ask about what it contains
The story is too long
There's too much pain

Of bloody fights and lost loved ones
Abuse, obsessions, hit and runs
Do not ask about what it contains

Full of please don't leave me's
And I have to leave you hon'
There's too much pain

Too much of false I love yous
Or baby our love is true
Do not ask about what it contains

Of secrets, deceptions, lies and rumors
Growing like weeds, fatal like a tumor
There's too much pain

All of this inside of me
Forget the mask the makeup and see
Do not ask about what it contains
There's too much pain

Maurice M.

One night I woke up
to find myself in a storm.
A very scary storm.

Windstorm
Cecilia R.

The windstorm
comes like
the tiger's
fast feet.

The windstorm
can come
any time
when it's
time for the cold.

Dayanara R.

I want you to be here.
Please come, please.
I wait for you an hour
but you won't be here.

I hear your car
I went outside.

You were here.
I was very happy.
Thank you for coming
to me.

The Snow
Deshawn B.

I saw a
white wolf
in the snow.

He looked like
he was bored.
He was looking up
at the sky.

He looked like
he was cold.
He looked like
he was crying.

Sun
Jocelyne H.

Sun is bright
as a dog's fur.

When a dog walks
the sun stays still.

When the dog goes to sleep
the sun goes down
and shadows come up.

Rain
Glarien S.

The rain feels like a little
dog's nose.
The rain travels
far under and
never stops. It comes
from a high cloud
and goes on and on.

Judith B.

The snow is like a puppy.
because snow
falls everywhere
and the puppy jumps
everywhere just like snow.
And when you touch the puppy
it is soft just like snow.

Jordan S.

I wonder who is
dancing with that silly dog
near the Taco Bell?

Life is For
Group Poem
Ms. Murtaugh's Class

Life is about love.
She is talking to him and the other man is talking to someone else.
She looks like she likes him and he does too.

Life is for families, is for eating good food.
Life is about singing. Life is for having a good time.

Life is for animals to live and to eat, to have green
bright trees and leaves.

Life is about not pretty on the outside but on the inside.
Life is like a couch, I want all people to have something to sit on.

Life is about a red, orange crab feeling lonely, wondering
If he should go to Belize.

Life is about sky.
Every time it snows you know you have lived another day.

Life is for standing still and being patient and quiet.

A woman is slicing lemons. She has a lot of lemons
because life is for lemons. Life is for pie.

Life is about singing to an audience and expressing
your feelings.

Life is for going into space.
Life is for acrobats, also tricks and danger.
Life is for getting in a crash.
Life is about courage and hopefulness.

Life is so blue, nothing else to do.
Life is about time, about watches, about sixty seconds.

Life is for flowers, for freedom, life is redish and pinkish.
Life is about a pretty turtle in the green grass.

Life is for flying and for being free, for beautiful things.

Life is about pink, confusion and weirdness
about green and in the ground, about yucky and fresh.
Life is about how things are.
Life is for understanding.

Charles Kozminski
Community Academy

Pam Osbey, Poet in Residence
Principal: Lionel Sr. Bordelon
Program Coordinator: Charles Washington
Teachers: Ms. Anderson, 5th; Ms. Englund, 7th; Ms. Taylor, 1st

Poetry Is
Group Poem
Ms. Anderson's Class

Unknown…
The poet's feelings.
Poetry to me is a snow cone in 105 degrees.
Spoken word with Kim Field's, that's what poetry is.
Poetry is like a butterfly bursting out the world.
Poetry is like relaxing on a summer day.
Poetry is like sadness or darkness.

Poemetry is like.
Poemetry is like a soul device.
Poemetry is a good sound method.
Poemetry is deep down in my heart.
Poemetry is like a hammer with no
Nails…hammering away.

Music…
Poetry is like music sounds
With emptiness closing down.
Poetry is like R and B, oooh
You and me!
Poetry is a writing process that makes
You happy.

Happiness is all up in the air.
Poetry is a part of people.
Life makes a big circle around the moon
That you can see in your dream.
You sleep and sleep well.

Sounds and Nouns
Poetry is like you can reach
Up to the beautiful sky.
And bring down the nouns and
Like a touch of a God and fell

off a nail.

How We Feel About Poetry
Poetry is like a soft pillow.
When you have a good time with your mom.
Poetry is like a spring day.
Poetry is like a good nice strawberry ice cream
Sundae.

Poetry is a person.
It speaks to me when I'm alone.
Poetry makes me want to shout, without a doubt.
It makes me feel like I'm worth 1,000,000 bucks.

Poetry makes me feel great like I just
Won a million dollars.
Poetry is like a dream cone.
True poetry is like an ice cream sundae.
Poetry is like love.

Poetry Is
Terek M., Jaynell S., Matthew H., Quintin T., and Robert H.

Writing a poem in a group is hard.
Poetry is ridiculous.
Everyone has something to say, in their
own way.
Poetry is stupid.
And everyone can't agree, they feel like they
need to do their own thing.
Poetry is dumb.
Poetry is tiring.
Poetry can tell about just about anything, many things…
Poetry is horrible.
Poetry is ugly.
Poetry expresses your feelings.
Poetry is hateful.
Poetry is threatening.
Can't you feel me?
You know what I mean.

How Colors Make Us Feel
Tyrice L., Lamarr B., Derrick W., Andrea D., Antionette H., Jasmine C., Shaniqua B., L.aShay M., and Erica H.

Color is currency meaning money.
Color is money because that's all I think of.
My favorite color is white because
I smile and brighten up the night.
Color is Green cause money is my

Favorite thing.
I picked the color Red because my
Life is in between.
The color Red is not dark or light.
My life is like the color Pink.
It is a kind of light color and it makes
Me feel bright because I am thankful.

How makes us feel…
White= happiness, rich.
Yellow = joyful
Red= reminds me of fire
Green= my life is in between
Blue= the color of the water it just swifts pass you
Pink= makes us feel pretty
Red= makes us feel special
Blue= makes us feel bright
Orange= makes us feel like a pumpkin
Black= makes us feel.
Yellow= makes us shine
Gray= makes us feel boring
Purple= makes us feel happy
White= makes us feel plain
Brown= makes us feel stupid
Beige= makes us feel like we are going to work

All the colors make us feel like the rainbow.

Poetry Is
Group Poem
Ms. Taylor's Class

Poetry is fun.
Poetry is a sun.
Poetry is a bun.
Poetry can run.
Poetry is a cat.
Poetry is a dog.
I like poetry because I watch
Poetry on T.V.
I like poetry it is like ice cream.
It's like a baby.

Poetry is my favorite.
Poetry is the best, like me.
Poetry is a butterfly.
Poetry is a kind of a friend.
Poetry is like a best friend.
Poetry is me.
Poetry is my Mom and Dad.
Poetry is a friend just like me.
Poetry is a star.

I like my poetry because it's a sun.
Poetry is a book.
I like my poetry because it's a look.
Poetry is beautiful.
Poetry is good.
Poetry never lets me down.

Poetry is my home.
I love the poetry.
Poetry is a house.
Poetry is my friend, Tony.
I like poetry, it's like a moon on fire.
Poetry is the house.
Poetry is good for you.
Can you find poetry?
Do you like?

Poetry is like a pillow
that takes me to heaven.
And takes me to my father, God
To send me to his angels.
He gives me toys.
And gold and a cat and a dog
and games and TV shows and
books and sends me to a baby.
Poetry is me.
Poetry is stars
and a sun
and poetry is science
and a tree and then it
snows.

Poetry is like a game.
Poetry is a flag.
Poetry is a girl.
Poetry is me.
Poetry is my favorite thing.
Poetry is a moon rise.
Some poems are scary.
Poetry makes people laugh.
Poetry is fun like games.
Poetry is like water blowing.
I like poetry because it is like TV.

Poetry is like a place.
Poetry is like a channel on my TV.
Poetry is beautiful.
Poetry are like babies.
Poetry is dad.
Poetry is Timmy and Me.
Poetry is a body.
Poetry is delicious.

Poetry is a big boat
In water and the sea.
But I do not like the water
And the rain.
I am happy today
and about me!

Spring Time
Don H.

I'm running in the water.
I'm biking for hours.
I'm playing basketball or football
For hours until I fall out.
I'm playing around all day.
Where am I?
I'm in Spring Time.

Spring
Xaki E.

I see sunshine in the spring.
I see ladybugs in the spring.
Spring is great.
I see flowers in the spring
I see sunshine in the spring.
I see butterflies in the spring.
I see roses in the spring.
I see black ants in the spring.
I see birds in the spring.

Words
Derrick W.

Words
Some are verbs
Who made up words?
Make me want to kick the curb!
Or use my words
I don't like poems
It makes me waste my words

I Wish
Jamerah H.

I wish I had lots and lots of money.
I wish for a bike and I wish for bubblegum.
I wish for a wizard and I wish for a cat.
I wish for a kitten.

A Land Of
Deandre M.

A land of love and zombies.
A land of love and queens.
A land of love and aliens.
A land of love and chocolate.
A land of love and flying beds.
A land of love and crayons.
A land of love and candy.

Song of the Eyes
Khaleelah J.

I sing these songs of the eyes.
The eyes see everything!
Nothing can get pass the eyes.
Eyes are everywhere, here and there.
You can't out run the eyes of mine or the blind.
Eyes come in different size and color.
Brown, black, green or blue!
The eyes can see you.

Spinning
Tierra J.

The world is spinning.
Time is going.
I don't have time to live my life.
Why is the world going so fast?
I just want time to slow down.
Sometimes I want to be a kid for life.
But I know I have to be an adult.
I will still be a kid stuck in an adult's body.
I just want time to slow down
because the world is spinning.

Time In Life
Sara K.

Not enough hours, minutes or even
Seconds to do things in life.
Not enough time to see new things in life.
I wish I could see my Great Grandchildren.
How they look.
How they act.
Nothing stays the same in life.
There's always changes around.
I wish I could see the world the way it is now.
But that can't happen because of not
Enough time in life.
(To: My Great Grandmother, on my
Mom's side)

Summer Is Fun
Dionesha B.

I like the Spring, it is very fun.
The sun gives flowers.
The rose are so pretty flowers.
At summer I see butterflies.
At summer I see bees.
At summer I see birds.
At summer I like to bike.
I like the rain and snow.

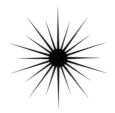

Richard Henry
Lee Elementary

Nannette Banks, Poet in Residence
Principal: Marjorie A. Joy
Program Coordinator: Erica Feldman
Teachers: Ms. Bourret, Ms. Catinella, Ms. Jamen, 7th

Thinking
Monica H.

So many things in my head worrying, panicking, I just can't go to bed,
tossing and turning the pillow around feeling the cool side on my head,
thinking about the day my problems, my fears, thinking about the solutions
or a way to get out of them, thinking about tomorrow how it's going to be.

Rising Eye
Damian C.

I twist and turn not closing my eyes,
I hear my mom and dad snoring out loud,
I hear the alarm clock as it makes its move,
I look out the window still no sun, I start to think
it's an eclipse but…one minute later, I see…the rising eye

Volleyball
Karen L.

I feel alone, when I'm thrown
I fear, when I get to the opposite team,
they will serve me, I don't want to go.

Hip Hop
Emaris

The flow drops down like rain
Beat after beat, rhythm after rhythm
It can't stop flowin' like a river of words
Poetry, stanzas, stories, strong, hardship,
disappointment, excitement, people talk about sex and games,
it's not all about that, It's about trueness and what's fair in life.

If Words
Roberto H.

If words were a bull take it by the horns control it, change its direction, deal with it
If words were a giant hole I would manage a way to get across with confidence
in the end words can be anything good or bad…No matter what you can always
overcome it.

The Power
Daniel V.

The power of the words helps you rhyme and sing,
they tell a lot of stuff and they say a lot of things.
They say I'm not going to make it, and they ask
why do I try; then I said because when I succeed
you are going to see me fly high.

A New Year
Melissa C.

I am laying here…I see a brand new year
what the future holds…I'll never know
whatever happens…I will not sink down low
whatever I do, I won't feel blue. ..I see a new me
loyal and true, all for the new.

Taking Back
Eduardo G.

I wish I could take it all back, get in a time machine;
go all the way back, because now I regret what I said to my best friend.

Me
Rebecca B.

Reasonable
Exciting
Beautiful
Encouraging
Caring
Cute
A lot of attitude

Rain
Gustavo P.

Life is like…rain
It comes down light or hard on you
you have to accept the way the rain pours on you.

Words Don't Hurt
Traveris B.

I can make it even if I was held down, even if someone makes me feel down
I won't take it, words are just like birds harmless, soft, like rice, I can eat them, spit
them back
 let them take the slap.

Happiness and Love
Amalie C.

Do you see the people walking down the street? They look at each other and give a smile they admire it for a while
They're walking and holding hands…he hears the music and asks her to dance in the street, he whispers "I'm yours to keep when I die,
 we may be apart, but you'll always be in my heart."

Gun Violence
Canaan E.

Gun Violence I see it everyday, once it stops I'll say hooray
You see peoples' tears; you hear them cry everyday you hear
a bang and a big loud scream, when gun violence stops I'll say hooray!

The Sun
Gabriela S.

Have you ever seen the sun in the sky?
Making me believe in what I see, planting the seed of my dreams,
I see the seed sprouting and spreading dreams, let the sun stay up forever to let my dreams grow free.

I Am
Vincent M.

Victorious
 In everything that I do
Never giving up
Creating a stronger me
Energetic and determined
Not stopped or discouraged
Tough enough to handle my school work

Quick Mind
Ramiro M.

My mind is spinning at the speed of light
It's getting faster as time goes on
I thought today was Saturday, it's Wednesday
I must slow my mind down.

Puzzle
Destiny R.

They take me and direct me into places; I don't want to be,
I push myself over to the place I want to be, they can see
I am not only a puzzle, I am an achiever.

Push it Aside
Natalia C.

People say words that they think will bring us down; they don't understand they are helping us to shine,
even though it hurts, push it aside, nobody can tell us what we are capable of.

Cocoon
Jesus P.

Sitting under the moon, waiting to be free, providing shelter, staying still on a tree, paying no fee, next to my family,
no matter what, I'll stay happy, I am a cocoon.

Cool Blue
Michael P.

I look at the sky, I want to fly
I'm going to the air force, everyone will hear my voice
some say that the sea is their life, the sky is my way
flying in the cool blue

Group Poem
Ms. Jamen 's class

The train came through the rain, like it was finding its trace
This misbehaving action gave me a strange reaction while I was eating my corn the rest of the track was torn
He did not seem to care that there was a tear; an actor was there to fix it with care
They still had to pay the train fare.

Group Poem
Ms. Bourret's class

The ocean's sunset makes the water look like an iron coin with tracks
on the tracks there was a crane where the white coat hangs,
they were playing a nice tone as near to a tear as time goes on we play the song,
the tone of the ocean sounds like rain there's nothing but pain in the song we hear
the reaction is heart breaking, as water crashes into the rocks the song will never stop
the melody of the tune makes the flowers bloom as the trio plays the riot will come,
deep as the sea I will find my answer key, the nation will race near this nice tone
we will race to the rice as the food perishes. Now this is deep and we will keep it as a treasure under the sea.

Group Poem
Ms. Catinella's class

I had a reaction when I saw the overgrown corn field
while on the race track that was not neat
It caused a riot when they saw Erica on the train
when the iron struck, it caused pain
and it started to rain near the train
and there was a tear on the train, then they hit a tire on the track,
she was in a trance she had to focus
until the tunnel she did not notice
while headed to the ocean.

Jacques Marquette School

Naima Dawson, Poet in Residence
Principal: Paul O'Toole
Teachers: Ms. Bryar, Ms. George, Ms. Schwarz, 6th

My Life
Kecheka M.

My life
I feel like a burning tree
A tree that is burning into pieces
piece by piece I'm dieing into ashes
when it is over they take my ashes
and drop them into the ocean and cried

My Thoughts Are
Jacqueline B.

My Thoughts Are...
in outer space
playing soccer
on the stars
in front of my face

To a Special Person
Antriana M.

A special Person is like a gift to me
It is like a person that gives me everything
It is like a guardian angel
Or like a very giving person
Or a person that cares
Or a person that loves me

The Limited Too!
Tiffany Z.

The Limited Too is the place
where all the girls go shopping.
Clothes, shoes, music, jewelry, accessories,
mothers with daughters shopping.
Pink, purple, green and beautiful walls,
fitting rooms, workers and fun for girls.
After all it is a girl's world!

The Space Out Back
Rudy P.

Old rundown, and wild animals all there
They are all there

Dead grass, porch with chipped paint
Rickety like it is going to fall.

Secured by fences and a garage
like it is trapped.

To This Girl I Once Was In Love With
David G.

I've known this girl for a long time
So this is how I say it from her heart to mind.
Let me express my love to this girl.
When I'm without this girl I am no longer someone.
I was in love with this girl for a few years.
One day you're in the next you're out.
I won't move ahead I won't!
I won't. Not without her.
I have to move on.
No! Not without her.

Ellen Mitchell
Elementary School

Erica Kholodovsky, Poet in Residence
Principal: Kathleen M. Bowman
Program Coordinator: Gin Kilgore
Teachers: Mrs. Deutsch, 8th; Mr. Palos, 5th; Mrs. Wipf, 7th

March - the Cold-Hearted Bully
Alexander G.

You're Strong
You're Fierce
A cold-hearted man
You fight
You defend
You blow like a storm
You scream
You yell
But March, you are fair!
Part lion
Part cat
Now spring's in the air.

Nighttime
Cody M.

The houses are haunted
By what I don't know
I hear a strange noise
And down the stairs
I flow

After running down the stairs
I turn the corner
Cross the hall
Looking at the fireplace...
Now I see them all.

INDIANS

They're dancing in the light of fire
This strange light aglow
Brings me higher
and higher
and higher.

Lego Collector
Marco M.

I checked the mailbox after school...

Oh no!

I still need the Star Wars lego collection
Searching through the catalog
Like a mouse

I have to
have to
have them.

Though I'll have to wait
'till January,
At least I have time to collect
the money.

RiZe
Christopher P.

Yes I'm on the RiZe
You cannot stop
me.
At the prime of my game
You cannot stop
me.

Think you're number one?
I'm taking your spot...

Yes, war,
I'm right up at the
front line.
I'm doing what I can
So don't try to
confront.

Time to take a break
for lunchtime.

A Bloody Poem
Diana M.

Evil, as cold as the wind
It frightens me
I run away

Bats everywhere
Evil...

Scary, creepy, deadly...

Luckily I got away

Nightmares
Stephanie B.

Have you ever dreamt
something so bad
A nightmare, a dream
Of Jason, Freddy, Chuckie
Or of monsters?

I've had a nightmare

At night the clock ticks
and the wolves howl...

A Colorful Poem
Marco M.

He sits in his
colorful room,
thinking.

More colorful ideas
Creations to put on paper
Many ideas
Many projects

He uses his
IMAGINATION
to create something new.

He wins medals
Many for creativity.
His creations relate to freedom
To the statue of liberty.

Untitled
Nick D.

In my yard
I have talking grass
And deaf flowers.
The grass always talks,
Never knowing
the flowers can't hear.
All day long talking
Not knowing.
I sleep thinking of

talking flowers
and deaf grass.

Thirteen Ways of Looking at a Leaf
Stephanie G.

1.   Aggravating (having to pick them up), useless and crummy.
2.   Inspiring—makes you do so many things.
3.   Beautiful—have many different shapes and colors and crunchy sounds.
4.   Fun, fun to make a pile and jump on them.
5.   Scatter all around without caring about life or its surroundings.
6.   Freedom of going anywhere without having to come back.
7.   Delicate, like a baby, soft as a baby's skin.
8.   Dry as sand in the desert.
9.   Flat as a table.
10.   Rough as rock.
11.   Light as a feather.
12.   Ugly and shapeless.
13.   Full of shape and color.

A Poem to Water
David O.

Oh water
you bathe me
you rinse off the germs
you wash the dishes
so I can eat again
you rinse my clothes
when I do laundry
I watch you splash
against the ocean rocks
I can swim in you
I take a glass cup
and drink the water in you.
I wonder, then I say
you are refreshing.

Guatemala
Romario R.

Oh! Guatemala
how yellow and hot
you make me glow at
the time of sunset.
I love you so
much
I would never
leave
you.
Oh! Guatemala
I love you so much

and always dream
of you.
Your mountains
so cold,
so shivering,
so icy.
Your sun so hot,
and burning my
eyes like pieces
of ice.
Oh! Guatemala
I here
right now
write this poem
to show my love
for you.

Ode to the Chocolate
Daisy A.

You, chocolate
you are so milky
once I put you
in my mouth.
You are so
sweet.
Your tastiness
just makes me want more.
You are the only
one I love
so tasty, smooth.
I just want the
Niagara Falls
with chocolate fishes.
Little pieces of
chocolate
you give me cavities
but no matter what sorts of stuff
you give me
nothing is going to make me
stop loving you.

New Skateboard
Stephanie B.

Come play

my skateboard is
new
do you like it
I do
let's go to the park

I think it's
time to go
we've been playing
all day
it's getting dark
we should go
home
come back tomorrow
and bring a friend
so he can play
with my new skateboard
too.

Shadow
Abraham V.

Darkness that lags behind you.
Always by your side.
Blending in the night with all the mischief.
Mimicking.
Also amusing, making different figures with them.
Harmless to people but
there and then there
always by you.

Night Time
Cody M.

The houses are haunted
by what I don't know.
I hear strange noises
and down the stairs I flow.
I run down the stairs
turn the corner across the hall.
I look to the fireplace
and see them all.
Indians dancing
in the light of the fire.
I see a strange light
and I start to rise higher.

Night Sky
Marco M.

Kids are sleeping comfortably
and are sleeping with the angels.
Grown ups are half awake and half asleep,
thinking of schedules
and burglars.
People in offices are still
trying to work
and are drinking coffee.

People are too alert
to go to sleep
and are scared.
Kids wake up with energy
and run to the kitchen
expecting breakfast
on the table but there isn't.
Grown ups now are sleeping
without energy.
What are children going to do
Without their grown ups?
They will be late for school.
The best thing is to stay with your parents
and make their breakfast and
give them a surprise.

Ode to my Toy
Melanie H.

Especially to my trollz doll
the way her hair waves
on the wind
the color of her hair
matches
the light of the sun
it reminds me of when I wake up in the morning
or
when I have a bad hair day
The way her eye
sparkles
The way she
smiles it makes me so happy
for the rest of the day.
When I am alone and bored
I play and talk to her
at the same time.

Bernhard Moos
Elementary School
Josh Kotin, Poet in Residence
Principal: Marilyn Leboy
Program Coordinator: Gloria Roth
Teachers: Ms. Becker, Ms. Morales, Ms. Santiago, 3rd

Homework
Jonathan R.

My work has been done
to experience the city.
The big city sits in
land. Far away from Chicago
sits Texas. To day
dream far away in a
land of big. Bigger than an
ocean. My eyes fold to
see a surprise so big.
I start to think I own
that place. I feel like I've
even been there.

Jonathan R.

The blue sky
upon a sun
moon
in its darkness
lightens
and it shines
upon people
and stars so glad and
so sad it
is a beautiful
sky for us.

Jonathan R.

The black shovel
    glazed in the
        sky
    watery in the
        dirt
    so much depends
on a beautiful world
    sparkles in the
    sun
    as shiny as
    a crystal.

Jahzae W.

Go to sleep little baby while the moon
is still shining and the lights click off
by the moonlight, by the shining
moon, little baby under the moonlight
in your cradle as the moonlight
shines on you.

Jennifer S.

Go to sleep
Little Baby
while I am
here to
see you
you must
dream so
beautiful
that when
you grow
you will
tell me
about your
dream.

My Friends
Jennifer S.

I went walking in the woods
I saw a monster in my mouth.

I was scared in my name.
I threw the ball into a book.

You can be a floor in your mind.
You can get a Kleenex in October.

I saw a tree in the windows.
I saw my friend in the tree.

Kittens
Araceli R.

The kittens are beautiful like
the water, pure like their mother.
They are not bigger than a
house or even little like a mouse.
They all drink milk but
don't think so much as
the people do. The people think
that they are going to attack them

but nonsense, they don't know
that they are cute just
like everyone.

Stars
Michelle P.

1
Some stars are so far away
that they look like a picture.

2
One day I saw a beautiful
cat in the sky with the
stars.

3
But then it went away
and there was a crystal.

4
And then it was night and
I saw a beautiful duck.

5
It was so shiny and
bright.

Geovanni A.

I
A blue jay is blue as the sky. And beautiful as a flower.

II
But I have only seen a baby blue jay.

III
I have only seen it once.

IV
It's a beautiful singer. It sings as beautifully as a person singer.

Four Ways of Tasting a Lemon
Abdiel G.

I
I lay in the Path of the Lemon
tasting yellow sour circle

II
The lemon is so sweet I can
taste the sweet and sour circle

III
The lemon has two lumps that is what
makes it so sour

IV
I lay in the Path, both my eyes
turn. I could taste the sweet
sour circle.

A Robot
Edwin T.

1
If you knock on a robot it will sound like tin.

2
A robot can be a square shape.

3
And he will be at my service.

4
And he will dance like a robot.

Samuel M.

I write of the future,
flying cars, flying people,
flying buildings, flying
everything, everybody
having every super power,
even flying water,
trees, and flying pets and then I
want water I just
get a straw and put it in the water
and drink and the
water is in the
air and we eat
in the air too
and there also
could be flying
clothes, beds, houses.

Florida
Nataly T.

Florida is fun to visit!
It has many things to see.
I wonder if a bee likes
to see Florida? It is
hot. It sounds like fun!
One day I will go

to Florida. And that will
always be my dream.

Jacky C.

I skipped school and sat atop an
ice cream sundae. Having day dreams
as light as cotton candy. This trend
setting girl likes to have fun and once
she starts laughing it is hard
for me to stop. I always blush
easily and I am a personality
as sweet as they come on.

In Mars
Janet F.

In mars there is no air.
If you go to Mars you
cannot come back because
Mars is very far away.
If you go when you
want to come back you
are not going to have
enough gas. But if you put
gas in the rocket then
you can come back. You
can put on an astronaut
suit so you could have
air to breath. You can go
to Mars with an astronaut
suit or on a rocket. In
Mars there are mountains.
There is sand in the
ground. There are rocks
in the ground too. Mars
is a planet.

Antonio A.

I would like to write about
a shark and a dolphin fighting
in the ocean and
they were trying to kill
each other so I had to stop
the battle then more sharks
and dolphins and all other
kinds of sea creatures.
And even if I was keeping on
stopping them they will keep
on fighting. And then I thought
of an idea. I brought their mother

and father and they stopped the
fighting forever.

Alexis A.

I wrote about clouds and monkeys first.
Now I'm going to write about
A dragon, baby dragons, playing with dragons.
I write about schools, homework,
learning, heaven. I write about
stores, family, food, flying in space
and the space was made out of
candy and everybody was eating it
and space was gone.

Auturo S.

When I come to school I see
trees cars faces walking and
pencils running to school.

I see camels I see balloons
flying beds walking I see ducks
swimming I see witches.

I see letters walking. I see the
moon moving. I see elephants. I
see snakes moving. I see stars.

**I Write of Planets
Fortino M.**

The moon is large. Pluto is small. The sun
is hot. But I am a dog. I am always wrong
and strong. I went to camp. I like to eat
stamps. The world is big and pink. The
moon is round like the rings. I like to
eat in the sink and when I want water
I only open the sink and drink.

Fortino M.

1
The money is green like the trees I wish the money
would be pink like the pigs some times it stinks like
my feet.

2
The money grows on the trees where the squirrels
live I wish I could sleep through the trees with those
other animals.

Jane A. Neil Elementary

Danielle Aquiline, Poet in Residence
Principal: Helen Wells
Program Coordinator: Bridget Kinsella
Teachers: Mrs. Collins, 6th; Mrs. Hardy, 7th;
Mrs. Mays, 5th; Mr. Rogers, 4th

John W. and Wayne F.

Why does fire burn?
It is really ice
What does ice freeze?
I made it
What color really is the Devil?
Blue
Why are we living?
We can
How many stars and planets are there in the galaxy?
None
Why does the wind blow?
It can't
Where did we come from?
We are vegetables

Myleena J. and Araina L.

Why is the grass green?
Because it is blue and brown
When was the sky made?
824,000,000 years ago
Do dead people come alive again?
Yes, they can live again
What is dirt?
Old dead and blue people burned up
Why do we sleep?
Because our minds wonder and rest like robots
Are we really alive?
I don't know, pinch yourself and see
I wonder the same sometimes
Why do we shoot people?
Because we are crazy red monkeys
and need life to live

On Top of My Ego
Amber H.

I swam on the ocean
with Moses, after we
were finished we went
over and helped Noah

with his ark.

I was the Queen of Egypt,
I was so thirsty I drank
the Nile and created the
Atlantic Ocean.

I fought Goliath and won,
I was made Queen for
many years.

I conquered the world,
not by fight, but with love
and I caused a huge tornado
to suck up hatred.

There was finally *peace*
at last, peace at last, thank
god almighty we have peace
at last!

Fly High
Antonia C.

I was born in Paradise
I discovered Jupiter and built
the Great Wall of China
I believe in myself

I designed Africa, Egypt and
more. I painted the sky blue,
the clouds are my footprints across
the sky, I fly high

I am Oprah's mom, I gave her
Chicago and she gave me
California, I fly high

I took the sky to the Philippines
I discovered emotions
I take a bath in Niagra Falls
I fly high

I mean… I fly high

Renga
Antonia C., Mylana F., and Kamora O.

Peace means to share
quietness, calm means
settle down.

Peace means quiet,
calm means still.

Peace means
a warm breeze
comforts you.

Peace means sure
enough to say anything.

Peace means music,
calm means hot
showers.

Peace means looking at the
ocean and pretending to be
a creature in the sea.

Renga
Keisha C., Asia L., and Aireka G.

Like a butterfly in the sky
Like fish in the sea
Like a god on earth

Like a man in a grave
Like a star in the sky

Like a girl in a house
Like a child in the sky
Like a monkey in the world

Like a crazy woman gone crazy
Like a beauty gone to beast

Like a tree in the jungle
Like a shoe in a box
Like a child asleep

Like an animal in
The sky.

I Seem/I Am
Matthew D.

People say I can't catch
But I can
People say I can't jump
But I can
My sisters think I don't like them
But they are like my friends
People say I can't pass tryouts for football

But I can
People think I can't jump and catch a baseball
But I can
People say I can't play sports because I have asthma
But I can do anything

I Seem To Be/But Really I Am
Christian H.

I seem to be a house cat,
but really I am a tiger
in the wild.

People say I am an immature
suck-up, but I am really a
tough guy.

Some people say I am lame
but I know I am not.

They say I can't jump,
but actually I can fly.

They say I am stupid,
but I am smart.

People think I talk white,
but I don't.

On Top Of The World
Zahira A.

I am laying deep in an oceano.
I am floating through nubes.
The loon in blanco and the cielos
are frambuesa.

My pelo is liberte and I feel
hermosa on top of the sol.

I felt like a nino who didn't
know what to do, and then I
woke up in the coche very
cansado with a vestido
and a cinta in my pelo and
it was frio and my nose was rojo
and I was laying deep in the
oceano once again.

Black Batman
Jabari T.

If batman were black
He might blend in better with his surroundings.

If batman were black
He wouldn't be captured all the time!

If batman were black
He might be Phatman or Trackman.

If batman were black
This poem wouldn't need to exist

Strange.

One day this will be different,
But until then I can only dream.

My Princess
Akilah W.

I want a fairytale where there are dark
Brown, light brown, light skinned princesses.
Not every princess has to be white and skinny.
They don't have to have long hair.

There are too many fairytales like Sleeping Beauty.

Snow White, I know why she is Snow White.

I am going to make a black princess.
A lot of people will like her.

Outside My Window
Arnell M.

Outside my window I see a bird.
Outside my window I see the bright, nice sun.
Outside my window I see kids having fun.
Outside my window I hear dogs barking.
Outside my window I see almost everything.

Arielhenleyi I.

I imagined that I was a slave.
I imagined being whipped.
I imagined my parents got whipped.
I imagined just because of our skin we could have equal rights.
I imagined pure cotton in my picking bag.
I imagined.
I imagined.
I imagined.

Off the Street Club
Toni Asante Lightfoot, Poet in Residence
Director: Ralph Campagna
Program Coordinator: Arnett Morris

What I Am
Ashley H.

I am 12 years
In the 7th grade
I go to school
Getting ready for

High school
I put on my shoes
I do my hair in a pony tail
put on my "baby phat" coat
I go on the bus
I play with my friends
At school I get A's and b's and c's
On my report card

I am the sound of a bird on the beach
I am a butterfly on a rose
I am in my favorite blue shirt and jeans at OTS club
I am jumping rope and beating up the boys
I am not a gangbanger and I will never sell drugs.
I am not a mushroom or a stalk of broccoli because I hate them
I love me.

Why I Write and Don't Write
Breana M.

I write because I feel the

             Flow.
I don't when I am lazy and watching
             TV
I write to express what I can't say
             Aloud.
I don't write when I feel writing is
             Boring.
I don't write because it reminds me of
             School.
And I don't write when I am well
             Relaxed.
I write when I like the way things
             Taste.
I write when I think of
             Poems.

Who Do I See?
Ciara L.

        Who do I see
               looking at me…

Some girls
       talking about me.
       Who do I see looking
              at another girl like me? Girls getting
                     talked about just
                       like me.

             Who do I see that wants to fight
             me?

Some girls that have beef

            with me.
                  Now I tell you

  who wants to fight me?
run up

       I'll give you stars to look at!

My Tebby Bear
Dominique M.

I loved my Tebby Bear

but I lost my Tebby Bear.

I started to cry

and I got mad at my family.

I said I need a car.

I need a person to drive the car.
Once I got what I needed,

I found my Tebby Bear in a store.
I asked my mommy to buy it back.
She said No!
I cleaned my room.
I took out the trash.
Then my mommy gave me some money.

I still didn't have enough to buy my Tebby Bear .
So I went to work to buy it.
I cleaned the car, yard and my house.
Then I had enough to get my Tebby.
I went to the store to buy back Tebby.
I did not because a little girl wanted it.
I felt sorry for her.

Besides it was time for me to give up my Tebby Bear.

Writing Is Fun
Rolanda S. H.

I write because I want to
           express myself.
  want to impress more people.
            to pay attention
I want to get good grades

When I write I feel
Happy like a flower that is blooming
Silly like a jumping frog
Original like my mother's cake

If I was on the radio I would

Say to pay more attention
To writing than playing games
Because writing will make you
Smart.

My Crush
Shalanda S. H.

My crush is, as pretty as the sunsets
My crush is, as sweet as Mr. Ogelvee
Asking Ms. Parker to marry her.
My crush is, as funny as Martin Lawrence
Saying his funny jokes.
My crush is, as crazy as jumping in a pile
Of falling leaves that fall from the tree
On Halloween.
My crush is, loving as to doves kissing on top
Of a paddle in a pond....

I Lost My Tooth
Shaquera S.

I lost my tooth and this is the truth,
It went for a ride. I wondered where it would hide.
As I was seeking I ate some meat, then
I began to run and heard a bug hum.

I thought to myself where is this mysterious tooth.
It could be in Africa or Japan or a new land.
As I looked I wanted to cook.

I walked down a lane I then took me 1 plane.
Then I wondered did my tooth land
in a clown's hand?
Did he throw it into a new town?
I wonder where it could have gone.

When I Lost My First Tooth
Talonna L.

Drip drop I think I hear a blood drop.

When I lost my tooth
I was happy at first
then I realized that I was getting old.
Then I was trying to clean my mouth
when all of a sudden my tooth fell
down the drain.

I know that it ended up in Hawaii
then a fish swallowed it
through the fish it traveled to South America.
There it was chased it to the lake.

To get my tooth back I'll have to con my mom
into letting me go to South America
So I can get it.
Then I'll get a dollar from the tooth fairy.

My Grandmothers
Tamarra B.

> *My grandmothers are strong…*
>   -Margaret Walker

My grandmother, Dorothy grew up in Chicago,
Got married, and had five kids

My grandmother works in an office
And buys me gifts for every holiday

She's the best Thanksgiving cooker ever!

My mama's mother was a hardworking mother
She was married, and raised six kids

She was as beautiful as a spring tulip,
Standing next to my grandfather in a picture

I want to inherit their good looks, courage,
Cooking skills and most of their love and caring

Dozen of Roses
Tyenisha T.

Well child I'll tell you life for me
aint been no dozen of roses.

Its been chopped down thorns
sticking out but still I keep growing.

I come from a place were we only saw cotton
there wasn't a rose in sight to inspire us.

We had to stand up for each other
and stick together and never fight each other.

Life for me aint been no twelve roses.

Its been planted in different places
and talked about by different races.

Well child I'll tell you life for me
aint been no dozen of roses,
its been chopped down thorns sticking out
but still I keep growing.

You Move Me
Group Poem
**Talonna L., Tyenisha T., Shalonda S.H., Rolanda S. H., Dominique M., Breana
M., Tamarra B., Ciara L., Ashley H., guest poet LaTasha Nevada Diggs, and
poet in residence Toni Asante Lightfoot**

You move me like Doritos on my tongue
like I'm a piece of hair
like Jell-O on a dish
like a car on a street

You move me like a bird in the sky
like a can of worms
like a silly dog on grass
like a 4 year old boy playing with his t-rex doll

You move me like my mom cooking when she's happy
like a writer's pen on a piece of paper
like a snake on the loose finding food
like a dancing river

You move me like a dino trying to eat someone
like waves on the sea
like a clock going clockwise
like a hulahoop

You move me like a setting sun
You move me like a rocking chair
at my daddy's house
You move me like young women
writing their lives out in the Westside
of Chicago.

Louis Pasteur Elementary

Danielle Aquiline, Poet in Residence
Principal: James Gilliat
Program Coordinator: Joann Fulanovich
Teachers: Mr. Anaya, 6th; Mr. Herbeck, 5th; Mrs. Shimkus, 6th

Ode to Mango
Miguel R.

The mango
is juicy as
the ocean.
The mango
is slippery.
The mango
is yellow.
It tastes
good. The
mango is
a fruit.
When you
put hot
sauce it
tastes
spicy.

Ode to White Rice
Maria A.

Rice comes
from water, it
is white like the clouds
in the sky, it is
sometimes salty
I eat
It with
fish with lemon and
salt, it tastes so
good,
rice is like snow
falling from the sky.

Ode to Apples
Jose G.

I murder
the apple
and put
some salt so

it could hurt
and lemon
too so it
gets pain
and the last
on is pepper.

Ego Tripping
Luis G.

I was born in heaven.
I was sent to earth by the blink of my eyes.
I snap my fingers and I have eternal life.
My parents tell me to stop but I say it is an addiction without a cure.
I stomp my feet and the Andes Mountains form.
I stick out my tongue and there is cause everywhere.
I cut myself and the blood that I lose goes to the dead and
When they rise they are my slaves.
So many people hate me so I get mad.
I travel around the world trying to make them like me
But they don't so I just give up trying to be another god.
It is just too hard.

Ego Tripping
Andrea C.

I was born in the deepest ocean
I built the largest mountain
I create thunderstorms when I am sad
I can walk across the sky
I built the largest pyramid in one day
I can become the fiercest animal on the planet
I created the ice age on the hottest day
I designed the little dipper
I created the greatest hero
I gave the moon the power to create waves
I am the queen of the world

Mr. Ego
Ramon P.

I was born in the Alps
I was born to stand all kinds of weather
To never be sick in life
To live eternal life
I give life to weather
I am the creator of the dinosaurs
I am the king of all kings and queens
I am so strong I make Hercules feel like an ant
I am the king of all the universe
I created Pompeii
I created all living things

My eyes are so strong I stared at a desk and it broke
My heart is so hard not even an atomic bomb could destroy it
When I snap my fingers I go wherever I want
I am a boy with the soul of a bull
I am myself and fire

Gloria A.

I was born in the Amazon
I am so perfect
I walked two moons
I crossed two oceans
I am so perfect my questions are answers
My spirit soars like an eagle

I was born to know

Kristian G.

I am thinking of a comic book
of spider man being Mexican
he would live on a ranch
his costume would be red
and green and also white
he would only speak
Spanish and have Spanish
enemies like the Mexican
Shocker or the Green
Snake Goblin and that
would be my comic book

Denise R.

I'm dreaming of a fairytale

Princess is normal
A Princess with wings
A Princess with black hair
A Princess that is any size
Just like you and me

I'm thinking of a fairytale

The end ends in a bad way
That is scary
That is horrifying

I'm thinking of a fairytale

That is different from other fairytales.
Instead of Cinderella dressing in blue and white
She dresses in green and purple.

I'm dreaming of a fairytale that is just normal,
Like life on earth.

I'm Thinking
Elizabeth G.

I am thinking of a fairytale
that is not pretty not
skinny not on a castle
I am thinking weird I'm
thinking different I'm thinking
a place near the forest and
near the waterfall I'm
thinking of the place you've
never been

I Wish
Rocio C.

I wish there would be love in the world instead of anger.
I wish there would be smiles instead of frowns.
I wish there would be light instead of darkness.
I wish there would be friends instead of enemies.
I wish people could be laughing instead of crying.
I wish there would be peace instead of wars.
I wish there would be all of this in the world.
I wish, I always wish, but the love never wins.

Lizzette V.

In the galaxy is a universe,
In the universe is a planet,
In the planet is a continent,
In the continent is a country,
In the country is a state,
In the state is a city,
In the city is a neighborhood,
In the neighborhood is a building,
In the building is a room,
In the room are students writing poems.

For
Marlene T.

For the sun is yellow
For the sky is blue
For everything I know
For the sun is the throne
For the gift I get
For the eleventh birthday
For the stars in the sky
For the daylight

For the moon I see
For what shines in me
For everything I see
For my mom and me
For what I believe
For Christmas Eve
For me
For myself
For my dream

Ester M. and Marlene T.

If a cat can whisper, what can a dog do?
Bark at the cat
If the moon is round what can the sky be?
It would be shaped as a square blue
If a turtle is black, what is a frog?
It would be rainbow colors
If the elephant is long, what is a giraffe?
It would be as long as an elephant
If the sea is simple, what is the ocean?
It would be a wrinkle
If the heart was white, what are your clothes?
They would be the color red
If the earth is triangle, what would my eye be?
It would just have one eye to see

Jose L. and Lizzette V.

Why are people happy?
Because they have no other choice
Could we discover ourselves?
No because we are too busy watching TV
Why do people smile?
Because they are too lazy to frown
Why are elephants fat?
So others can get scared when they make fun of their trunks
Why do stars light?
Because they feel like it
Why is Pluto so far?
Because it is embarrassed of its size

Fidel V. and Maria A.

What is the fattest animal?
The turtle
Where does God come from?
The sky
What color are God's pigeons?
Pink
What is the juiciest fruit?
Pears
How old is love?
15,220,150
Can the sun stop smiling too?
Yes, at night it stop

Ferdinand W. Peck Elementary

Nannette Banks, Poet in Residence
Principal: Okab T. Hassan
Program Coordinator: Marie Clouston
Teachers: Ms. Cirrintano 4th; Ms. Martinez, 6th; Ms. Myers 8th.

Today
Rafael A.

Today is filled with normalness
normal things happen everyday-
everyday in unison, like time will never stop
my day is going over and over in some way
there is playing, working, and the bad people
that has been hurting and killing.

My Mood
Jorge G.

A bullet describes me
It is dangerous ferocious and powerful
locked away from everybody…

Open the door
Francisco L.

I see the mistakes I have made
I see how I must obey
I see that the past will not return

Love
Viviana Z.

When I open the door I see the wonderful sun
Rising through the sky I see love…

New Things
Claudia A.

 When I open my eyes
new things are discovered within
things I thought would never be, discovered or seen
I open my eyes I see the person, I care for
I see the real person inside of them

Keep Going
Yesenia C. Raymond L., Sandy R., Anthony M., and Rodrigo V.

Even if you know you're weak
if you feel like letting go don't give up
on your dream on your future or your life
for success, no matter what happens
whatever the situation keep on going

If
Juan M., Abraham R. , Andres B., Adrien, and Alajandra

If your dreams don't come true
If you don't make the team
If you can't achieve your goals
If you can't solve your problems
If you have bad grades
try hard, work hard and keep going

Hip Hop
Alejandro E.

I teach you how to think, expand your mind
I send you to places that are the truth
These places show struggle, people with no hope
I tell about people who try anything to reach the top
I am hip hop

Who you are
Jonathan R.

I am your reflection
I show no rejection
I am here to talk to you
I show you who you really are
I don't care if you have a fancy car
I am there for you

Pink
Stephanie R.

I appear on your cheeks when you laugh
I am the color of your lips when you smile
I color your face when you are shy

Storm
Karina A.

The wind wooshes around
Rain clattering down the window and on the roof
It whispers woo…wooo…wooo

Rain
Alejandro C.

A rainy day is like
having to eat green peas
my t.v. is shut down
I want to frown

The Panda
Fabiola P., Cynthia G., Cynthia G., and Juliza A.

White fur reminds me of snow
black fur reminds me of a night sky
Morning crawling like a panda
I see the panda with its cubs
crawling in the meadow.

Six
Lorena D.

It was my birthday 2001 the twin towers fell
exactly on my birthday September 11, 2001
I was sad, I did not want that to happen
on my birthday.

Winner
Uriel B.

Uriel has a soccer ball
he plays on a winning team
he kicks and kicks
he always wins.

Storm
Ericka S.

There is a storm in the cloudy night
The wind blows, thunder is in sight
I can't see the night

Thunder Storms
Group Poem
Ms. Cirrintano's Class

Scared of
Thunder I shout
Oh my God I see and hear
Rain so I run to my
Mother

To
Norma M.

To really hot days
To really rainy days
To listening to music
To walking around, eating big macs
To talking to my friends
To summer

By Myself
Sanjuana M.

I close my eyes
I am windy clouds in the sky,
I am a kite flying really high
I am whatever I want to be
and anything I care to be...

Wear the Mask
Nicole Q.

I wear the mask of fear and confusion
not knowing what to do, the fear of violence
people being killed, to many things going on around me.

My Mask
Andres B.

I wear the mask when I take a test
when I am sad
when I have a task
when I don't show my feelings being hurt

The Mask
Jorge G.

I wear the mask to hide my identity
to make sure I am not a hypocrite
and become someone else
I wear the mask to hide the pain and live without it

Snow
Abraham R.

Is sometimes yellow
You can sometimes eat it
It comes from the sky

Helen C. Peirce School of International Studies

James Shea, Poet in Residence
Principal: Paula Rossino
Program Coordinator: Maria Perryman
Teachers: Ms. Foster, Ms. Handschuch, Ms. Ponce de León, 3rd

Javier V.

I saw a person.
I saw a roof.
A ladder.
A slide.
A secret door.
One humungous machine.

A Sestina
Ms. Ponce de León's class: Rona A., Jennifer C., Michelle C., Alex D., Nicole F., Theiry H., Daisy J., Mitzi L., Diestefano L., Paige L., Nancy M., Sherwin M., Elo O., Jasmine R., Daniel R., Dellinger S., Rayan S., Ryan So., Ryan Su., Hieu T., Javier V., and Alfonso P.

I saw the sun.
The bird has a nest.
We need a map.
Let's run
really fast. I can dream
I saw a wave.

There's a big wave.
The sun
shines brightly as a dream.
I saw eggs in the nest.
I run
really fast. We need a map!

If we need a map,
we can just look in the waves.
I like to run.
It's a big sun.
The robin is sleeping in the nest.
I have a dream.

Winter Haiku
Alex D.

The mountain
It was fast
Snowmobile

The Last Leaf of Winter
Dellinger S.

I was on a foggy bridge
icy dead trees with long dull
sticks gave me one more leaf
I saw a shape in the clouds
         The bad and fun place
A little lake is not a lake
in winter. It sometimes is a fun
place. But someone fell in.

Poem
Elo O.

Dog! Dog! Burning
bright in the backyard
of the night. Why do dogs
chase the cats? Dog! Dog! Jumping
tall, I hope you don't fall.

Dear Robin
Jasmine R.

I am going over
to South America.
You can come along.

It will be warmer
over there but
colder over here.

So come come
with me to feel
the warm air.

Sincerely,
Cardinal

Nancy M.

Leaf! You fall from one of my petals
Humming birds are taking my pollen
Rain is falling all day
Bugs are living in me
That day you were due
Yours, Rose

3 Collage Poems
Daisy J.

A Ghost Is Born & living like almost the day we returned from The Faith Factor

Paige L.

Wonder
Ful required
Peace inside

Nicole F.

Who'd ever thought of Continuous
Safety the voice said
we have the biggest thing ever
Keep life on the way
help was
out there

Unicorn!
Maria C.

Unicorn, how do you heal?
   How do you shine?
Did you come up from the sky?

How do you live?
   How do you shine?
How did you come from the sky?

Did you come up from heaven?
   Do you live to be eleven?

Time Power
Davon B.

I can go to a lot of cities and
I could go back to time when
my mom was a kid. I could go
back when I was 4 so I could see
what I was doing because I
forgot what I was doing. I
could go back when I came out.

Renga: Walking Outside

There's a panda outside my window.	**Leslie P.**
In my pool, I dream I'm in my bathtub.	**Jim C.**
Michael Jackson dances well in a movie.	**Najee E.**
I saw a mango on an apple tree	**Pablo G.**
in the sunny summer of Chicago.	**Hugo Y.**
A butterfly flew into my window.	**Stephanie V.**
I was in a fancy bathtub outside.	**Genesis C.**
My name is Sammy Sosa.	**Luis G.**
An orange sat on top of a car.	**Yasmin H.**
I saw a limo sitting on a person in New York.	**Shakur G.**

Judith C.

I went to the black aquarium
and saw a sea horse.
I saw a jade green shark at the beach.
I saw a blue lion on the football field.

A Real Poem
Kevin T.

I saw a light brown puppy
in Ecuador and it's mine when
I am in summer vacation and
I will be so happy that I
have the light brown puppy
here and I will take care
of my puppy.

Four Winter Haiku
Fernando H.

You need mittens
and I don't

Aja B.

hail storms
coming this
way run

Ivan S.

We start
to cheer for snow

Loc N.

Snowmen roll
down the hall
and stand back up

Dear Lilies
Lily X.

How did you grow up without food? But you
could drink water from the rain?

Quiet Night Thoughts
Guadalupe R.

Before bedtime,
I look out the
window and I see
a shadow through
the other window,
and say that was
weird

When I Fall Asleep
Elizabeth B.

When I sleep in the car
I feel like I am at home
but when I wake up, it
seems like I'm in the
middle of the road.

Abdulwasi H.

I am a silver shark that lives in the city.
I am a black panther that lives in the kitchen.

Ashley R.

I am a
shark charging
through the redness
of the ocean.
Now the ocean
is dark black
for every step
I take every
thing burns.
When you cross
my path you
vanish. Gone.
Out of my

sight, gone
forever, never
to be found.
You Can Never
See The Light
Of Day!

Laura B.

Banana! I am so sorry that
I ate your sister. Well, I will give you a new tree.

So do you think I will eat you?

I will never.
Yours, Monkey

Jeremy C.

The striking shocking booming lighting
while falling rain
and the glowing warm moon
The moon is like a star
and a white paper
and silver legs of chairs.

The Rock and the Crystal
Alex M.

Dear Crystal
I told you to come to rock island!
Your crystal friends came to
see famous rocks. On the third
we are going to crystal island.

Your friend, Rock

Jose V.

I am a fierce black puma who lives in a turkey.

Renga: Walking Outside

Walking and walking a bird flutters.	**Ashley R.**
When I lie in my bathtub I feel so warm.	**Frank A.**
Eminem has cool songs.	**Christian Z.**
I'm walking outside with a mango.	**Geminis C.**
I love the city of Chicago where I live.	**Anibal G.**
The sweet smell of the color red.	**Cindy G.**

Yue D.

The keys are
stolen by a bear
I could not
find them
anywhere

The Control
Adriana S.

Control,
I know you
are under
the couch
They can't
reach you
DVD control
is here,
Your friend, TV

Concepcion S.

A key to open a door to the
way to a mountain
and to fall in water
with sharks with
underwear.

Three Winter Haiku
Jocelyn V.

Mittens cover my
five fingers
that's perfect

Kathy C.

It's really chilly
out in the mountains

Teague I.

Tea coffee naked trees
nobody outside cozy blanket gloves
hot cocoa snowing snowflakes

What I See
My-Lien L.

I see a ship
that is shaped like a sword.
I ask you, how can this be?
When I see the letter M.

I ask you again, how can this be?
When I see the number 11.

I see a person
that doesn't have an eye.

Renga: Walking Outside

One day a snake was in a forest
and his tail got tied in a knot.   **Luke A.**
When I was taking a bath, my dog
jumped into the bathtub.   **Caitlin S.**
Don Omar was walking outside with an
ice cream cone   **Eliani R.**
with a mango.   **Alex M.**
Chicago is a special place.   **Vladimir M.**
And the whole world was black and white   **Luke A.**
except my hamster and me.   **Caitlin. S.**

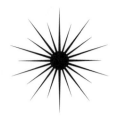

J. J. Pershing Magnet
School for the Humanities

Michelle Zaldonis, Poet in Residence
Principal: Katherine Volk
Program Coordinator: Catherine Tanner
Teachers: Ms. Mosely, 1st; Ms. Sileo, K; Ms. Sutherlin, K

Erica J.

Blue makes me think of sea
Blue is sky
Blue is hopes and dreams
Blue makes me feel good.
Blue is cool.
Blue is smooth
Not like the other colors.
Pink is girly
Boys don't like pink
Pink is like a water color
Pink shows
Pink grows when you color
Pink is like red
Yellow is WOW!
Yellow is sun
Yellow is bright
Yellow shows like pink
When you mix yellow with green
It is yellow
Black is old
Like back in the day
Black is ugly
Black is dark
Orange is pretty
Orange is lovely
Orange shows

Kenneth H.

I am in New Mexico
flying on an air ball
My glass is full of paper
I don't have a brain or a head
I steal toys
And my mother smells like snow
I eat bricks and bugs and windows
I lick windows
I still scribble on the wall
My head is full of chicken

Destiny M.

Cheetah!
Where did you get those spots?
They came from a bird
Where did you get your ROAR?
Under a rock where spiders live
Where did you get your run?
From exercise

Mehki C.

I used to be a cookie, but now I am a chocolate chip
I used to be a frog, but now I am a chicken
I used to be a girl, but now I am a boy
I used to be a rainbow, but now I am a donkey

Khanyisile Z.

I used to be myself, but now I am a heart
I used to be a watermelon, but now I am a sun
I used to be a girl, but now I am a boy
I used to be bows, but now I am a skirt
I used to be hair, but now I am bald
I used to be you, but now I am a dot
I used to be a face, but now I am lipstick
I used to be raindrops, but now I am a puddle
I used to be a bear, but now I am a goose
I used to be a pencil sharpener, but now I am an eye
I used to be apples, but now I am a grape
I used to be trees, but now I am a bird
I used to be leaves, but now I am a bed
I used to be a pencil, but now I am a sticker

Destiny M.

I used to be a girl, but now I am a boy
I used to eat trees, but now I eat rocks
I used to drink mud, but now I drink raw eggs
I used to eat cats, but now I eat dogs.

DeAndre A.

I want to live on Jupiter
And I want to dance on the rings
And lay on the rings
And hug Jupiter
And kiss Jupiter
And say "thank you"
For letting me go on you, Jupiter

Jamiere C.

I would like to live in a berry house
Because I could eat my house
I wouldn't have nothing to live in
But I'd be full
I could climb the house
And touch the sky
My neighbor is a worm
He lives in a dirt house
His school is in the sky
He is a good neighbor,
But he dirties my house
His helpers are dogs
I love my berry house

Brielle L.

I live in outer space
I would float in space
And see a rocket ship
And grab a star
And go up to the moon
To play catch

Breyjon D.

I would live on the beach
I would lay on the beach in a chair
Sipping coconut juice
And I would go swimming
With my best friend
We would lay in the water
And then lay in the chair
And sip more juice.

Ronald B.

If I lived in a clam, I'd be safe
Safe from a shark
I would open his mouth door
The pearl would be my chair
It's dark in there
So I'll have a flashlight.

Tyler B.

I live in a heart
Living in a heart with my family
Living in a heart, I play with my baby
Living in a heart, I wrestle with my dad.
It's fun to live in a colorful heart

Aolani S.

I live in Heaven
They have milk and honey buns and soda
It looks like a safe place to live
People have fun and go on roller coasters
It's so much fun in Heaven
Almost everybody wants to live there.

Sabria C.

A name tag is like a ticket
A heart is like cherries
A window is like a ladder
A basketball is like an orange
A flower is like a rose -- Darnesha
May is like an apple tree
A flower is like a butterfly
A cloud is like a pillow
A sun is like a balloon with sticks
And grass is like itchy hair.

Brielle L.

A pea is like a little head
A moon is like a sucker
Colors are like a rainbow
Art is like a masterpiece
Firecrackers are like sparkles

Breyjon D.

I want to be a superhero
And speed fast
Like the dairy cow
I will save the world
If a baby was trapped in a fire
I would fly in the window
And bring the baby to safety

Atukwe K.

I am the best cha-cha dancer
It's a lot of fun
I drink champagne
It takes a lot of practice
You have to have the best techniques
And I got a sexy girl
Dancing with me

Kelli B.

I have trophies for being the best artist
I'm the best because I am listening
I can draw what I am thinking
I was the best artist in the whole entire world

Aolani S.

I am the best bike rider
I ride so fast the poles fall down
And the school breaks to pieces
All the food in the store falls out
And falls to the ground

Jamar D.

I'm the best break-dancer
I can do back flips and handstands
And do back flips with one hand
Or with no hands and my eyes closed

Devin P.

My eyes are made of wood
My ears are made of ice cream
My hands are made of cardboard
My face is made of jelly
My nose is made of octopus
My legs are made of hats Peterson
And my forehead is made of an apple

Erika J.

My hair is made of whip crème.
My face is made of cards
My room is made of strawberries with sugar
My house is made of clouds
Ice cream is made of metal
Tissue is made of glass cleaner
Boxes are made of tracks
Trays are made of wood.
Lockers are made of greens
Books are made out of mail
Posters are made of cars
Apples are made of Hershey.

Keyshawn B.

How kites became purple
It flew out of the sky
And how the grass got green

A turtle splashed his green on the grass
And before the sky came blue
And before the rose came red
Red paint splashed on the rose
And before the leaf came orange
Orange rain came down
And before dark became black
It was yellow

Isaiah J.

The bird get a tree
And made him green
The cloud fell on me
And made me white
The sun fell on a chicken
And made him yellow
The apple fell on the dog
And made him red.
The sky fell on the boy
And will turn the boy blue.

William H. Prescott Elementary School

Parry Rigney, Poet in Residence
Principal: Avelino Martinez
Program Coordinator: Jen Paterimos
Teachers: Mrs. Buttle, 4th; Ms. Hines, 5th; Ms. Jacobs, 3rd

Sun to the Moon
Angelica C.

Sun! I miss you
why aren't you here
the sky is back
but not you
what happened
on your trip
to Japan
the clouds got home yesterday
everyone's here except you
so come on
          your friend, Moon

The Redbud Tree
Alexis G.

Beside
a slanted like
tree
your eyes
can
see
the heart of its
family,
pink or hot pink
blossoming
the air
people come
visit to see
its blossoming hair
it blossoms head
to trunk go up
then down
if you listen
the flowers blossoming
you can hear the
sound
the flowers maybe
grow up or round that's what makes
the flower pretty, pretty in sound.

It Rains
Francisco C.

It Rains It Rains It Rains and Rains
     It rains day and night
When It snows there's snow all over.
When It rains the rain is talking
to the snow. Snow why do you have color
White? Rain why are you Invisible!

Karina H.

This morning I saw myself
in the mirror
        I saw
a young girl being like a mouse
        so quiet
This morning I saw myself
a girl looking for freedom
        like deers
live in the wilderness
This morning I saw myself
a girl running like a jaguar
running
running
running for my life.

Sad and Happiness
Jamal P.

I saw sad flying
over the sky into the
clouds.

Sad stopped on a
wire singing all day
long a sad song.

I take him in my
house and give
him food and
then he was
singing a happy
song so I changed
his name to happiness.

Hello Sir!
Marissa G.

Hello sir fire—
it's me Mr. Candle—
I see that you're having much fun—

but too much to handle

As you see that I'm crying so hard—
Can you just go out please—
Because my tears are starting to begin
to freeze—

Please just turn off I can't hold it anymore—
It feels like I just going to drop on the floor.
Mr. Plate now knows that I am crying—
He stopped all the helping and pretended he
was dying—
But plates can't die
unless they're cracked up and broken
Now please Sir fire no more talking
because I have spoken.

Life
Jessica B.

three
people laying in
the sun.
just in the
neighborhood.
can you get the picture?

Ezequiel E.

I heard stories about my grandfather
he was cool
a gentleman
he was strong
he had black hair
he had brown eyes
and every lady wanted him as a husband
he lived in Mexico
and he had a wife named Coco
and he always liked to play soccer
he was very good at it
and I guess you could say I got
the good looks from him.

Bananas
Jazzlyn G.

Bananas remind
me of summer
Karisma eating piece
by piece
getting dirty
Bananas giving me

strength to run
to ride my bike,
scooter
good tasty inside
you can make
banana cream pie
it's like
eating a
banana shaped
moon when
I eat it
I feel like
A monkey
swinging in the
vines.

Guadalupe B.

Happiness
you usually don't feel happiness
when it stops
raining
and the sun
comes out
you feel
happiness
when you put water on
a flower
it stands
straight and you feel happiness.
When the fresh air comes
through
my hair
and my face
and I feel
happiness
so happiness is a good feeling to feel.

The Fruiting Wahoo Tree
Oswaldo L.

Fruiting wahoo tree
your leaves are sweet.
Tall branches tall roots,
how do you get your fruits.
The smell wakes up singing
birds and your taste is so sweet.
Smell better than the
redbud tree and your leaves
are as sweet as honey.
Fruiting wahoo tree you're so
so sweet.

Estrella V.

This morning
this morning
       I saw
       my
       self
In the mirror
with the bush
of hair in my
head pretty
and with
my school clothes

I saw myself
in the mirror of my
lipstick cap and
with my red
glossy mouth
       I looked pretty
            pretty
      pretty good.

The Little Boy
Tyrek W.

Watching the day go by saying hi to the sky the birds sing all around the ring oh little
girl watching the day go by looking at the birds sing all all all around the ring good
day on the beach watching the birds go under the sun set around the ring in to the
park sing sing all the way there all night on the beach all day and night sing sing all
the way there.

Talking
Evelyn G.

The computer is talking to the
keyboard, and the keyboard says, "are
they punching you too?"

The chair is talking to the desk,
the desk says "man someone warm
me up!"

A bridge is talking to the river,
the river says "don't open."

The couch is talking to the T.V.
the couch says "you talk too much."

The flower is talking to the dirt,
the flower says, "I'm colorful, and
you are black."

Maria G.

yesterday sun you were
very bright and I know that
we do not have nothing
in common but you
are still my best
friend.

Sincerely, the moon

Mexicana Naranja / Mexican Orange
Gustavo P.

Mexican Orange you bring me Mexico. Mexican orange why are you named after
a colorful color? Mexican orange you bring me life extra life. Mexicana Naranja
Mexican Orange you are so sweet. Mexicana Naranja Dulce you're so juicy. You are
my Mexican Orange. Tu eres mi Mexicana Naranja Dulce.

Dad
Maria M.

My dad is strong like the
tree and like the buses.

Jennifer S.

From Mexico come the Mangoes. Juicy inside, familiar with the summer. The
mangoes come green, dusty but delicious. Adore it, when you have it in your hands
eat it with love put lemon you will adore it more. Eat it in a day windy but sunny sit
down in the tree it will be more delicious and juicy.

The Hotdog and the Game of Baseball
Tony G.

The hotdog
coming from the hotdog stand
hearing the roar of the crowd
from the White Sox stadium
laying the mustard onto the golden hotdog
in the summer time
hearing the crack of a bat against the ball
taking a bite
the returning team
against the enemy
a homerun remembering
what really matters
loving the game
and remembering…
what you were doing
and what you remember is the good luck charm
and the warm up meal
and the hot dog giving you a fuzzy feeling

Casimir Pulaski
Fine Arts Academy
Tracy Zeman, Poet in Residence
Principal: Leanor Karl
Teachers: Ms. D'Andrea, Ms. Jackson, Ms. Sagami, 8th

Delilah G.

I dream of going to heaven and walking on the shiny golden path.
Here is like a rule always having to do your best.
My mansion had been waiting for me on 777 N. Cloud.
Here is having to work for food and paying for what you want.
My scrumptious buffet with nachos and cheese. I can't wait to see it, I can't wait to eat.
Up there in heaven is not like down here.
It's graceful and good and there's nothing to fear.

Thayra O.

Winter is like a Sunday.
Winter is like a teardrop dripping down
my face. Winter is like a day in
heaven. Winter is in my heart. I love
winter, the snow flakes dropping
from the sky. Winter is beautiful.
Winter is me.

Anthony L.

I am like winter cold and windy as the dark skies.
I am like a dead bug that sways in the wind
when winter's dreary skies blow above my head.
I am like winter because like snow, my thoughts
and emotions stack up, with each snowflake that drops
is like blood or tears that drop on to the cold
and lay on the lonely sidewalk of the lonely winter days.

Emily T.

Summer is like a hot relaxing bubble bath.
Spring is like doing math.
Fall is like a rake.
Winter is like a frozen lake.

Glen R.

To walk through the days
when the days go dark
at five o'clock. When

the street lights shine on the
red leaves which brings memories
to the silent deaths in
the streets of this threatening
neighborhood. To fall into
the darkness of a light
can you read the colors of this theme.

3 Unspoken Things
Geovanni R.

As I feel the breeze while I sit on the ocean shore:
as I watch the sunset. As I see sailboats sail by I lay
in the sand and dream, dream of things I can't even imagine,
things that make me feel every emotion, but when I open my eyes
it all goes away. All the emotion I felt disappears,
all things I dreamed of "gone" but I still feel the breeze,
I still watch the sunset, I still see sailboats sail, and I still dream of unspoken things.

As I stare at the ceiling a light. I see as I stare at the light
I lose my sight. I feel lost…lost in a place I've never seen.
People talking a different language. All of a sudden I can see again.
I still see the light on the ceiling. As I drift in at the light I lose my sight again.

As I sit on a hill staring at the sunset I wonder.
I wonder to the sky. I imagine myself floating on something…
while I float I stare at the sunset and I wonder am I in heaven?
but I'm back on the hill and I think I'm thankful to be alive!

Sky
Beatriz M.

The sky is like an endless path.
It's like walking on the clouds without seeing the end.

The sky is like a path of numbers
you may say 1, 2, 3, 4, 5, 6, 7, 8, 9, 10 but what goes at the end.

The sky is like the circle of life.
You may see a lion eating a zebra and the next day it's all the same.

The sky is like a space.
People see one thing but they never see the rest.

The sky is like life,
you are born but you never know your end.

Michael R.

the brain can be
looked at in so
many ways,

some are crazy
or insane, it
can be complex
or it can be simple,
it's like a building
with so many
elevators, all
of them going
up and down,
it can go slow
or fast as the
levels of places
pass, it never
goes one speed
at a time, like
a car the brain
can shift gears
and you're the
one behind
the wheel,
you're in control
you steer the
wheel, a brain
is complex like
a picture from
Picasso every
color is unique

Oranges
Stephanie M.

I live in my fairy tale land where a sweet
odor intertwines with the wind.
Everyday I look out my window and I grab
the sweet taste of heaven.
I cut the heavenly product in half that reveals
the juice of earth's gift.
As I bite into it to suck the juice
tiny buds slip into my mouth.
I let the bud roll around in my mouth until
I finally bite into it and a slash of sweet water
surprises my tongue.
As I peel parts of my orange sweet juice rolls
down my arm looking like a river, rain.
I drink and drink and drink 'till the orange
is dry and empty and when that
happens I find myself at my windowsill
once more reaching out for another orange.

Love
Jamion B.

Affections touching across time
two beings flying in sync as one but not alone.
The castle of love hidden through
the looking glass, two beings
reigning as one in love and happiness.
A love that transcends time.
A love whose love knows no bounds
obstacles flying beyond the
grips of space beyond galaxies.
The legends of love from the
vast plains of an ancient
kingdom two beings focused
on each other in a synced and
fused state ruling as one.
Masks never separate in a Masquerade
always knowing their lover always
love that holds no equal
moving the earth manipulating
fire moving with the flow, love
controlling and holding the
wind in a net of fire and
passion. A love that can
always transcend time.

Hello Stranger
Merrean R.

Hello Stranger.
Walking down the street like people
seeing families enjoying themselves,
shopping, having a good time.
Why am I, you, kids, adults so alone?
Can't do the things that we want.
Walking down the street. I hear my
name calling me. I turn around.
I see nobody walking, more, I hear
it more louder and closer. I turn
around I see somebody that has
been missing in my life. I try to
hug them but they disappear.
Why did they leave? Why can't
they stay here forever. Leaving a
rose to remember where they
go. A different way to follow.
Hello Stranger. Hello World.

Ashley M.

Dark ashamed
don't care about anything.
Inside burning with fire letting the smoke
out angry full of pain not even water could
wash the fire out.
There's no place to go stuck in the middle
of nowhere lost cause I'm like in a black hole that has no escape.
The only light is the lighting bugs flying
to brighten up this darkness but there's not
that much light there's no room for brightening up this hole.

The Raising of Lazarus
Diana Q.

Raising somebody from the dead is like raising a ghost
and their unfinished business. Somebody who raises
someone from the dead is a miracle worker.
A person who has God on their side.
A person who cares for others even though
others don't care for him. Raising someone from the dead
is showing that they still have a chance in life,
that it wasn't the time to die.

Fantasy World
Giselle F.

In this fantasy world,
where dreams are as clear as a pearl,
and living things enjoy life with no fear.
Where beautiful colors,
surround your dreams,
and people with two heads,
walk down the street.
Where you can fly with an umbrella,
as high as the Eiffel Tower,
if you would like.
In this fantasy world,
anything is possible,
all you have to do,
is close your eyes,
and dream.

Winter Ocean
Alex O.

Ice runs across
the rivers

When the wind
blows a quick shiver

Ships sail across
this winter ocean

Everything is frozen
nothing is in motion

A blizzard had fallen
on the land

The view is very
beautiful like a
wedding band

The snow is
white covering
the ground

The winter ocean
is a perfect sight
around the town

The Winter Ocean
is a sight to
see

There is no other
place to be

Pablo D.

The sound of the massive rain
on a land, harness
The sun rises in mid dawnness
Nocturne sky is bliss with morning chill
But the descent of light
Won't lift the spill
Blue and silver
Creates overwhelming stabbing
Shivers
The rage of the ocean
crashes the side of the shore
But the darkness settles the score

Sonnet
Claudia G.

We stand near the mountains
the wind whispering around us
suddenly I remember another day
another day in May
you said the wind
was like the voices of the beloved
always there but not actually there
now I say the same thing to you
hoping that it'll help you heal,
you smiled, eyes like the sea.
We walk away, hand in hand
leaving them behind in the wind
but they will come back to us
they always do.

Philip A. Randolph
Magnet Elementary School
Lee Glidewell, Poet in Residence
Principal: Joan Forté
Program Coordinator: Ayanna Mitchell
Teachers: Mrs. Baines, 3rd; Ms. Bell, 4th; Mrs. Smith, 7th

Asanta C.

I have taken a toy that
was not mine. I am so sorry I say I say.
But I said I had fun playing
and playing with it. It was a
action figure of GI Joe with
the pop out gun. I said I like
popping out the blaster inside
the gun.

Rottweiler Trouble
Darius M.

When I woke up my dog was licking
me in the face. Next thing I know that dog
was chewing on a slipper. And I told myself
oh that dog has to go. When I bent down to
pick up my slipper that dog jumped on my
butt and then I screamed. My mom said,
honey, what's going on? She ran in the room,
seen the dog chewing on my butt, she ran
and got the cord. She grabbed that
dog in her room and when she got done
with him he didn't never bit anybody's
butt again.

Dear Emuni,
Tyreea J.

I am sorry for making you fall out of your chair. Please forgive me, okay,
but it was funny.

Sherriana R.

I have ate all of my mom's
Candy. It was all chocolate
and good, also delicious. When
I had ate my mom's candy bar
I had said sorry sorry, wonderful
sorry.

Deshaun A.

I'm so sorry that I was
talking in class so I will apologize.
But it was so so so fun
it made me do it some
more. But no I won't do it
again. This is the funny
part about it: I just
keep on doing it but it's so so
bad. And I'm so so sorry
because I fought in the
classroom with Amonte B.

Keshawn J.

Lion! Lion! How did you get so big? I wonder, how did you get big paws, how did you
get so big eyes?
I am the king of the jungle. How do you expect me to be?
I don't know. But I have to get like you.
No, you won't get like me! You can try. But you will not get like me. Unless you
exercise any you will not get like me.

Jazmine J.

The dog of the
the night
how can he
attack a poor little
cat of the night?

Dog's running after
a little
kitten in the rain and
of the night. Here's
the sun
bright, here's the
sun bright.

Now dog has to
run, before the kitten
get tough.

Jerome T.

Sharks live down the blue sea.
Please sharks don't bite. I'm just
a little boy that cannot swim,
so please sharks don't bite others.
People want to live. Sharks, why
do you bite? I said. For a moment
the sharks didn't answer, but the
sharks said "I'm hungry."

Six Ways of Looking at a Redbird
Vinnnasia W.

I
among the tall mountains
was the red bird

II
I was on my Summer
break thinking like a
cat in which was a redbird

III
the redbird was whirled in
the blue sky when the wind
blew.

IV
a baby and a child
is one
a father and a mother and a
redbird

V
a red bird and a white bird
eating worms at the same pond

VI
the wind filled the long
window with snow in ice,
the shadow of the redbird crossed
it, to make a snow angel.

Peace Comes Dropping Slow
Darsha L.

Peace comes dropping slow with the flow
desires. Peace means quiet or not a
sound,
but in my case it means quiet.
So desires probably means to do something.
Raining cats following down touch
the sky when you fall all together.

Part 2 of the Cheese Eaters
Chyna M.

When they'd wake up in the morning
they would ask for more cheese. I'd
get tired of making the same thing
every day. So when they wake up for now
on, they would have more than cheese.
And that is how I solved my problem
of them eating cheese.

Jason R.

I am sorry for doing what
I did. I couldn't resist the
watermelon. It was so red,
green, so ripe, and so big,
juicy, delicious, and so
nice. I am so sorry but then
I'm so happy, about what
I did. If I could replace it
I wouldn't. So don't get mad at
me, that stuff was good.
Don't be hating you hater.

Holla!!!!

Delano B.

Walking to the store
Throwing snowballs at the cars
Hoping to get chased.

Doneisha W.

The picture was laughing
when the camera had made a
nasty face. He said, ha ha ha.

Travis C.

The moon is running
To a place far, far away
The moon has made it

Necole S.

I wish I was a millionaire.
I wish I was famous.
I wish I was popular.
I wish I had a car.
I wish I was a teacher.
I wish I pass all my grades.
I wish I pass all my classes.
I wish I had a magic pencil.
I wish I had a magic carpet.

Jasmine M.

As she walk down the street, she
greets everyone she sees. She smile
always with her big green hat.
People watch her eat trying not to
hear her smack. She is a good
person to talk to, but live next
door to her I'm positive you will try to
sue. 99% to me you will lose. And
people will look at you as if you're the
fool. That devilish laugh she
has, I'm 100% sure it will take out
a football crowd.

In My Wild Dream
Diamond D.

In my wild dream I had
the night before I called Michael
Myers name three times and when I got
to sleep I had a dream that
Michael Myers was chasing me
and tried to get me. He put
a scar on my face. I woke
with a scar on my face.

Asanta C.

As I'm dreaming I see
the seas are green and
black and red at the same
time. As I see the seas I think.
I need something to eat
so I make a pig into
bacon.

Doneisha W.

You had a dream that an elephant was dancing
In a pink and yellow tutu while juggling
a mouse. While the elephant was juggling an
alligator came and did the chacha
slide, and he started pop locking. Everyone
had laughed but the elephant said my turn,
So they turned to 107.5 WGCI and "Lean
Wit It, Rock Wit It" came on. And he did lean
wit it, rock wit it. So then everyone joined in with
the rest of them.

Jamila S.

He finds himself in a park and he is sitting
and talking, but not to anyone particularly. But it
turns out to be a dog. While he talks people
can't believe the dog is saying words. Now a
cat comes along and the dog wants to fight it.

Now you find out you are dreaming because
you are now in a pool with a singing shark,
and when you get out the shark grabs
you and starts dancing with you.

When you wake up in real life your
pet snake is now dancing to the music
on tv. And you join and you have a ball
with the snake.

Derrick P.

You go flying down the
street on your bicycle, dodging
people left and right. Your brakes disappear,
are gone, so you can't stop going faster
and faster, you feel the air rushing
past you like a tornado. Next you
are in a race car, the clock count's
done, taking off with speed, a straight
neverending track. Your steering
wheel turns into a little monster
biting at your clothes.

The Pizza Eaters
Angelique W.

I eat pizza all day. I love the
pizza so much that I can't
stop lovely pizza. And when I
was eating pizza my pizza
fell on the floor. And I eat
pizza for dinner. And can no-
body can stop me from eating
pizza. Because I love pizza
So much. Why I love pizza?
Because of the cheese.
And that's why
I love pizza.

Malcolm C.

I am a running back
The quarterback throws
the ball to me I catch it
I'm running, I spin left
Someone tries to tackle
me, I spin right, I dive.
Touch down. We won the
game, we are in the
finals..

Sherriana R.

I wish I was grown. I
wish I was popular. I wish
I was smart. I wish we
didn't have to do homework.
I wish they will find the
people that ran away from their
home. I wish I was a
doctor. I wish I was a teacher.
I wish we can stay at school
for one minute. I wish I
had a car.

Paul Revere
Elementary School

Pam Osbey, Poet in Residence
Principal: Shelby L. Taylor
Program Coordinator: Frankie Hall
Teachers: Ms. Goff, 5th; Mr. Lazar, 7th; Ms. Shabazz, 7th

What's Inside of Us
Group Poem
Ms. Goff's Class

I have bones they go cricket and crocket.
I wish I could run like a cheetah so when they
teach Jazz I could run…
I'm funny in my own way like David Chappell.
I'm so funny I made Snoop Dog do the crop walk.
I see myself as a car or a cheetah.
Inside my body my feelings are gold, and bright
As the sky.
I'm a lot of things. A lion, a King of all Kings,
When you see me you'll know I'm a lot of things.
I see myself as a nice angel.
I'm entertainment.
I can dance so good.
I have Energizer batteries inside or a guitar
I can make beautiful music.
I'm a lot of things, A lion, a King of all Kings,
When you see me, you'll know I'm a lot of things.
My heart beats of four cats.
Some people make me laugh.
Some people make me smile.
There's a girl in my life.
It's just me…
There's a king and a God in my
Soul, and bones that are red.
When I'm in school my brain goes super fast like a motorcycle.
I'm a lot of things, A lion, a King of all Kings,
When you see me, you'll know I'm a lot of things.

I Don't Like Sports That Much
Tatiana P.

I like Tennis but not Basketball.
I like Volleyball but not Dog ball.
I like Bowling but not Hockey.
I like Skating but not Soccer.
I hate Football and Baseball –
Two but that's ok.

Why We Write
Group Poem
Mr. Lazar's Class

Poetry is a group of stanzas that sometimes
Rhyme not all the time.
Poetry is like God flowing through your ears
On a Sunday morning.
Poetry is like unstoppable bond between you and the
Pen and paper.
Poetry is something that goes on through life.
Poetry is good, good for your health.
Poetry is bright like the sun and it's also nice like my Mom.
Poetry is an emotion that I feel inside that I write on white paper.
I write poetry to express my thoughts on red colored
Flowers with pink paper…
I write because I'm mad, angry, or depressed.
I write so people can learn how I feel.
I write to express myself.
I write what I think is right.
My poetry shows how long I've fought.
Dark dreary dreams are loose at my seams.
Spill and flow quick.
Poetry is like I'm at home doing nothing.
Poetry is like love and hate and it's what twists
Your mind out of place.
Poetry is like a beautiful sunset.
I write because I'm free.
I write to get thoughts out of my head.
Poetry is a group of stanzas that sometimes
Rhyme not all the time.
Poetry is like a bunch of words of stress.
When you write too many you make a mess.
My pen writes stories that never lies.
That's one thing I want people to realize.

I Am
Chondra C.

I am a darker woman.
I am strong.
I am proud of my color.
I will stand tall.
I am a darker woman, not your slave.

Poetry and Expressions
Group Poem
Ms. Shabazz's Class

You can't always say what you want to say, that's
Why from this day I write night and day.
I write to get stuff off my mind because I don't want
To talk at certain times.
I write to release my mind and leave all the bad
Things behind.
I write to escape from out of my way, or maybe
Because I'm not having a very good day so what
I do is take out a pen and paper and read it later.
Poetry is a rhyme of thoughts when I do bad things
And it's all my fault.
Poetry is nothing but a bunch of words just waiting
To be heard.
Words are powerful like the hot burning sun.
It sets like steaming words.
Words are powerful like the stars in the air.
Words are powerful because you can express
Your feelings.

Poetry comes deep from the heart.
But sometimes you just don't know where to start.
Poetry is like the soul, it never gets old.
It's just like rapping, you got to go with the flow.
Poetry is my heart, my soul.
Poetry is something I will hold, tuck in my heart forever.
Poetry is important to me, it lets me express myself
And lets me tell others how I feel.
Poetry is something that is precious that expresses
Your feelings.

Poetry is very lovely like a bouquet of flowers.
Poetry is
Powerful
Outstanding
Energy
Trait
Real
Your Feelings
I write from my feelings, not from my heart.
I write madly like when you're throwing darts.
I sometimes wonder how the paper feels,
Hardly pressed on like the judges appeal.
My pen expresses my feelings.

The "Do You" Lesson
Shanice S.

A noun's a person, place or thing.
A verb's what you do.
So don't do nothing stupid, just do you.

A verb's your actions.
Yeah, you can say it's what you do.
So don't care what people say about you.
Just do you.

Yes, some people might try to
stop you from doing what you do best.
But don't care about the rest.
Just brush your shoulders off and clear your head.

Because in a few minutes that person might
be your friend and what you were arguing
about will soon be old news, the past.
It'll be dead!
Like I said, just do you.

When people are messing with you
just say "Yeah, whatever", or "that's cool"
cause when you think about it, they just looking like a fool.
See, it works when you just do you.

You might have hard times.
You might sometimes cry.
You might even ask the Lord why.
Just keep your H.E.A.D. U.P.
and never G.I.V.E. U.P.
and you'll see.
So just do you.

Have you ever heard that word
"Karma"?
Yeah, just think about that.
What goes around comes back
and don't think that goes for one person,
it goes you too.
But it won't go for you, if you just do you!

Praise
Malaka S.

Praise my Mom for being strong.
Praise my Dad for not leaving me alone.
Praise my Mom for accepting me as her daughter.
Praise my Dad for not giving me a quarter.
Praise my parents for raising me right.
Praise my Mom for having me that night.

Wright K.

These words will have no dreams
it will be filled with rhymes.
No dreams but nightmares
fill these lines and take your precious time.
The claws that scratch my sleep.
They've cut this skin too deep.
An overdose of Kleenexes,
fuel this pen and paper link.
The flares that set this flame apart
can burn the most naive of hearts.
So you can't breathe.
So you can't talk.
The loss of strength,
it makes a mark.
When they ask you
"Are you fine?", say yes.
Note this: your nightmares can depress.

Rock Bottom
Jamil G.

I want my old life back but I can't have it.
I want to stay positive but my mind won't let it.
I hit rock bottom and I can't come back up.
I'm drowning at the bottom because mind seems to be stuck.
I ask for help but no one cares and all I get are crazy stares.

I sit in bed thinking of my terrible past.
And thinking of how bad things happen so fast.
My heart's been shattered.
I'm caught in a trance.
I've got somewhat of a wounded soldier's stance.
Now nothing holds significance.
Nothing holds relevance
because all I can search for is true intelligence.

I've gone from hero to a zero in almost 10 to 12 days.
I don't know what happened, it's all in a daze.
I can no longer speak my words have no meaning.
From no where my pen does the true speaking.

I am less of a man and more of a boy.
For the pen is my game and the paper.
My toy.

I am an artist who's entirely lost his way.
I think my heart aches almost everyday.
My heart aches because of the pain I've been through.
Now there is just one thing left for me to do.
I must start over and begin anew.
Erase all the pains that fill my soul.
And tried once more to fill that dark hole.
There's plenty of reason why I wrote this.
But the main reasons are my hearts broken.
Soul empty and I'm seriously pissed.

If I Were
Simone H.

If I were a school, there would be ice cream
and cake for lunch.
If I were a school, I would make it so there
were no more reading.
If I were a school, I would be in the sky.
If I were a school, there would be no vegetables.
If I were a school, at the end of the day
we would watch a movie or play
video games.
If I were a school, kids would always
be good.

Ice Cream
Destinee H.

Ice cream, Ice cream.
Everywhere.
We have chocolate, strawberry, butterscotch.
What other flavors can you guess?
Oh yeah, that right, we have Vanilla too.
You can buy it anywhere, at the
Gas station, even at the candy shop.
You can guess any other stores.
Can you guess?
Oh yeah, that's right.
Save-A -Lot!
That's all I can guess.
Good bye, everyone I'll be back
So you can tell everyone your other flavors.

Song of My Soul
Ashley T.

The song of my soul is the body of the feel
that gave me pressure.
The song of my body gives me a beat to my heart.
The song of my soul of my body, celebrate the day I was born.
The song of my soul of my body, makes my day happy.
The song of my soul, gives me the best poetry I ever told.

My Community
Earnest H.

Drive by.
Hear guns shot over time you try to say "Hi."
Bums in the alley, that's not good.
Try to think to myself, *"What's really good?"*
You got a good school.
Drama is what we go through.
Get shot just because who you with.
Only healthy snack is a bag of chips.
No help when hurricanes are killing.
Whole house flooded.
Bush don't care.
Black people on the ceilings.
Mr. Comer helps.
Keeps us all tied up like a belt.
Houses turned into offices.
We need new leaders.
We're a good school.
We should be called, The Achievers.

My Community
Martinez N.

My community, we stick together
We have fights and we try to make peace.
We have community tournaments.
We have the drill and basketball teams.
My community is called "Pocket Town"

Philip Rogers
Elementary School

Adam Novy, Poet in Residence

Principal: Joel Bakrins

Teachers: Mrs. Airo, 5th; Ms. Jackson, 4th; Mrs. Neyman, 4th;
Ms. Reese, 6th; Ms. Schoenfeld, 6th; Ms. Wilkins, 5th

Anoosh Siminovic
Anoosh S.

Anoosh Siminovic
Is a wolf in lonely woods.
Maybe she is a black star
In darkness
Never seen
Never heard
She may be a wild dog
Made to kill
She may have beady eyes
Which can't stop staring at
You.
Some say she's a wind
That throws you off balance.
Some say she's a spider
That crawls on dirty ground
She is like a broken heart
Pasted up
Some say nothing can prevent this girl
From being her.
Anoosh Siminovic,
She's nothing
But unbelievable

Linval R.

Moonlight
I hate the night.
I wonder what light
Does at night.

Light of the night
Why are you in the sky?
Please, night,
Don't bring that mean old night out!
One day I will
See that light
I promise!

Brains
Nicholas M.

They look like pieces of chewed gum
Put together like a larger
Version of your tongue.

Sometimes chewing gum
Makes you feel like
You lost your mind
And you're trying to eat a brain to get it back.

Poem
Ashoor M.

The heart or not!
The heart is right
The brain can be bright
Like the heart isn't.

Blue Pen
Connor M.

This must be
A gift from the ocean.
When I write with you,
My paper holds an ocean.

When I erase the ink,
Only water remains.

Friendship
Yetunde O.

Friendship
Is beautiful
But dies out like a flower.

Poem
Mary T.

A dim light leads the way
On a very dark night.
I shine my lamp in different directions
Stopping
On a cat
At the edge of town.

Shoes
Anoosh S.

One old shoe
With no brother
One side ripped and dirty
Stepping through mud
Walking everyday
It will never be
Reunited

Scissors
Andreea S.

New born twins
With heads like shapes destroyed
Poor things,
all with one leg

People
Tear their legs apart like

scissors.

Paper
Kevin N.

Paper
Is bright like heaven
But sharp like a sword

Like a devil
Sent to look like an angel

Winter
Yetunde O.

Winter
Snow, white like a dove
Snowflakes
Like white roses
I am walking on clouds

Haiku
Rabia I.

Sky
Give me a shining blue thought
You are prettier than a scissor-cut bird

Plate
Jasmine V.

A plate
Resembles many things.

A frisbee
That flies and breaks

A wheel
That is hard to move

It resembles a sun
That will never be hot

A moon
That is hidden by clouds

It resembles a world without continents
A soccer ball without a sphere

But it would be best
As a flat dish.

Wind
Anoosh S.

We can't see it
We can feel the
Unbelievable
We know it's there
We hear
The whistling
Of the wind
Like the moving river
Pushing its way out
Like a person crying
Or walking down a path
Wanting something so bad
It will do anything to get it

Haiku
Janice R.

Teenagers trying to act like bears.
It's even funnier than the last time
They acted like bears.

Five Poems About Sleep
Ursus G.

Sleep in a dizzy way

Sleep when
You are not asleep

Dreaming
In an active way

Going sleepy
When in danger

Getting sleepy
When you're bored

Jack C.

In the moggy swamp
You hear the bullfrogs burping
See their chins bulge
Their smooth and bumpy skin
They splash when they jump in the water
Who would swim in that muck?
They catch flies on their tongue
Who would eat that?
Why call them bullfrogs?
They are burping frogs

Clayton D.

An owl sits
On a post
Waiting
For something to happen
A man in church
Sitting
But not praying
A girl waits for her boyfriend
He never comes

The Birth Stone
Hirangi P.

In deep ravines
Are there stones
That no-one ever visits?

I went up the mountain
On steep pathless slopes
To find the stone that no-one sees.

This stone all thick with moss
Was only born
The moment I saw it.

Poem of Flowers
Yenedid S.

Flowers against the grass
Near the flower
Smelly flowers
Especially the roses and the yellows.
Flower
The lily smells the best
Different than the
Purple yellow pink
I don't know which to choose.
Daisies beauty of daisies
The color and the scent
the shape
daisy
I see it every day
Sunflowers, the bees
Sit by you.
I would like to be a bee.

Poems About Cheese
Dani S.

Among fifty blocks
Of cheese, the only
Moving thing was the
Scent of the cheese.

The cheese
got eaten by
a very hungry
hobo.

It was a giant
piece of
parmesan.

A foot and a toe
Are one.
A foot and a toe and
Cheese are three.

I don't know
Which one I
Prefer, but I think
I'd prefer the

Cheese because
It is very tasty.

Cheese melted
In the microwave.
Its beauty
Splattered all over
The microwave.

Cheese doesn't
Walk.

The cheese sat in a window,
Waiting to be eaten.

Connor Moore
Connor M.

Connor Moore is a bat on the ball
He's a tiger in the dark
Hunting sleepy animals
And I worship him.
He's only one percent soft.
Bother him in rap
And he'll tear you to bits
He should be hung from the sky
Or put on a ship to Pluto.
Let's just say one thing about this beast,
He will be mad at us
For these actions.

Chop Sticks
Micki C.

These strange wooden objects
Came right from Bejing, China.
They resemble tiny wooden stilts
Tiny people use to see.

Hold them in your hand,
And you can imagine
The rest of the bird you are eating.
An ostrich:
Its head is such an angry fist.

These strange wooden objects are mysterious!

I Wish I Could
Carol G.

Go to Antarctica.
Feel how cold it is.
See many animals:
Polar bears, seals, and walruses.
See how they survive
The snow, ice and winds
I know I could die
But it would still be better
Than doing homework or chores.

I Wish
Devante K.

I wish I could be a grown-up now
I wish I didn't have to die
I wish I could be with my friends and family forever
I wish I will die in my sleep
I wish I will go to the NBA
I wish I could be a lot more brilliant
I wish I could do everything I want to do
I wish I knew my father
I wish I could see my father

School of Entrepreneurship
at South Shore Campus
Pam Osbey, Poet in Residence
Principal: William Gerstein
Teacher: Ms. Matti, 11th

Black Rose
Matthew B.

I am the black rose.
Strong like a tree deeply
rooted in earth.
Though winter will come and
I will surely die my seeds
will grow strong and flourish.
I am beautiful though I have a rough
exterior.
The world around me may crumble but I will
still stand.
I am the black rose.

Hood
Darius B.

Black and Blue/what's good
in the hood/nothing for you
Cause you about to be laid
out with no gym shoes and
you don't have to prove you
about to lose and maybe.
be now or never but me
I 'm going to always be on my
cheddar and my name like
K West cause it's going to last
forever.

Chicago
Eric D.

A city where gangster's famous
to the Soldier field...United Center
where the project is deteriorating
and the block is always full
A city where you have to bundle
to the people that give you coldest stare
where police harass young people everyday
to drug dealer and city workers stand on corners

My Chicago
a place where you can live here you can make it anywhere
crisis reign supreme bloody murder people
turn devil's by green
a place where it is not safe unless you have a familiar face

Dedicated to a Mother from a Child
Sashay S.

I dedicate this to that one person.
That's always there no matter what.
You help me with my every need.
Nothing would ever tear us apart.
Without you I cannot be.
You always push me harder and harder.
Just to make sure I will succeed.
No one else could ever take your place.
I talk to you for hours at a time.
Just so you can know what's on my mind.
More like a sister then a mother
but I know what's the limit and I dare not go over.
You're always there to show how much you care.
I dedicate this to that one person.
That knows my every need.
Sometimes I get mad when you go through
my things, but I learn to get over it.
We laugh.
We play all the time.
That's why I think of you as more of a sister
than a mother.
So I dedicate this to my mother.
With love from a child, to a mother.

Quiz
Bonita A.

Life is a quiz.
But it's up to you to study real hard.
If you study hard then you will pass.
If you don't study then you are bound to fail.
Fail, a quiz, test or even life.
Study hard and you will get good outcomes.
Outcomes that will follow you the rest of
this quiz - life!

The People Cry
Jacques S.

To Haiti, I go.
Where for Christmas, it never snows.
It's hot all year round.
Faces filled with frustrations and frowns.

Infants infected and no injections to help 'em heal.
So they stay ill, no doctors to prescribe pills.
The government is corrupt.
The presidents make life tough.
They kill the ones who speak the truth.
And the crime rate's through the roof.
But they always get away cause there's
never enough proof.
Kids are given guns and forced to fight and kill
More and more mothers bury their sons
atop the hill.
The little girls are raped.
Their bodies found in lakes.
You'll make a lot of money
if it's coffins that you make.

Family
Moneet B.

What is family?
I used to know what family was when
I had one at the age of
twelve.
But that all changed and I...
No longer had one.
Now family is my grandpa.
I also have a grandma but she is
not family because she is mean.

When I thought I lost my family,
I was like it was all over.
But now I have someone else who
loves me.
And that makes me feel like I have
FAMILY.

Why I Write
Briana G.

I write to release pent-up energy.
I write to express creativity.
I write to reveal my innermost desires.
I write to be free.
I write to remove the hurt and pain from my life.

Poetry is an expression of self.
Poetry is a reflection of self.
Poetry is a release of feelings.
Poetry is a world of verse.
Poetry is a way to vent creatively.

My pen tells stories of hurt.

Tells stories of pain.
Of love.
Of joy.
Of dreams.
Of hope.
Of sadness.

I write because words are powerful.

Tycelynn T.

Children getting killed in their own homes.
Mothers running home from the message on the phone.
Your daughter has just been shot.
The bullet, an innocent child.
Not living to see her 12th birthday.
The mother will heal someday.
Not knowing that it would be her
Loud music, cakes, children, then this....
Not giving her her last kiss.

Gang bangers stop killing innocent children
Cause they are the future.
Put the guns on the desk.
And please, please, put it to rest.
Children can't even enjoy life
Worrying about who the next bullet will hit.
Not living to see what their destined to get.
Stop stop stop.
Can't you see this hurts
Innocent people?
If it was your daughter what would you do?
You'd walk around not having a clue of what to do.
Stop wasting your money on guns and bullets.
Spend it on a child's education.
Stop standing on the street's corners.
And stand at the alter.
And be forgiven for your sins.
Stop selling cracks to feens.
Sell homes to queens.
Stop killing people
And fight for better jobs.
Stop going to jail for violence.
Go to school, college or take up a trade.
And when you look back on everything the
Two little children could've stayed.

What is Inslavery
James A.

Inslavery is being enslaved by someone who not knowing.
Inslavery is children getting killed on their birthday from a mindset of gangwar.

Inslavery is chefs beating people on nation T.V. and getting away with it.
Inslavery is police beating and dealing as well as the drug dealers getting drug from their vendors.
That is Inslavery.
Inslavery is…
The rapists
The murderers
The gang bangers
The injusticed people
The low pay jobs to no pay jobs
The video chicks
Etcetera etcetera
Inslavery is starting to come back
And we are too blind to see that it's slowly
But surely come back in effect and I think
We should be aware.

Life Is
Group Poem
Ms. Matti's Class

Life is everything you make it.
Life is the lessons you learn.
Life is always worth living.
Life would be fair when we all have peace.
Life would be fair when I'm on my own.
Life would be fair when everyone earns what they work for.
Life will never be the same without my love.
Life will never be the same if I didn't have my family.
Life will never be the same as it was when I was six.
Life and its uncomfortable emotions.
Life and its tragic seasons.
Life and its complex notions.
Life and its abstract reasons.
Life and its moments.
Life and its exasperations.
Life and its nonchalant attitudes.
Life and its difficult lessons.
Life and through it all.
Life's sunny mountains standing tall.
Life and its sacrificial obligations.
Life and its eternal occupation.
Life is full of lots of pain.
You got people selling crack cocaine.
My life is a very hard challenge
You can't even walk the street
without witnessing some damage.
People shooting and killing.
Don't have respect for the willing.
Because everyone is dope dealing.
And every time you turn on the news someone is dying.
And witnessing the parents crying.

Wondering...thinking how life is.
When I'm sitting there laying in my bed.
Thinking of the good times
I had when I was a kid.
Life is too valuable to waste.
So get up and find your place.

Young, Black and Trying
Robin I.

As the day goes on, I become
stronger but with the new
day ahead, I'm still trying.
Trying to make it through life.
Trying to be the best I can be.
I try everyday to help others
in every way that I can.
I try to be that young black smart student.
So that soon I can be that young black crime
scene investigator.
I keep trying and trying in every minute,
in the day.
I try to keep going every day
even with harm and danger in my
way.

Back in the Days
Shapell T.

When I was growing up I was
Older than what I was.
Doing what I'm doing
But more of it.
Rats and things you could say
That was the hood.
Other people getting robbed and shot.
I don't think that have an end.
Every time I see a fight just wondering
If there is a murder.
But the fact remains that it would never
Change.
We never had green grass let alone
Perfect in the house or outside of it.
Being the house was so old, I thought
Ghosts was kicking it with us.
I can't lie, I hated house but my
Lifestyle was cool.
Best believe that thing is priceless, with no
Price tags.

James Shields Elementary

Larry O. Dean, Poet in Residence

Principal: Phillip Salemi

Program Coordinator: Assistant Principal Gerardo Arriaga

Teachers: Ms. Coyne, Ms. D'Andrea, Ms. Dennehy, Ms. Farrell, Ms. Fialkowski, Ms. Graefen, Ms. Hughesdon, Ms. Michel, 5th

Trouble
Jose A.

My family was short, big,
and famous. Once my dad
rode the biggest bull and beat it.
Once I rode the lawnmower into
the house, drove the golf cart into
the pool and filled it up with lobsters,
the cake with firecrackers. My family
is wired.

The Painting of Mona Lisa
Angelica A.

It is on an afternoon where a
lady stands with her sweater.
In back of her you could see
a river, mountains and dirt. The
sky looks blue. Her eyes look
like she was hiding something
from you. If you take a
closer look you may see that
she has a scar on her head
close to her hair.

My Self and a Scissor Stone!
Yesenia A.

It's a hot day with no one to play
with. My dad sends me to cut the lawn.
I take the big heavy scissors and
cut. They make a clicking sound. Big and
gray they're still over 2 pounds. I run
in, my dog follows me and I do
my projects. "But wait!" Where are my
pieces of paper? Oh I found them.
My dog was stepping on them.

5 min's. Later I go outside and
trip over a big smooth but cold
stone. I didn't get a cut because, it's
not too rough. So I try to move

it instead. I call my dad and
he pushes it away. When he pushed
it I knew it was heavy, I could
see his veins. Well that's what
I did ....

The Past!!!
Crystal B.

The girl who was my neighbor long ago.
Hot summer days playing in the water. Getting
a tan, walking and talking and going to the store.
Playing dolls, very hot, no water because too fun
to stop playing dolls. In the park, swinging on
the wheel, playing around the park. So much
fun in the summer but not to more!

My Uncle's Car
Rocio B.

In the hospital while I was being
born my uncle had finally fixed his car
after two years trying to fix it. He got so
excited in the alley all people who saw
him thought he was crazy already. Then
he heard the big news I was born. He
quickly called everyone in the family,
if they wanted a ride? Luckily no one did 'cause
he popped into a pole. The ambulance came
and took him to the same hospital
where I was at.

Lunch Time in School
Elizabeth C.

Everybody is with their friends and
you hear different conversations
and some people are quiet and
just eat without
friends to talk to
but that is
how life
is

Colors
Arminda C.

Red sounds like a big, loud trumpet
Yellow reminds me of the bright sun
Orange reminds me of the crunchy
leaves of fall
Green looks like the freshly cut
grass
Blue looks like the night sky of
summer
Purple reminds me of my mom's
favorite dress
Brown is like a spoiled banana
Black sounds like a rainy day
White reminds me of snow
Black also sounds like when
you get a bad report card

The Sweetness of a Heart
Yudith C.

Your heart is tender, so sweet,
so kind. Your heart is the one who
keeps you alive. It's sweet like honey,
tender like the wind. Peaceful helping you
to live, red and blasting dark red blood.
It doesn't matter at all what people say, it
only counts what your heart says. No matter
what, your heart is sweet and makes you
bleed. No matter what, your heart is
sweet it looks like a red gum drop
you can eat.

My Room
Alejandra C.

Where I concentrate and play. Where
I always want to stay.

The floor is white.
The door is red.

Where my brother snores.
Where his tiger toy roars.

The walls are pink and blue
and where my homework flew.

My favorite room is
my room.

Halloween
Andrea C.

Halloween, you scary day
you shine my heart with your
scary moves. You scare my face
with all the things you have. My
hair goes up and stays there. My
eyes fall off and stay all alive.
I faint and you laugh and
you make me loose. I become
a loose person without bones.
I'm all wiggle and I scare
people with my wiggle stuff.
My eye bumps out with your
scary night. My night was
terrible and I was dead
like a zombie.

Stomach
Jose D.

　　　　My stomach, it's a hungry lion
looking for food.
　　　　My stomach is a hill going up and
down.
　　　　My stomach is where a bear hides
his food.
　　　　My stomach is where pirates dig their
treasure but they never covered the hole.
　　　　My stomach has an X to mark
the spot.
　　　　My stomach is a blanket
that covers my heart and lungs.

Living Room
Moises D.

The way the floor creaks when
somebody walks by. The couch when
you sit on it, how good it
feels to relax. The TV we all watch.
The curtain designs shine on the floor.
The Playstation 2, how it lays on the
bottom right next to the TV calling
my name. The things in my living room
all make a part of the whole house.

Chicago
Adeyanira E.

You are like a flower letting
out fresh air. We have many

sports that we play in you. Many
people love you and call you
"land of opportunity." We
have many shops to buy things
from with your money. You also
have so many beautiful things
surrounding us.

Cousin Jennifer
Daisy G.

Cousin Jennifer
so tall so bright!
So nice, so furious
like if she woke up on the
wrong side of the bed! So damp
outside, she stays in, feeling left
out. She's wanting to go outside
and have fun but still. Remembering the hard
times and good times, laughing
and giggling, oh my gosh? She falls
asleep and forgets everything. Still
slouched on top of the couch.

Opposite
Judith H.

I am so tall I can touch the
clouds.
I see the trees flying and bouncing
off the ground.
I have a pet alien.
I am a no belt in karate.
My jacket has an automatic zipper.
I have a star on my forehead.
My hand reads books.
I wear my clothes on backward.

Monica H.

I remember
when I was
playing with a
cat and I
fell to the
floor and
the cat that
I was playing
with it was
a girl and my
tooth came
out and the

little cat
was like
sad and crying
and she went
to my grandmother
and brought her to
the patio and
then I went
to the hospital
but I was
good and I
was on the
bed in the
hospital and
then the cat
slept with me
I love that cat.

Raquel H.

This picture is about when my sister
graduated from kindergarten. She was
wearing a pretty sparkling dress with
little high heels. The date was June
15, 2003. She looked excited. She was
in front of the closet door.
You could see the top of my
hat from the closet. Her dress
is purple.

Remembered
Ruth H.

I remember my baby niece
yelling so loud that could blow your head off.
I remember her chubby face looked all swollen but
it's just fat. I remember her loud farts that
could make you faint because it smells so bad.
I remember her saliva all dripping down to your
mouth when you carry her high in the air. I
see her clapping to every song she hears. Her
name is Brianna, my beautiful Brianna.

Alex L.

I would like to give
my mom a puppy. She will
like it. The puppy will jump
on her and start licking
her. She will be laughing
when the dog gets dizzy.

Jessica M.

In the morning
my living room smells so
good like hot chocolate that
my mom makes. I
feel so comfortable in my
living room because I
can hear my favorite
radio station, B96.3.
I have a square
room, with a round sofa.
I have wooden tiles in
my living room. Man,
I wish my living room
was my real room.

A Cruise Around Mexico
Alehandro M.

My friends and I were taking
a cruise around Mexico. On a
pickup truck, a red pickup truck. My
cousin picked her friends up to take
them home after a day of soccer. As
we drop them all off we take a ride around.
The driver's name was Rosa. She was
driving crazy, my head kept bumping on
the side of the car.

Karina M.

The big horse
is bored
trying to jump
to make me fall

Me happy not
realizing,
the hot weather
dry and messy

The horse
with the long
hair and the
air making
it grow more

It's so sad
seeing the
horse tied up
with the stirrup

Game Room
Jesus M.

The floor is marble, shiny
and white, slippery and nice.
The computer is gray and
black and has a cool printer.
The TV is on the next
corner and it has a PS2;
it also has a Nintendo 64
but it broke. We have a
big palm tree on the next
corner. The sun comes in
sometime in the morn it is
warm because we have a
heater. The chairs are
black and they spin.

Paper, Scissors, Rock
Pedro M.

Paper is always so blank. Never anything. Always
blank. Some with lines and holes and some
just lying there, waiting for you to write on
it.

Scissors are always colorful with its
mouth always moving, ready to cut paper.
The two finger holes, always looking like
eyes.

Rock is always just there. Never moving.
It is always lazy, never wanting
to move at all. It's probably on vacation.
Paper, scissors, rock.

My Brother
Lizbeth N.

He was five years old.
He liked baseball.
His name is Eddie.
It was a Saturday.
Eddie sat on my aunt's fluffy seat.
Eddie has grown.
Now he is twelve.
Eddie will be thirteen in December.
Eddie's glove and baseball were so soft.
His hat is red and blue.
His hat was a Spider-Man hat.
He has a bat now.
He was so cute.

He is staring at you.
He has Hercules shoes.
He dressed so nice.
Eddie still has that shirt.
The hat he gave it away to Brian.
Brian is his cousin.
My brother's friend hit me with a bat.
It hurt me so much.
I went to the hospital.

Pumpkins
Cristina P.

Pumpkins are green
pumpkins are orange
pumpkins are good
once you make
me a pie.
You carve a pumpkin
you make a face
but you don't
scare me.
You can make
it scary, make
it your costume
if you want.
Still you don't
scare me.
The only thing
that scares me
is not going shopping.

Ode to My Favorite Sweater
Uriel P.

My sweater which is so warm
when I put it on it is warm already
the color is also nice
I like it because my best cousin gave it to me
When I got it it was so big and I looked funny
now it fits me just right
In the winter it warms me really good

The Opposite of Me
Laura Q.

I'm always writing backwards
I'm writing with my left hand
I have 3 pairs of glasses
I can jump off a cliff
I live alone with 27 cats
I live in the corner
My life is missing!!

A Bed for Mom and Dad
Alejandra R.

I wish I could buy you a bed but it is
too expensive, so let me buy you some
snow boots instead so the snow would
not get in your brand new shoes.

Ode to the Pool
Isabel R.

O how I love the large cool blue
square of water called a pool. Underwater
nice and quiet as if, I was in a dream.
The floating motion I feel as I spin
like a dolphin. In the showers steaming
hot, but in the pool cool enough
to refreshen.
The splash of dives in my face
as if I was in the lake or ocean
a swimming motion
a snake.
Swimming speed underwater
almost as a slow motorcycle
in one position the second position
as if flying in a cool sky like the
evening dark. From above to look is almost
like a mirror.
O how I love that blue
square looking like a blue Jell-O.
That cool blue pool.

Poem of Me
Kristina R.

My mom told me that I was
eating under the bed. I imagined that
the bed sheets had real flowers. I was also
taking a break from running away
from my brother. It looks like I
was stopped from trying to get on my
mom's bed. The wind is moving my hair.

Lunch Break
Megan R.

The loudness of
    the kids talking
        laughing and joking around.
            My friends make me
                laugh till I'm red
        sometimes I laugh through the
whole period of lunch. Crazy things happening.
            Crazy people and normal
        people sitting and sitting till
        we leave.

Paper, Scissors, Rock
Jessica T.

Paper → Homework, tests, poems, all those things
        we use to write on paper words.
        All those words make head
        aches. No wonder the teacher
        in 411 has a big head. Ouch.
        I poke my hand with a
        pencil. Hmmm...... I wonder
        how it hurts the paper.
        Poke, poke, poke. Damn I
        never knew paper was the
        problem. I get too much home-
        work. Hey paper go back to paper town.
Scissors → Scissors are sharp. We use
        them for cutting and
        they're coming to getcha!
        zzzzz Oh it bit you
        on the nose. Oh. No now
        you're bleeding seriously you
        better go to the doctor you
        have a pain.
Rock → Rocks hit you they getcha.
        And you need to protect your
        self. I know why don't you
        call it laser and by the
        way you need to ask those
        doctors how to get rocks off
        your back.

Ode to My Bracelet
Sara T.

My bracelet slides up and
down as I move my arm.
The tickle feeling on my
arm tickles the small
hairs and gives me
goosebumps. So thick, silver,
bright, stand out color.
Pretty silver charms swinging
making music when
it jiggles in the air
or on my desk, a
smooth, funny noise, sounds
like someone says shoo,
shoo, shoo and the
silence breaks.

Maria V.

I look like I was happy
my mom took my picture
I was not looking
I was with my mouth
open and my shoes looked
cool my hair looks
like it was sitting up
with one big rubber band in
my hair. I was wearing
a jean jacket with a pink shirt
and my buttons are pink with hearts.

Opposite of Me
Stephany V.

I don't understand anything
in class. I don't do my homework.
I never listen to my tea-
chers. I hate school. I
think I don't
know much. My desk is a
mess. I can't even sing or
dance. Is this
the real me?

James Shields Elementary

Erica Kholodovsky, Poet in Residence
Principal: Phillip Salemi
Program Coordinator: Assistant Principal Gerardo Arriaga
Teachers: Ms. Breen, Mr. Koclanis, Ms. McCormick, Ms. Storino,
Ms. Vazzana, Mrs. Vilchis, Ms. Wiegers, 3rd

The Happy Cat
Brenda R.

My cat's name is lady
She plays football
She's a happy girl
I feed her too

She's cute and happy
and that's why I like her

She's smart
Everyone in my family likes her

The Best Grandma in the World
Diana H.

My grandma is the best
She's nice, fun, and pretty.
She's my favorite grandma

And she knows how to cook really well -
Like tamales, pozole and eggs.

I love my grandma
And my grandma loves me too.

Wishes and Dreams of 2006
Julissa S.

I wish that there were no guns
I wish to go to school
I wish that my parents love each other
I wish for a present
I wish to go swimming
I wish mom gives birth to a boy
I wish for a cake -
I love cake.
I wish love to my teacher

I love you.

Blizzard
Carlos Z.

One day it was
sunny.
I went outside
I barely opened the door
to find
a blizzard
outside!

The blizzard
made me laugh
because when I
opened my mouth
and the snow fell in
It tickled.

The blizzard made
me cry
because I couldn't go outside.

Grandma Bertha
Analiz F.

My grandma Bertha likes to cook,
She's just like me.
My grandma Bertha has brown eyes,
She's just like me.

My grandma Bertha's really active.
She always says,
"Lets play popcorn!"

Grandma Bertha is always
really, really happy.

Teachers Are Smart
Megal M.

My teacher is smart
I think he knows everything
He really does know everything

My teacher is smart
He's as big as a tree
I think he should be on T.V.
Because he's funny, and sings well

My teacher is smart
He gets mad sometimes
But that's okay
He's still the greatest teacher

In the whole world

Grandmas
Keith D.

My grandma is strong and happy
She cooks rice and beans

She's healthy and has strong bones
And sometimes she plays with me

She worries about me
She helps me

She is a special grandma
And I love her
so, so much!

Riding A Bike
Diana R.

In the summer and winter
I race down the sidewalk
Riding my bike

It doesn't matter if I fall
'Cause I'll land on the
fresh cut grass
It'll feel the same as the snow.

I ride my bike down the block
It feels great having the air
blow in my face.

Art
Jonathan R.

Art is fun,
You can imagine...

Clouds are cotton candy pink
Penguins flying in the big yellow sky,
Different colors, different shapes,
Different sizes in my face.

Mexican, American, and so much more...
Sculptures from all over the world.
There are stories left behind from art and love.
There are many kinds of arts -
Singing, dancing and painting.

I like art because it is so fun
to imagine blue trees, dark red water,
Horses riding on people...

My Mom
Cynthia G.

My mom is sweet
She loves sewing
She also cooks
She's always smiling

She has pretty eyes
She's a nice lady

She is kind to everyone
She is the best!

Raindrop
Alexsa P.

Let the rain go down
your nose.
Let the rain hear you talk.
Let the rain make puddles
on the sidewalk.
The rain can makes sounds
like drip drop... drip drop.
The rain can tell you things
Like jump in the puddles.

5 Ways I Look at My Cat
Anonymous

1. I look at my cat's eyes and they look like marbles.

2. I look at my cat's tail and it looks like a furry snake.

3. I look at my cat's ears and they look like mountains.

4. I look at my cat's mouth and it looks like a cave.

5. I look at my cat's body and it looks like a forest filled with hairy trees.

Aileen R.

I can touch my pencil when I am
Writing.
I can taste the fresh apple on
my mouth.
I can hear when they're calling my
name.
I can smell the fresh baked
cupcakes.
But I can also see you.

Colors
Andrew L.

Red is good red is great
Blue tastes like carrot cake
Purple is cool
Yellow is hot
Green is like a lot of snot
Silver is cool it looks like glitter
But when I eat something pink it's bitter
Gold is really really shiny
Bronze is like a baby crying

Andrew L.

Martin Luther King was a great man to me.
Rosa Parks didn't have to give up her seat.
If Garret Morgan didn't invent the traffic light we would all crash.
If we crashed it would be a big smash.
If the Sox won I would be glad.
If the Astros won I would be sad.
If we didn't have school I would be happy.
If we had school forever that would be crappy.

Angel R.

My mom smells like a nice red
cherry. When I taste the cherry
it reminds me of my mom.
When I look at my red
shoes it reminds me of my
mom because of her smell.
When I look at something
red it reminds me of my
best mom ever.

Bianca S.

My favorite book is the Magic Tree House.
The water is like a dark jewel.
The ship is big like a whale.
The people look like ants.
The dog looks like a cat.
The dog has puffy hair like a puffer fish.
The dog's paw looks like a paw print.
The dog's nose looks like a cow nose.
His ears look like a big fish.

Damian A.

I am a little bit short like eating beans or
fries. I am a little bit brown of my skin. I am
a little bit braggy. I am a little bit hairy with
a lot of hair. I am a little bit short and a
little bit noisy. But I am great with
that. I have no glasses or grasses but
I do have legs or eggs. I do have
a mouth but not a bouch pouch. I do have
eyes but not beyes.
I do have everything.

Damian A.

The music feels like a drum and a trumpet to do a song. I heard a lot of noise like a musician like his playing a song at a show. The song makes me write faster and faster like an airplane.

I hear a trumpet and a

and a drum and a flute that reminds me of a tornado swirling over Iowa dancing like a show or a song like something.

I hear a flute, and a piano, and a guitar. It reminds me when my two birds when I was little one died and one flew away.

Daryl C.

Some people are short some are
tall but it does not matter. Some are
brown some are white it does not
matter. Some talk some are shy
it does not matter. Don't climb a
mountain without your safety stuff.

Eddie L.

The sky is blue. The lake is blue. The cat is blue. The houses are blue. Everybody's eyes are blue. The park is blue. The witch is blue. My whole body is blue. Kevin's nose is blue. The monkey is blue. Leslie's hair is blue. Samuel's foot is blue. The lightening is blue. Everything is blue, even the whole universe is blue too. Also the sun is blue, and the stars.

Sun and Earth
Jose P.

Why are you color blue?
    That's the water.
Why is there oxygen?
    So the people can breathe.
Why did you put it so the people could?
    That's just the way it is, said the Earth.
Why are there strange things there?
    Those are buildings.

The Dog
Letica R.

I.   There are six
mountains and
we walk the dog
up with him.

II.   The dog goes
up the stairs and barks.

III.   My mom sees
the dog drinking water.

IV.   A man and a woman
with a baby and seeing
the dog that it needs a family.

V.   My mom does not
know what to prefer
a dog or a cat.

VI. The shadow in
the water sees the dog's
face.

VII. I could imagine
a talking dog.

VIII. The way how the
dog is what size.

IX. The way if it's
fat or skinny.

X. The way that
he barks at people.

XI. The way people
looking at him.

XII. The way that
we take care of him.

XIII. And the way
that he sees the snow coming
from the south pole.

The Alien and the Boy
Ricardo R.

Who are you?
>My name is K.O.
>I am from the planet Mars.

I'm from Earth. My favorite
color is green.
>My spaceship crashed in
>a mountain. So can you
>help me fix it?

Yeah, but first let me get my
tool box, o.k.?
>What is a tool box?

Let me show you when we're
finished.

My Dream
Richard Q.

Once I had dream
I was in my room
In my dream I was eating my shoes
When I woke up and was eating my shoes I knew my dream
was true
Chew and chew I did to the shoe.

I Remember
Group Poem
Ms. Koclanis' Class

I remember running very fast I was fast.

I remember when it was my first birthday and they said "bite the cake bite the cake!"
So I bited the cake and guess what, someone pushed my head and I got cream all
over my face. I was so mad and embarrassing.

I remember getting my first shoes but now they quite smell.

I remember the first time my sister played with me and lost.

I remember the time I got my library card.

I remember when I beat all of you.

I remember: a silly hat I used to wear and the kids were teasing me about it.

I remember: my first day of school that we did not have homework.

I remember: Halloween when Mr. K was a pirate and now a cowboy.

I remember: when I went to Mexico and rode a horse and drove a car.

I remember going to Chucky Cheese when I got a free cup.

I remember winning a goldfish.

I remember running from a cat.

I remember the day that I drank maple syrup.

I remember Ms. Warren's funny three eye hat.

I Remember
Group Poem
Ms. Marfise's Class

I remember I went on a slide that never ended.

I remember when I first touched a flower the color red petals soft like a blanket.

I remember the first day of school I was shy.

I remember when I got adopted by aliens.

I remember when I got adopted by lions.

I remember when I got adopted from tigers.

I remember the day I went on the ferris wheel and a man fell off.

I remember when my teacher slipped on the ice two years old.

I remember when my dog got bit by a dog.

I remember my uncle's wedding in a nice church so brown.

I remember when I rode a flying motorcycle in the air and the air puffed right through my hair.

I remember when I was adopted by a dogcatcher in light blue he looked ugly too.

I remember my dad woke up looking like a frog.

I remember my grandma got struck by thunder.

I remember when I wore 500 hats.

I remember when Santa put me in his bag of presents.

I remember when I was reading 1,000 books.

I remember when my dog licked me when I was asleep.

I remember one day I went to my cousin's house we made blue tamales.

I remember Ms. W. had a meatball hat that was brown.

I remember I saw Santa Claus and he fell down.

I remember when my sister was in my mom's stomach.

I remember I hit my sister with a snowman's head.

I remember when I got on a swing and it couldn't stop.

I Remember
Group Poem
Mr. Heredia's Class

I remember when my dad works.

I remember when I was the only one crying.

I remember when I was a little boy and I threw food on the floor.

I remember when I got run over by the Mystery Machine and Scooby Doo was in it.

I remember when I was playing my game and every time I lost I said a bad word.

I remember the time when I went to the zoo a tiger that wanted to get out.

I remember when I saw people fighting over a piece of cheese.

I remember when I saw a monkey with a dress.

I remember when I was trying to talk to a squirrel and the squirrel got up and started touching his chest ready to attack.

I remember cuando (when) I got hit by a dictionary.

I remember when my brother would sleep the whole day in September.

I remember a dream when my family and I were in the sinking Titanic.

I remember daydreaming all morning. (I still do.)

I remember when I had carefree worries.

I remember when I didn't want to take a bath.

I remember when I fell out of the swing in Mexico.

I remember the time the pot of tamales that I carried fell in the sidewalk of Mexico.

I remember when I was running in the mile run in first and second grade and I had the fastest time.

I remember my dog playing jingle bells.

I remember Joaquin dancing the cha cha slide.

I remember when I would get yelled at in library.

I remember when I ate cake by myself.

I remember the time I rode a horsey in space while eating toothpaste.

I remember the time I gave a dollar to a hobo and the next day he was in a Hummer.

I remember the time I became an astronaut and fell asleep in space.

I remember when I was adopted by cows and trained how to give milk.

I remember when my dog bit me on the toe.

I remember when I saw an astronaut saying weeeeee while he was flying.

I remember I ate a whole chocolate cake and blew up.

I remember when I got a house and rode it in space.

I remember my brother was being shy.

I remember when my cousin first laughed.

I remember when I was the first girl with two pony tails.

I remember when I heard English music for the first time.

I remember when I was the only one with white shoes.

I remember when I was the only one wearing a blue dress.

Smyser Elementary School

Dave Rosenstock, Poet in Residence
Principal: Jerry Travlos
Program Coordinator: Heidi O'Toole
Teacher: Ms. O'Toole, 8th

Papá's Revolución
Alexis G.

Papá has improved himself.
Now, he dresses in fine clothing.

No longer does the stench of *tobaco*
surround him,

selling cars, having his own *mercado*.
An event of pride,
La Revolución of his own....

Instructions on How to Do Your Nails
Amelia B.

Begin by choosing a color, one or
two or eight or ten. Too many to choose,
pinks, reds, blues, greens.
Then you see the color yellow
and you smell the bitterness
of enamel rotting away.
Then just to look beautiful
you stroke an endless stroke,
the color brilliantly shining
and all you can do is wait
for the color to dry.

I Remember
Alexis K.

I remember when my cousin opened the lid
to a public ashtray, and a mass
of smoke drifted out, making us cough
and choke on the strong fumes.

I remember when I made cookies with
too much brown sugar, clumps of
sweet grains in every bite.

Dear Prisoner
Mariam K.

You are trapped. You are lonely. There is anger and sadness in the air. It surrounds you. It lives in you. You breathe it. You feel it crawling around in your mind. The world doesn't see you. You live in despair. Your world fades away, day by day....

Smell
Tasha J.

Spirits invisible but not immaterial. Muffled accompaniment of an Indian march. Everywhere darkness is absolute, with the least lapping of sea-green.

The Streets
Jasmine P.

When you walk down the street.
You always see a sheet.
People crying, people dying...
Will you survive
in the grind
you gotta' hustle
to get through the puzzle.

Dear Prisoner
Monika W.

Penguins are black and white. They have a white belly and orange feet. Chubby and cute. I feel bad for you little penguin, because you have no freedom. You sit all your life in that cave, not knowing how wind feels. All crumpled and crowded your home is. So many others wanting to escape. We all gather to get some food, if not now then not later.

Sleeping
Ernie D.

Everyday you wake up
With all these things on your mind
You work, walk, run, and play
So you can wake up the next day

With all these things on your mind
You lay your head on the pillow down
So you can wake up the next day
While your mind dreams and plays

You lay your head on the pillow down
And you wait until the sun will rise
While your mind dreams and plays
You wake up the next day and smile

How the Diamond Ring Came to Be
Andrea O.

A long time ago a cave woman was mad at her husband. She pouted and yelled
until she left the cave. The husband needed something to calm down his wife. So
he jumped up and down until the ground caved in. Underneath the rocks were shiny
diamonds. He gave her the diamonds and she chilled out.

Instructions on How to Beat Yo Kids
Mariah R.

take out yo belt
tell yo kids they betta
get inside dey room,
den go inside dey room
wit da belt and make sure
yu ain't holding the part of
the belt dat got da
buckle on it. And make sure
ur kid taste the belt
hurting dem.

With Its Beak Open
Krystian C.

The egg that is rounded
In the nest and is bounded
By straw and hay and is shrouded
By it's mother's warmth

The egg that is rounded
Cracks like a broken mirror
The chick pecks for freedom
For hours and hours

The weak chick loses energy
As it tries to break from the hard shell
The baby chick makes it out
With its beak open
and heart stopped

Moon
Matt L.

The moon is bright as a shadow. It follows in the night like a peeping tom. All are
engulfed in madness, never the same again. See more light coming from the
swamp than the moon.

Black Rose
Amanda C.

I would give you a red rose
But because I hate you
      I won't
This rose suits you
      Just right
You have a black heart
      and a wilted soul
As this black rose is dying
      so are you
As it falls apart
      And the petals become
               Dirt
So do my feelings
      Just like this rose
Dark, wilted hate

Dear Prisoner
Isela M.

I am a prisoner. In
my basement. Surrounded by
little kids. Running around.
            Screaming.
Sitting there. Without a
window. Babysitting. Being
punished. For nothing done wrong.
Watching boring shows. Waiting. Waiting
for adults to come.

Dear Prisoner
Tetyana V.

I love and miss my family
Also, my friends
I want to be all the time with them
But the life is very hard now
I must be here in America
And on Ukraine I can just call
It's very hard for me
But when I come to Ukraine
It's will be a very good time
I believe in the happy future!

Me
Emily C.

Its fangs pierce my heart
Bringing me closer to the dark.
Its bat wings grow bigger
Making the light dimmer
I search my
Eyes for proof
Glaring at me
As if somehow it knows
We share something—
The same fears the same tears?

A Red Malibu
Natalia G.

A red Malibu
parked next to *el mercado*

A man inside the car smokes *tobaco*
and listens to melancholy boleros

wandering off into space
thinking about his love

tears falling down his cheeks
while his hands shake

Lichon
Nathaniel S.

I remember eating lichon with garlic
after I slit open the pig,
cleaned out the blood and guts till there
was only meat, then put all the
spices and veggies in the slit
open part and sewed it all up. Then tied
the arms and legs to the stake
and stabbed the metal stake
through the pig's butt and out
the mouth.

Instructions on How to Watch TV
Jun N.

Begin by smelling where the remote is.
When you find it, press the tongue button,
then search for what you like and
just put your ear to the TV and
stare at the program.

I Remember
Jenny D.

selling lemonade in front
of my house, people loved it and
always came back for more
little cups and homemade signs
25 cents

My Mom
Diana B.

My mother is working
Trying to finish fast like a
Running train
Exhausted as if she were going to die young
She works with people
Fixing their teeth to make them
Feel beautiful
"Smile," she says.

What
Maritza J.

Anxious to see what it is, what it does, who it is
Three more bumps wander all around where the shadows end
Ending the noise, disappear into a clear night
Vultures suddenly appear and the weary sky
Endless words with fear and cries

Thunder
Paulina R.

I am gray thunder drip drop
Boom I came drip drop
Boom I come light light
reflects on the water pooled
on the sidewalk
Oops my fault drip drop drip

My Dad
Becky D.

My dad works in an office
and types away on a computer
in the light of the sun
with nobody to talk to
but the guy sitting next to him
all of whom are broken
and on light duty
instead of transporting food
all over the city
they're sitting at a computer
organizing data
for Sysco foods

Her Papa
Maggie K.

Her papa, so big and strong,
has the kindest heart of any man.

His room, smelling of tobacco,
would be the favorite one in the house.

The radio working day and night
played boleros to create a thinking mood.

As he took me to the carnival in his Malibu
we laughed and we sang, leaving no time to waste.

Proverbs I
Agatha B.

You are generating windows of your soul
Good news will be and the evil is ignorance
Your first choice is always your best investment

One Day an Alien
Stephanie K.

One day an alien was playing with G.I. Joe and a Barbie Doll. A storm was on the
way and the alien left the two dolls on the lawn. A surge of lightning turned the dolls
into people and the rest is in the books.

Tombstone
Edwin E.

When a soul dies
another is born.
A tombstone is born from a woman.
She cries and cries as a tombstone lives
another soul dies.

Age
Jacqueline A.

Jogging along the beach
youth is holding on by its
fingertips. Night has arrived.
Get home as fast
as you can and sleep.

Pain
Allyson L.

No one understands the pain but you and I
If they did it wouldn't be just our pain but theirs too
They don't understand going across town to see our mother
They don't understand having to choose to hate or love our father

If they did it wouldn't be just my pain but theirs too
They don't understand why I cry myself to sleep
They don't understand having to choose to hate or love our father
They don't understand how I got in over my knees

They don't understand why I cry myself to sleep
These people I call friends I don't know if I should trust them
They don't understand how I got in over my knees
They don't understand why I feel like no one's home

Hannah G. Solomon
Elementary School
Becca Klaver, Poet in Residence
Principal: Susan Moy
Program Coordinator: Allison Lasner
Teachers: Mrs. Edelson, 3rd; Ms. Goode, 4th; Mr. Sandlass, 5th

Turnips Haiku
Group Poem
Mrs. Edelson's Class

Turnips and water
And what song would you sing, bird?
Spiders sing a lot.

My Wolf
Cristina T.

My wolf is as fast as a cheetah.
My wolf is as furry as my winter clothes.
He is as mean as a cat.
He is as curious as me.
My wolf is like a fur coat.

My wolf eats like he's royalty.
He is as black and white like
a pattern. My wolf acts like he's
in America again. My wolf's ears
are as pointy as a mountain.
He is as Romanian as me.

I Am A Seedling
Aimee P.

I am a seedling.
Because I am so small.
Even if I drink lots of milk
I'm still my same size.
It seems like in 10
years I'd grow.
A seedling takes many years
to grow into a tree.
I think I'll grow that way too.
So I'm a seedling.

Don't Tell Me
Nick C.

Don't tell me what to do
Don't tell me your shampoo brand
Don't tell me what time it is
Don't tell me your great grandma's favorite perfume
Don't tell me to write an essay
on how global warming has
affected our caterpillar growth
Don't tell me to wake up
Don't tell me to do my homework
Don't tell me your favorite color
Don't tell me to go to bed
Don't tell me to drink that medicine
Don't tell me

The Light Grave
Ruben V.

Dedicated to my father

I remember my father's grave.
I remember the shocking death.
I remember the crying day.
I remember the dark fire.
I remember the dark cemetery.
I can't sleep.
I can't eat.
I can't write.
I can't tell people.
    I need a father.
    My father is dead.

I've Never Been to Greece
Liam D.

I've never been to Greece,
But I know it must be
Full of locomotives
And lots of things to see.

Shishcabobs and statues,
And building of all sort,
Feta cheese is yummy,
I think there might be a port.

Tick And Tock: The Clocks
Alex B.

One day a clock named Tick
lost his tock and everyone
laughed at him. A clock named
Tock lost her tick and they
met each other and went
tick-tock.

Don't Tell Me
Rhys B.

Don't you dare tell
me anything I can't do

Don't tell me not to make
a time machine to bring a
dinosaur to eat some possums.

Don't tell me not to buy cards.

Don't tell me not to waste
a ton of money on winning
the lottery.

Don't tell me that I can't
eat a ton of soup.

Don't tell me not to destroy
the TV.

Paella
Camila M.

I turned the shrimps
into jumping shrimp

I turned the rice
into evil shine

I turned the chicken
into a dress

I turned the spices
into magic glitter
turns the age

I turned the paella
into everything

Loss of a Tooth
Benjamin S.

We lose a tooth. We grow
one new. That we keep forever.

A shark loses a tooth
he grows one back again
and again.

Sooo … Da-na, da-na, da-na
da-na …… crunch

Love is a CD
Katarina J.

Love is a CD if you listen to it too
many times you get sick of it and
if you listen to it only once in a while
whenever it comes on you think I love
this song.

The Table
Eleanor H.

It's four frightening legs
wrapped around yours when you eat
Food under tables
not the best place to hide
the pride of a wooden monster
It seems so magical in a woodcutter's
house

A half rectangle it makes my
heart tangle

Bad Boys
Salmaan H.

The sins.
Eight at the warehouse.

The sins. We
punch people in their chins.

We cheat on tests.
We're the best.

Cousins
Lubna A.

And old cousin
Big, old
Came to a big stop.

They have gone out of my life
This god has sucked them up.

Now another one comes
living, lying down, last and
lonely. Ready to be passed
on to the little one
Just barely beginning to
walk.

There Won't...
Deiarra T.

I remember when I had to
listen to my parents.
But now everything has changed.
There won't be any do your chores.
There won't be any go to your room
        or can't go outside.
And definitely won't be any you
        can't wear that shirt
or those jeans.
There won't be any do
        your homework.
There won't be any time to
        go to school.
There won't be any eat your
        vegetables.
And there definitely won't
        be any save your money
                for later.

I Never Saw the Arctic Circle
Calum B.

I never saw the Arctic Circle
But I imagine it like this.
With ice fields longer than life
and the sound of the wind,
        more tune than a pipe.
The lights of the lunar sky,
so peaceful and dazzling to the eye
I wish I could fly
        to the Arctic Circle.

Balls
Mohammed A.

Balls are a version of the earth. We play with them almost
every day. Sometimes they hurt as if you were bombing into the earth's
hardest rock.   When you throw it around it's like the earth rotating
around the sun. When kids have balls playing with them
is like a planet rotating around the sun.

Who Am I?
Nathaniel M.

I am a flower on a sunny day.
I am a police officer in a donut factory.
I am a teacher in a room of apples.
I am a 5-year-old in a chocolate factory.
I am a cat on catnip.
I am what I am.

My Computer
Mark A.

My computer is slow like a snail.
My computer gives me bad service like an old motel.
My computer is big as a giant.
My computer is black like nighttime (without the moon and stars)
My computer smells like Febreze-scent stories.
My computer has a voice like a tough man's voice.
My computer is wide like a white board.

Haiku
Rose C.

What a strange shadow.
Big fat tall scared and strong, open the door,
Father is shadow maker.

Haiku
Jimmy T.

Water is very light
Oceans cry like waves go by
We run, the water runs

The Necklace
Lemonia M.

The necklace has pearls
from deep inside the ocean
It can be beautiful but
it can also be foul.
It can come alive
and choke you just like
a murderer that murders
for no reason. For their
enjoyment. It can look
at you straight in the
eye and choke you.
So you can never know
what to expect from a
pearl necklace.

Untitled
Ethan V.

I was born three minutes ago. I opened my eyes
for the first time. I look at myself black
skin frizzy dark brown hair. I hear my mom
call me Menilik. My mom gives me
milk I hope she never leaves I will be scared
if she does. I am in Africa. It is hot
so I cry. I love to cry. The doctors helped me
get out of the womb. I want to be
a doctor. I am crabby and small but I am
Born!

A River Goes Fast
Emanuel C.

A river goes fast like a cheetah running
as an ostrich running for its life
as elephants running a stampede,
as a monkey swinging on vines
as a bird flying fast
like a wolf chasing its prey
as a crack in the ice
cracks fast. Huuuu! Whoa!
That's how a river runs fast.

William Howard Taft
Academic Magnet Center
Dan Godston, Poet in Residence
Principal: Arthur N. Tarvardian
Program Coordinator: Maria Asvos
Teacher: Mrs. Asvos, 7th, 9th

Poem
Dino B.

Festivals never been to, rain washes away
the leaves. It brings the smell of flowers,
and suddenly fall doesn't seem bad.

Fearsome Winds
Alejandro D.

Fearsome winds on a stormy night, unable to see
and unbearable to stand. The flashing of lightning
is the best of all. The sound of a thousand trains,
just hearing fearsome winds, would make you think
it is the end. Louder and faster it gets. There's no
escape, for the fearsome winds it's a game.

Chewing Gum
Jeoneva E.

You buy a pack of gum,
Then you take a piece out.
You unwrap the piece of gum
and you put it in your mouth and chew.

Then you take a piece out.
The best chewing gum is Extra,
And you put it in your mouth and chew.
People tend to stick their gum under the desks.

The best chewing gum is Extra,
that's why gum is not allowed in school.
People tend to stick their gum under the desks.
Therefore chew more gum!

That's why gum is not allowed in school.
You buy a pack of gum.
Therefore chew more gum!
You unwrap the stick of gum.

Atlantis
Ezell H.

1. Those who live in the sea will return to the shore.
2. Technology is the key to our future.
3. The angry will sink to the bottom and drown.
4. The happy are those who follow the chosen one.
5. A heavy burden for a heavy heart.
6. The blessed are those who see beyond what's really there.
7. When there is a problem the ocean is the solution.
8. The sun predicts the time. The time predicts our future.
9. As the tides change so does our lives.
10. You must become one with nature and technology to ascend to the lands.

Grass
Nenad L.

We play on you, like sports and stuff. You grow
like hair, and you're cut again. You're green,
and you smell good in the morning.

Watching the Fire
Shane M.

As I watch the fire I watch the colors burn and burn,
I watch the embers soar away. As the logs begin to shorten
and the flames begin to dull I watch and wait
for the shortened logs to fall.

Zombie
Kevin N.

I am a meaningless figure, I wander the night under the full moon
and the bright stars. I am a breathless creature without a purpose whatsoever.
I feed off the living and stay with the dead. My eternal world of torture
has no meaning, walking from place to place hoping to find a purpose,
but I don't. I am a zombie, a breathless figure.

More for Less
Slawomir P.

If you have less you have more. If you're rich, you're a poor soul.
If you're poor, blessed be your soul. If you're poor, you'll leave in peace.
If you're rich, you're a poor soul. When you die, you'll be dismissed.
If you're poor, you'll leave in peace. You'll have the kingdom and peace.
When you die, you'll be dismissed. If you're poor, you'll leave in peace.
You'll have the kingdom and peace, if you're poor and rich in soul.
For being filthy rich you'll be destroyed. You'll be forgiven forever,
and you'll be remembered... If you are poor and rich in soul.
For being filthy rich you'll be destroyed. If you have less, you'll have more.
And you'll be remembered... If you are poor—blessed be yourself.

The Ocean & Me
Stella S.

Swimming softly with the waves
our bodies move as one.
I take this moment to my head to save.
I think of the next swim that is to come.

Our bodies move as one.
I splash all the water around me.
I think of the next swim that is to come.
I splash so high I cannot see.

I splash all the water around me.
I hit the water slow, then fast.
I splash so high I cannot see.
I step to look at all that I have passed.

I hit the water slow, then fast,
Swimming softly with the waves.
I stop to look at all that I have passed.
I take this moment to my head to save.

Leaves
Dorothy W.

They come in different shapes. They are wonderful to play with.
They have wonderful colors of the rainbow, a crunch sound in the fall.
They all fall in the fall. The best thing you can do with leaves—
put them in a pumpkin-colored bag, use them at Halloween.

Poems: A Way of Life
Wasif A.

Poems are body parts used to express thoughts that cannot be at risk
of getting cancer, that cannot be cut or fractured. Poems are body parts
that are carried around everywhere. Poems are body parts with thoughts
as bones, figurative language as skin. They are nourishment to you,
but they can't be digested. They give blood to veins, without danger of loss.

Additive Adjoining Adjectives
Raymond A.

Rapid revolutionary races, rickety rackety riots,
many multiple mice, long leggy lines, fully flanking flowers,
masterful monstrous marbles, extravagant elegant elephants,
fictional fake flies, atrocious, attentive ants, wistful wishful wasps,
blank boring base, creative crateful creates, explosive exiting exit,
hopeful happy hogs, Additive Adjoining Adjectives.

Life
Elyse D.

The earth is like a child, growing like me. We are the universe.
We came from the stars. The stars are our ancestors.
Every time we go to sleep we are sleeping with the universe.
We wake up with the universe. The universe is life.

Freckles
Katie D.

The galaxy is a child of the universe from which all things are made.
I am like a freckle on the face of that child. The child is a small part
of a larger family which continues to grow every day.
The universe knows more about itself than I do,
And it will always have its secrets that will be well-
hidden from my knowledge until the end of time,
until everything disappears and is forgotten forever.

Houses of Words
Kamil K.

The house was made of wood, *The Iliad*, the Queen of England,
the Coca Cola can, the Ides of March. Mozart's piece, Mark's trumpet,
Beethoven's piece of tape, Homer's *The Iliad,* The city of Chicago.

Poems
Mary L.

Poems can be a tedious passion or backbreaking labor. For me poems
are hard to write because sometimes they just don't come out right.
A poem can be thoughts and feelings from me, or maybe a stanza or two or three.
Poems take time because you have to think and write and you feel
like you're researching the history of meteorites. Researching meteorites
is hard to do because sometimes they pop up out of the blue. Yet for others
it's like having a good dream that you don't even have to think about to do.
It's all peace and easy feelings that don't bother you at all,
as if you're dancing at a ball. Everything runs smoothly, quickly, dandy,
but for me, "Would they really come in handy?"
'Cause quite frankly to me poems are just backbreaking labor.

A Poem: Touching Flow
Nick S.

A poem is a song that sings in one's head. A poem is emotion
on paper. A poem will go through your body, then it will soar
till it touches your soul. A poem is a river, a poem is a lake,
it has a calming flow. A poem is a leader, a poem is a lion,
it is a model for inspiration. A poem evokes emotions, a poem is a daisy,
a poem is a rose, it shows great beauty. Strong and beautiful,
touching and moving, it touches with lots of emotion,
like an amulet content inside, surrounded with feelings.
Hard to resist, its amazing lure will break through you and touch
your heart. Beautiful and graciously it flows. Like a song it flows.

Ars Poetica
Dominic S.

A poem is fire burning with details to the very end.
It has sparks flying everywhere. A poem can move
from side to side like a river, shift gears like a car,
or make no sense whatsoever. A poem has a center
of balance that keeps it a poem.
It may have words you don't understand, or
sentences that don't make sense.

A Poem Is...
Emichelle V.

A poem is a homemade picture of words, wanting to be heard
like a flying flock of birds. A poem is a mirror looking back at you
coming closer and closer. A poem is a feeling that you get
when you live. It's part of living and being. A poem
is like candy, so pretty and sweet keep it or eat it.
A poem is a poem. There is no limit to it. Just respect it.

The Art of Lying
Kaity B.

The art of lying isn't hard to master;
so many people don't look like dorks
but when you find out the truth it's a big disaster.

Tell a lie every day. Accept the grounding
after saying your dog ate your homework.
The art of lying isn't hard to master.

Then practicing less, lying less:
about friends, money, and maybe even rings.
All of these will bring disaster.

I lied about cleaning my room. And look! My
room is messy, and I can't find many things.
The art of lying isn't hard to master.

I lied to one of my friends, then many good ones,
and many didn't want to look at my face.
I don't talk to them, but it wasn't a disaster.

Even though some lies weren't a disaster,
I shouldn't lie in the first place.
The art of lying isn't hard to master,
though it may look like a big disaster.

How To Make a Nail
Chris F.

You will need metal and plastic. First make a mold.
No, first start a fire. There should not be too much metal.
The mold should be able to fit in your hand. Put the metal
over the fire until it is liquid. The hard part is not too hard.
Pour the liquid into the mold and you have a nail
as perfect as a nail can be.

The Art of Dreaming
Megan G.

The art of dreaming is an art indeed—it's not just leisure;
it's something we all need. It takes imagination and effort too—
To dream big dreams and make them come true.
Sometimes dreaming is left to the young.
Seems like when folks grow older, their dreams fall unsung.
To be what you hope for, to be your best—
Dreaming is necessary; it gives you pleasure and rest.
Just close your eyes and let your cares slip away—
You can do it at bedtime, or at the dawn of day.
Let your worries slip away while your dreams wash over you—
You'll feel relaxed and happy, like someone brand new.
I like to dream of my favorite places, and then build from there—
There's no wrong way to do it, it's your own private prayer.
The art of dreaming gets more beautiful with time—
It's your own private melody, a colorful rhyme.

The Planets and Me
Michelle K.

Mercury, though "little" in size, is burning hot, like my face
if you get on my temper. Venus, surrounded by deadly clouds,
mysterious like me as if I'm wearing a cloak. Earth, a cool relaxed pool of blue,
like me, unlike when I am at school. Mars, cold and red, I might be buried
there when I die. Jupiter, a giant gas planet, reminds me of when I caught a fish
in a net. Saturn, its rings are made of ice, reminds me of how I love Icebreakers
liquid ice mints. Uranus, it has a weird name, it's true, reminds me of the bathroom.
Neptune, god of the seas and his planet, reminds me of the swim team
I'm on here at Taft. Go Polar Bears! And Pluto, last but not least,
reminds me of my favorite cartoon character Mickey.

The Universe and Me
Sofie K.

Sometimes I feel it loves me...putting us directly in the right position

for human life to live. Sometimes I fear it hates me...when I hear of black holes

or when thunder boomshickles along. Sometimes I think we're fine.
The universe 8 other planets in our solar system to scare and tend to.
Sometimes I don't know what to think. I wonder, and my thoughts
become confuzzled. The universe likes to play mind games.

The Universe
Eduardo M.

I don't think that we are supposed to know. If we knew
it would be boring. Some people might not even like what they are.
We are who we are and we control it. We make the decisions
and we take responsibilities for it. There are unlimited ideas
of why we are here. I think we are here because we chose to be here.
I also believe we are here so our spirit can feel the greatness of life.
I am happy to be here and a lot of people take life for granted.
If people realized how lucky they were they wouldn't hate
so much and they would enjoy things more. We are the bosses of our lives.

Postcard Poem
Aileen N.

The feeling you get when someone remembers you
when they're having the time of their lives. Postcard.
When people give thought a time, 2:30, 5:20,
7:30 p.m. When my Aunt smiled in front of the ice
topped mountains. Postcard. When you reply
just think about the picture they gave. Postcard.
But the thing that always is the same is how
every reply ends in this was a very nice postcard.

Far Deep in the Sea of Stars
Nicole P.

1. Far deep in the sea of stars are unidentifiable creatures who have to be kind to others.
2. The greatest form of being funny is touching someone's shoe.
3. If a chicken laid an egg, then why isn't the finger here by now?
4. Never lick the window because the vampire was already there sucking souls away.
5. Shoes are completely good scented toward one's nose.
6. Cheese cubes are the number one vehicle.
7. Yoyos can't be inside the speaker.
8. Everybody has nine candles without wax.
9. Bomber bob is the king you must hail.
10. Five toes and eight pinkies to play with the keyboard.
11. Never make sense.

City of Fallen Flowers
Elizabeth S.

1. Serenity is the ruler of all.
2. Respect can be lost with actions.
3. Admire your elders.
4. He who murders will spend 10X the number of years the victim lived at the time of the murder.
5. All must be familiar with the crescent moon.
6. The West Side of town wears gold.
7. The East Side of town wears white and silver.
8. Must be able to accept the world's diversity.
9. Verbal attacks are prohibited.

The Light
Anjan U.

In the darkness of space, and in the planets of planets
there is a light far beyond reach. In the cosmos of the universe,
splendorous heat surprises us and show us the path.
The beauty of the universe is far beyond explanation,
and the stars of the galaxies are the light of our lives.
We are what we are and we cannot change
it but we should expand our knowledge of the universe.
I realize the world's beauty and I am thankful.

Tarkington
Scholastic Academy

Richard Meier, Poet in Residence
Principal: Vincent Iturralde
Program Coordinator: Assistant Principal Elizabeth Kastiel
Teachers: Ms. Cruz, 7th; Mr. Dunlap, 5th; Mr. Green, 5th;
Ms. Herrera, 6th; Mr. Kimbrough, 5th; Ms. Mitchell, 5th

Abecedarian
Mayra A., Jocelene C., Rafael C., Daniela C., Andrea C., Jairi C., Naschely D., Paola D., Miguel E., Jacqueline G., Victor G., Cynthia H., Victor H., Francisco H., Janet J., Ahmir L., Ofelia M., Marco M., Amalia O., Jonathan P., Lorena P., Gloria P., Ariella R., Manuel R., Gabriel R., Guadalupe R., Luis R., Alejandro S., Jaraea S., Salvador Z., Alejandra Z., and Ms. Kate Mltchell

Apples under the world and the color
black are evil apples, poisoning
children who eat them.
Decimals are killing the numbers
eight and seven because they
fought a war over the flag.
Grades are important and good and bad.
Hot fire on Ms. Mitchell's hat
injures little girls' and boys'
jackets.
Kites fly and
lonely people sit on the grass. The
moon stares at them.
No one goes wild
over school.
Power for tomorrow: the
Queen steps on the King.
Rest in peace.
Softballs
turn into unlikely variables.
Water
xylophones versus saxophones
your own very
zoo!

Inside of Me
Marco M.

Inside of me there
are big clouds of cotton
candy. The fountains throw
chocolate. A house is built
of candy and the river is
of orange juice.

My pet it is a humungous
pet. There are dinosaurs fighting
each other. The numbers in
the alphabet are up side down.
The sun is bright in the mornings.

Inside of me there is
a playground with slides and monkey bars.

Inside of me there is gold
stars that shine in the night and
you need to see them close because
they are small.

Inside of me there is a
tree with fruit candy.

Never Mind
Mayra A.

I don't feel like going outside
Not like an artist who draws
Not like going to play catch
or falling from the sky like a drop
I feel like an orange
wearing orange every day like
writing orange on the wall
people who fear
crying in places like being alone
      like going on a visit
      my sister a pillow
my brother the cover and
me I am a bed so tired
crying for them because they
are not here with me and
me alone in the rain
waiting for the sun to shine
all day because I haven't
felt good all day
I wish I was happy but never mind.

All Day Because
**Diana A., Jessica C., Oscar C., Adonis D., Johan E., Jonathan F., Denise F.,
Yasmine H., Maricela M., Erika M., Brandon M., Cruz N., Javonte P., Jermaine
R., Edward R., Jorge R., Rocio R., Marilyn R., Arturo S., Angelique S., Roldan
S., Bianca S., Gregory S., Tierra W., Shanice W., Jose Z., and Mr. Derrick
Kimbrough**

Because the cats were abandoned on 74th Street,
Because the dog bit the girl who hit him,
Because the girl got stuck in the tree,
Because the one star in the sky was shining bright,

Because the ice cream truck ran out of gas,
Because the guy on the corner was playing beats,
Because the homeless man asked for money at Walgreens,
Because the dog was chasing the cat, and the cat broke the lamp,
Because the bullies were chasing the girl,
Because the pencils are being thrown in the garbage,
Because the men fell in the crocodile pit,
For this, only for this reason, I hit my teddy bear.

Memories
Cruz N.

I remember my dog
when I used to talk
to him. I remember
the trees that I used
to see. When they
were so many differ-
ent colors. And how
dark the bark was.
I remember see-
ing the raccoons in
when they were
so furry. And when
their tales used
to wag so much.
I remember
in the zoo when
I screamed be-
cause the snakes
were so scary.
I remember
at night in my
room when I closed
the door and
the light was
on and I was
staring under
my bed to check
for monsters. I remember
being outside and watching
the birds because they were beautiful.

How I Feel and Other Things
Shanice W.

I don't feel like Dr. Seuss
and Thing One and Thing Two
eating Green Eggs and Ham.
Or Mr. Kimbrough teaching us.
Not my mom frying egg shells.
Not an Earthquake Shaking

in a Circle.
I feel like the Sears Tower
Standing tall, like the world
Spinning.
The moon going up and down.
My father the crocodile and
my mother the small one.
I feel like a reading book,
math book and Cat Woman
saving the world.

Pain Poetry
Javonte P.

At times you go mad
Because your control vanishes and you have to
Close the doors to everyone and have a
Desire to do anything and everything.
Even hate has more joy at times
Forgetting the things that you love
Getting away from everything
Hoping that someone won't catch you your
Ignorance overwhelm you
Junk in your mind
Killing your self from the inside
Leaving home and never returning
Marking your territory
Not feeling
Putting a price on life
Quiet deaths
Resting forever
Stop wishing for happiness
Tearing memories away
Ugly is that place
Vaporizing loved ones
War against everything
X-rays of pain
You hate everything
Zooming away till a new day.

Myself
Samia A., Irais A., Emmanuel B., Isaias C., Omar C., Lucero C., Leslie D., Malik D., Elizabeth E., Javier F., Vanessa G., Karina J., Shanica J., Armon L., Jazmin L., Jennifer L., Alexis M., Trevelle M., Brandi M., Demetry M., Jawon P., Jasmine R., Allison S., Marcus T., Marzaree W., Marquise Y., and Mr. Joseph Dunlap

I am alone in the desert
in the afternoon
with rocks sinking into the sand
and a mirage lake
in the distance of my feet.

I am alone in the closet
because nobody wants to talk to me
in the middle of the night
with coats like strangers.

I am alone at Christmas
when my whole family is there
eating tamales
and ignoring me.

I am the solitude of a flower
with petals coming off.
My loneliness is like a magnet
getting all my energy.

By Myself
Shanica J.

I am by myself in the store
in the day time.
I am buying limes and lemons.

I am by myself in the candy aisle.
All the candy is turning blue with sadness
and anger because I am by myself.

I am by myself in the bread aisle and the bread
turns away and turns to ash.

I am by myself in the juice aisle and the juice
melts to stone.

I am by myself in the cake aisle.
I am like a piece of cake being sliced in one and
being thrown in the garbage with the rest of the piece of
trash. I am by myself as some juice being spilled
on the counter and wiped away from existence.

In Imaginable Heads
Jawon P.

In Imaginable Heads
there are stampedes of
rhino's and snowstorms that
make houses white.

And there's an alien planning
to take over our new world.

In our new world everything
is free and there are oceans
that come to you.

But there is one thing
you must know your
multiplication.

There are wings you can buy
to make you fly.

I believe that
kids dreams cannot
be destroyed.

ABC Poem
Jasmine R. and Vanessa G.

An incomplete homework that day
Boys disobeying their parents
Cars nonstop for red lights.
Disliking the sand in the park
exclamatory sentences that
faded nonviolently.
Giraffes eat all the leaves from the tree.
Houses disliked by people who are
imperfect to be around with.
Just unperfect going to the concert.
Kids poetry unequal to
love for impossible nonsense.
Marquise jumping off tree like crazy
nut head eating bananas.
Oppum's nonviolent behavior.
Popular dishonest nonsense.
Queens have not
ruled the world
since
the king left her.
Unuseless nonsense after letters at the
Ven machine
with a
xotic
young mouth strategies
Zebra's eating the next day on.

Inside of Me
Iniki A., Jovanna A., Leonardo A., Erik B., Guadelupe C., Shevell C., Shawn D., Paris D., Fatima E., Lauren F., De'michelle G., Angel G., Veronica G., Jazmin G., Fantasia H., Consuelo H., Alexandria J., Kassandra L., Lamont M., Amanda M., Bobby M., Izamar M., Daniel M., Nakeara P., Joshua R., Vanessa S., Anahi S., Ivan I., and Ms. Lilly Cruz

Inside of me
there are no empty
spaces, no spirit.
There is rain

on midges and flies,
a mansion
with ten floors.

Inside of me
there's a person
sitting on the floor
meditating.

Inside of me
I'm taking a walk
and picking flowers,
balloons are flying
up in the air,
somebody's getting shot.

Inside of me
elves the size of my fingernail
walking around on my organs
and Winnie the Pooh
eating honey.

But beyond this weird place
of fire and everything upside down,
there is room enough
for one apple,
one me.

I Remember
Fatima E.

I remember my Bug's Bunny coat
hanger with its thorns out, and falling
down the steep, dark, long stairs,
screaming for my bottle and laughing
because of me falling down Dominick's.
Pretending to be a Powder Puff
girl long time ago looking back at dogs
behind me. My Mom in the hospital
with my brother by her side, sweating
cause of the hot blazing sun in my
yard, my wall with my Virgin Fatima
hanging looking at me. Waking up from
the nightmare and suddenly I know
how to spell my name. I know more
but I forgot.

Abecedarium
Anahi S.

Art, my favorite subject
Being yourself is tough sometimes
Criticizing is what bothers me
Drum banging music
Everything is always going wrong
Freak is what I'm referred to as
Grades stressing me out
Having second thoughts about a friend
I'm falling asleep during Social Studies class
Just standing and waiting
Knowing there is something out there
Living in fear of finding her out
Maybe someday things will change
Never knowing when the time will come
Optimistic about the future
Posers and liars everywhere you look
Quiet and shy doesn't describe me
Rock and alternative music is what I like
Saying sorry for laughing at her
Time to say goodbye soon
Us being afraid of who we are
Violence everywhere taking over us
Why is life so harsh?
X-rays for injured people
You know you're hiding something
Zebras are black and white

Pretending
Iniki A.

Apples, oranges, bananas, and cake
different kinds for Easter day
faking to sing great music at home
when really I had the radio on
just too late to kick the hay
lost my nice hair in an oval cake
prepare to quit running
I think I'll sit
today or tomorrow Vegas calls
what's excellent is. . .
All these things I dream up today
in my fantastic way
will probably all go away

The Alphabet
Kassandra L.

A lot of animals
begin to
count many ways.
Don't worry
everything should be okay.
Freak as it sounds, we're
going through many places like
here and there, mostly everywhere.
I'd hoped to be in a
junkyard by the time you get done with me.
Kangaroos will be hopping all around.
Lullabies will calm them down.
Making little noises through the day,
not only me but
over the city of Chicago.
People here and there.
Questioning why the
roses never bloom.
Shaking water through the bucket
though it splashed me all over my
unhappy face.
V. a little lame, I never liked her
wished to be gone
exactly out of this world.
You can imagine all the
Zing Zang up down my life is gone.

Love on First Sight
Lamont M.

When you see a girl you just stop what you are doing and just look at her

And when you want to talk to her you can't because you are
scared of what her reaction might be

But when you finally ask her she says that she has someone

And when you hear that you just pause and walk away

But when she is alone she suddenly wants to talk to you but
when she asks you you say I have someone and then she feels
salty because she didn't talk to you when she had the chance.

Inside of Me
Marisol A., Carlos A., Yanet C., Stephanie C., Alma F., Cesar G., Brenda H., Michael I., Devante J., Kypa J., Ariana J., Christopher J., Carolina M., Dalila M., Clyde M., Nancy O., Eduardo O., Alexander P., Rodolfo R., Jalonnie R., Elizabeth S., Robert S., Devonte S., Johnny T., Erick V., Rickaiya W., Ricardo A., Kelly M., and Mr. Jerome Green

Inside of me
there is a bobblehead
with his eyes closed, shaking his head,
and birds singing on a rooftop,
people swinging on a swing.
I'm being strangled by anacondas
with ninjas around me.

Inside of me
there are pyramids
and hot sand.
I'm searching for cool water
under hunted trees.

But beyond this zone
of scorpions and desert quicksand
there is room enough
for one raindrop,
one piece of pie,
one glass of lemonade.

Unknown Questions
Brenda H.

Why do trees dance in the wind?
Are they protecting their property?
Why is the sun so hot?
Is it because it has a fever?
When the snow comes,
does the grass get sick?
When the trees lose their color and their leaves,
is it because they got a new hair cut?
How would it feel
if we had no feelings?
Why do avalanches happen up on the mountains?
Is it because it dropped its milk while eating breakfast?
Do earthquakes happen
because the Earth is angry at us for living on it?
Why did they call
one of the planets Neptune?
Is it because a guy named Neptune
ruled this planet once?

When I was Little
Eduardo O.

When it was snowing
I thought god spilled salt.
I remember I used pillows
as villains.
I tried to spell my
name with alphabet soup.
I used to break out of my crib
because I wanted to watch TV.
I thought teachers lived in schools.
I remember I broke
a glass cup but my sister
took the blame.

I Am
Ernesto A., Myriam A., Moises A., Salvador A., Martha A., Deriknesha B., Nekeisha B., Essence C., Maria C., Alfredo F., Cecilia G., Yannick H., Robert M., Jesus M., Osvaldo M., Daniela P., Angelica P., Isela R., Juan R., Joshua S., Alberto S., Sheila S., Ryan S., Jamal S., Desiree V., Aaron V., Dawud Z., and Ms. Ana Lucía Herrera

I am the nerd reading the dictionary.
I am the dictionary full of words.
I am the fairy changing the frog into a prince
and the frog waiting on the lily pad.
I am the wind that moves the tree
and the tree swaying.
To the wind I say: stop blowing.
To the trees: stop complaining.
I am the smile on the Mona Lisa.
I am Leonardo painting.
The volcano about to erupt,
and the gentle snowflake
falling down from the sky.
The forest and Hansel and Gretel
dropping bread crumbs.
I am the world and the unseen galaxies,
the fact and the opinion.

An Alphabetical Feeling
Essence C.and Nekeisha B.

After Katrina I caused
Big
Commotion I feel like a
Drought
Expecting more water
For the damage I caused, feeling
Guiltiness is not a good feeling
Having no need of self esteem my
Ice cream has
Just melted and
Kids are
Laughing at
Me
No more crying now
Oh goodness said my tears, my
Portion of happiness is a
Question I'd rather not know, the
Symptoms of my sickness is
Taught
Underneath the
Veins of my arms
Why is the
X-ray of me matching
Yours
Zebra-like costume?

I Am The World
Jamal S.

I am the shine from
the light
I am the shadow
from the darkness
I say to the foot:
don't move
And tell the Earth
to rotate

I am the Earth's
gravity
I am the solar system's
moon
I am the one of God's
tears
I am the face that's
exploding

I am a father waiting
for my check
I am a school desk
with heavy books
I am the whole galaxy

Deep Inside Me
Myriam A.

I don't feel like snow white running
away and living with seven dwarves

I don't feel like little red riding
hood out in the dangerous woods

or birds touching the sky

I feel like leaves falling from a tree
I feel like a jar of peanut butter
trying to make its way to the bread

clouds hopping across the sky

My father is the milk my mother the
cereal and I'm the spoon

I feel there is another
person inside me hiding

Lyman Trumbull
Elementary School

Carina Gia Farrero, Poet in Residence
Principal: Robert J. Wilkin
Program Coordinators: Kristin Acierto, Jill Zver
Teachers: Ms. Acierto, 5th; Ms. Antoniadis, 5th; Mrs. Ashlaw, 4th;
Ms. Patterson, 4th

Music Poem
Syrene M.

Happy
On Friday
Pink

dance
Saturday night

Full moon
A little cold outside
Gold

Windy
Brown
Saturday afternoon

Friday afternoon
thunder
Black

Joyful
Frankie S.

If I were green I would be joyful.
I would be the grass and the leaves on a tree.
I would be a frog or a lily pad.
I would also be tall hills.

Dream
Max C.

Dragons
Rats
tropical beaches
People
My dark side
My grand parents

Music
Kyle M.

Sad
pink
crying
afternoon
winter
hard
roller skating

clapping
white
dancing

007
black
2stepping
boarding
water
slow
hitting yourself

yellow
afternoon
African
soft
sad

Maribel L.

una reina

las reinas son bonitas
por eso yo quiero ser

una de ellas

Communicating flowers
Brandall C.

The flowers communicate
When they   need   advice
to grow.
When   they   need   to
feed   their   bees.
When   they   fall   off
of trees.
When   they   are
carrying seed.
When   they   need
water, sunlight   and   other
flowering needs
When   they   are
fainting   and   almost
gone.
When   they   are
hanging   past   their
knees.
Flowers communicate.

Chalk
James M.

Chalk unhappy
      eaten by the chalk board

      I am a chalk
      an unhappy chalk
      eaten and eaten away
      by the chalk board

Pink
Natasha E.

I'm pink
I'm sweet
I'm me
Pink clouds wonder in the sky
Pink cars fly
Pink fashion statements run
Pink people walk
Birthday passes by pink cake,
Pink balloons pink every thing
I am pink
I wear pink
When fashion statements run by
I wear a pink skirt a pink blouse
And a girly pink blazer
I drink
   eat
   sleep
   talk
   walk
   sing
   ring
   pink   because I am pink

Saturday Song
Bianca A.

people was clapping
so raven, four aces. The night
time in a raining light.

a Wednesday song this is a
storming night in a tornado
time.

a happy Friday morning
is also a James Brown.

Coral Reefs
Lourdes D.

Rough, soft
dirty laundry
nothing
beautiful colors
salty

Music Poem
Denise F.

People dancing.

First it's sad then it's like a bad guy
chasing someone.

People in love.

Winter
Xuan Y H.

Winter
cold as the ice
wind as a blizzard
chilly as snow.
Dark
Freezing as a Ice
            and the best of
all we could have
a snowball fight.

Polar Bear
white as a snow
fluffy as the cloud
and the color of
piano keys

Poem
Sam S.

I am a dog

I am a fast car

I am a bug

I am a bee

I am a cartoon

I am a cat

I am a worm

I am a block

I am a number

I am a rock

Jeans
Blanca V.

When I wear my
cool jeans
they say
I love
your jeans.

Hurricane
Jose R.

Hurricane
is deadly
and hurtful.
it's rough like
a dog. When
I see a dog
I think of a
rough hurricane.
When a dog moves
I think a hurricane
moves.

Table
Lilianna M.

      Table
       I
    hold items
    tired
    sad
    dirty
    quiet

When I am a table
I feel
tired, sad, dirty, quiet.
I feel
      lonely.

Jesus P.

sadness and a story dance or
like a story with no words just music.

violin, and fast dance and fast play and
musicians and a play with no words
and just music. People dying and someone
dying.

musician music, guitar, words, mariachi
dance foot dancing.

blues, rock, drums, cymbals, dancing
electric guitar.

Isaac C.

spring / happy / tranquilo / azul
de 1985 / de fiesta / de muchos colores / night.
opera tranquilo / night / fast / red
a locos / caliente / rojo / James Bond.

Walter Payton College Prep High School

Cecilia Pinto, Poet in Residence
Principal: Gail D. Ward
Program Coordinator: Eileen Murphy
Teachers: Ms. Rodriguez, Ms. Murphy, 9th-12th

Where I'm From
Candice M.

I am from plastic slipcovers on the couch,
Antique pictures hanging on the walls
(broken time and again).
Where cans of reused grease, almost over-run by their contents.
Where the number of television channels doesn't pass the boundary of nineteen.
Where hand-woven quilts provide consolation.
I am from the times when friends were no longer friends,
But rather acquaintances.
Where children laugh and play in the rain wondering where the rainbow ends.
When streets were paved with glass.
The times when it takes the police an hour to respond to calls of "domestic abuse."
I am from times when you know your life is only temporary.

My State of Mind
Darryl T.

My mind state stays focused on the state of my nation.
I state the facts as they come to my mind that's racing.
My mind hits the page as I ride down State Street.
And the lady next to me asks me what my state-ment?
If Bush don't care how is he the head of state?
My state of mind changes as I contemplate what she stated.

José S.

My spirit always harbored a dark boat containing my past
as loneliness was the only demon i feared
like the birth of a falling star
it was a sudden moment when u appeared
u made everything worthwhile once again
replacing cynical thoughts with self esteem
i see a future through ur crystal eyes
as my mind recovers and begins to dream

One Word
Rodney S.

Amazingly
One word can change the world of a sentence
One statement can change the mind

One word can change the document

Inserting tools into the chain of thought
One word can create a network of places
Just one word on a page can spark an imagination

Her
Stephanie Rose P.

How she talks
And unconsciously makes a difference
How she walks
And immediately attracts followers
How she stands tall
Though everything inside may be collapsed
How she smiles
And is unaware of how many lives she has changed
How I admire the woman I call Mamí.

Turquoise C.

It's the one thing that holds it all together. The custard. If I keep spinning it'll all come down. None of us realize the true importance of these little things. She changed it. No one remembers the old ways of how things were done. We hail from beautiful Georgia where our ancestors lived. I have no idea of how the past came to be. Lemon, make sure you add only a little. The arguing stops, it dances around their tense shoulders. Such a tradition needs to stop. It's almost done. Is this what our family truly is? You'll be the last one, will you take it to your grave? I remember now a childhood of laughter and loneliness. Just like hers. Now I hold the key that keeps us together that keeps us alive. It's done.

Gabbi K.

There were rings, rippling outward from where the small stone had plunked into the water a second earlier. It seemed as if the water had swallowed the stone just as the people swallowed the words they wished not to speak. The ripples kiss the shore, rise up and slowly fall back down into the depths of the water as if telling the shore a quick secret and leaving it to contemplate the short message.

Secret kisses fall on her lips. She swallows deeply and looks shyly away. The quiet person who watches swallows his rage and turns away. He slips off the ring on his left ring finger and trembling, slowly shuffles away.

Secrets told, kisses refused, words swallowed, eerie silences, a piercing scream, sobbing families, carts wheeled away, burning hears, troubled faces, confused ideas.

Index
Carlos T.

Castillo, Pedro ix-xxiv
Birth 1-2
Adobe house 3-9, 270

Destitute 10-80, 270
Heading north 82-84
Crossing 85
Foreigner 36-98
Finding work 99-119
Assimilation 120-250
Finding love 251
Love lost 252
Eviction 255
Alcohol 260
Understood (or not) 2-262, 270
Loneliness 253, 265, 270
Heads back south 269
Finds adobe house in need of repair 270
Finds no one in adobe house 270
Lost 270
mid-life crisis 271
Buys a horse 271
Horse dies 272
Stares at the stars 273
Last words heard by no one but the barrel of his gun 275

Shoes
Yesenia A.

They sit there and they wait for tomorrow.
Because they were there yesterday.
Because they were there the day before
when I had to give my history report
when I had to climb through my basement window
because my keys decided to stay home.

They stayed with me. And now
we sit in silence, and now we think
in silence and now we sleep.

Noah's Dove
Jasmine H.

You loved me
But I held back
You comforted me
When I cried
You took me
Despite the things I lacked
And opened me up inside.
I hurt you but you were there
I dismissed you my first true love.
I drowned you
In emotions with care
Now sent my heart as Noah's dove.
She writes you

To clear the haze
Of doubt that clouds
Your mind.
She hopes you'll
Fly again today
She yearns for your love to bind.

Esoteric as it Gets
Jose A.

Don't hesitate to hate because what you thought was love was bait and gives
you every right to shove.
I did it again, surreptitious and repetitious
Until you couldn't tell I was the good guy anymore.
So take my habits sing grand theft auto
And say, got 'em, because
In the end you'll know who I am
And what I did.
I'd feel regret but then my life
Perfect in its bubble, would be reduced
To rubble and you'd get to tell the world
About the xanthochroid boy who broke who broke your heart.
Instead I'll let my pen be the fist rising
Through the mist
Of all my spoken pleasantries
Because black ink won't be
Afraid to hurt your feelings.

Where I'm From
Gabriel T.

I'm from Luke 1:19
From God and the Blessed Trinity
I'm from Vaselined faces
On Sunday morning.
I'm from down in the delta
By the wishing tree
On which my ancestors
Wished fro a dream of freedom.
I'm from peppermints and cigarettes,
From January and Winter.
I'm from the mommas
And the daddies,
From grannies and papas.
I'm from Tupac and Biggie.
From Nikki G. and Lauryn Hill,
From the mysterious flo child.
I'm from Doris Day and President Tyler,
Burnt caramel and Milk Duds.
From the people who fought
For my freedom,
And the country that is blind.

In my house, there ain't no crystal stairs,
Nor any mahogany floors.
No peace and calmness
To cover the surface
And hide the truth.
I was made by dreams,
Dreamed before I screamed.
All these things, they make up me.

Out of Sight
Seth C.

She likes to see him.
He likes to see her.
She likes to see his friends too.
Something is wrong.
It's time for a break.
The break is killing him.
She is cool and indifferent.
She wants to see him during her break.
He has to see her but he knows he shouldn't.
They see each other,
But only for a night.
The next morning he is cool and indifferent.
He is killing her.
Another night she wants to see him,
He wants to see her too.
He sees her seeing someone else,
Therefore he flees.
She is angry that her ride home has ditched her,
He is cool and indifferent.

Rosey M.

I am from Rosemary,
Who brought hope and light to a cursed family.
I am from knowing of one race.
Who brings trouble with difference.
I am frijoles and rice
And meat only on the day my dad gets paid.
I am from sisters and brothers,
They are my models and advocates.
I am from house to house
And every day, a better one.
I am from appreciation and support,
That they can always find.
I am their desire of accomplishment,
I am theirs and mine.
Along time ago they dreamed

And one day, that dream came true to be me.

George Washington Elementary

Margaret Chapman, Poet in Residence
Principal: Craig Ergang
Program Coordinator: Andrea Eichhorn
Teachers: Ms. Culkin, 3rd; Ms. Ferraro, 5th; Ms. Petrassi, 4th

I used to be a Cocoon, but
Teresa R.

I used to be a cocoon, but
Now I am a butterfly

I am very cool.
And also impressing.

Look at my colors
They're very neat.

Oh but crack
Here comes the babies.

What I took
Octavio G.

I took your
book Captain Underpants
off your desk.

Which I know you
bought at the
book fair.

I'm so sorry
I just realized
you loved it
but it was so boring
when I read it.

Nobody Knows the Ocean
Jackie L.

Nobody knows the ocean
would rather be pink

although they have so much
fun being blue.

The river would rather have
a secret to tell.

I would too.

The Sea
Horacio P.

Into the water or into the sea
I will see sea creatures
going in and out through the coral reef
fishes giant
and small but in the sea.

I wanted you to know
Amy C.

I have taken
your spot
in the
white house

you probably
want your
spot back

I'm sorry
but I felt
so powerful
and so important

The Leaves Turning Into Money
Juan B.

A rich person
having fun catching money
and he's happy because he's getting more money
and he's suspicious
because he wonders where it all came from

Lemon Cool
Mark N.

I have used
your toothpaste
that was on
the sink

that was
probably
very
expensive

because it
was the new
lemon fresh
flavor.

I Used to Be Short and Blue
Adrian D.

I used to be short and blue but
now I am tall and tan.

Better if I was taller, tanner
and famous.

Nobody Knows That Aliens
Nikolina M.

Nobody knows that aliens
 use Venus aftershave and
 they double dip nachos

Nobody knows that boys really
 want to go to the moon
 and be opera singers.

Nobody knows that a baby
 is really a top secret
 spy from the CIA at Pluto

Now do you know that humans
 are really dogs in disguise
 so bark.

A Whirlpool Exploding
Jacky L.

A whirlpool exploding
My family gets scared.
A river was in the whirlpool.
The Sears tower is as long as the river -
all the green grass is getting sucked in.
A bad way to start spring.

George Washington Elementary

Joris Soeding, Poet in Residence
Principal: Craig Ergang
Program Coordinator: Andrea Eichhorn
Teachers: Mrs. Harrigan, 6th; Mrs. Rengal, 6th; Ms. Schlansky, 8th

The Wind
George M.

When I leave my heart fills with sadness,
I say my goodbyes to you and you say it back,
I rejoice the day when I see you again,
my heart breaks when I take my leave,
my soul feels shattered
I made this decision,
I brought this upon myself,
my dear loving mother.

Marissa F.

The flowers red mixed with yellow
look at the beautiful land
the wind blowing through your hair

A Lesson in Driving
Kathrine P.

So there I was in the backseat of an ugly grey van, full of useless crap
nobody would ever need. I stared out the window and watched the other cars. All of
a sudden, I felt the car jerk. My aunt begins to swear up a storm. I hear words I've
never heard of. As I watch, it becomes clear to me, that one day that crazy woman
will be me.

Change the world
Jeremy D.

I am looking into a photograph of pain + anger. O I wish I could change
this world of ours. To get rid of war and murderous people behind police bars.
Throughout history great people have been killed first a Kennedy, then a King, and a
beatle who didn't die of a plane crash. All of these people had one thing in common,
they died because of society and man. If I could change the world where would we
be. Since I can't change the world I'll change me.

My Family
Megan F.

My family is very big
there are 4 kids
it is a bad thing

with so many in ways
but that means I will
never be alone
when I need to go in the bathroom
it is usually in use.
Then I have to wait
until it is my turn
with 3 teens
not including
for the fact being
6 days till my birthday
there is lots of arguing
between my brothers
and me
but in the end
it is worth having
a big family
lots of love
and lots of hugs

The Call
Melissa S.

My dad was at Iraq, fighting to save the United States of America. Wrote letters to him everyday and waited, waited for him to write back, or maybe even call. When the phone rang my brother and I like a bull and the phone, a man with red. Dashing for the phone, I get it and, hurry for Melissa. A man with a strange voice said, "Hello, is your mom, Pat, there?" "Mom, it's for you!" "OK!" She came running and yelled with excitement, that dad was coming home. I thought that call would be a telemarketer. But it was actually my dad.

Ode to Cheerios
Joshua M.

They talk to me oh no doubt
when I look at them they have no mouth
I don't know why they talk to me and no one else
maybe one day my friends will see them and hear them talk
after they're gone I'll hear
their echoes
forever alone in my side saying oooooooo

Sporks
Jessica J.

These are some questions that many people might think of? What are sporks? Are they a spoon, or is it a fork? Or maybe it is both? All we know is that they are shaped like a spoon, but has three points like a fork. I suppose we will never know!

My Dad
Maira A.

I never got to meet my dad because he died when I was one. But, day after day my family always shares memories about him. At times I remember when I was five my mom showed me some pictures of my dad's accident. Which was terrifying for me so I cried. Many say he was a great dad to his children he always played with us, took us on vacation, and did lots of other fun stuff. Every time I see a picture of him with me I start to cry but that will stop very soon. When people come up to me and ask me where my dad is I always respond saying he is having a good time in heaven with all the angels.

Alfonso P.

My dearest wish will
finally come true. That finally one
day I'll be with you. I wish
and wish that my wish will happen.
Even if it's for 30 seconds I'll be happy.
When I'm with you I'll never want to cry.
I'll find release from my concerns and
have a good time.

Bleeding Mascara
Isaura V.

Tears fall from unopened eyes
as my bleeding mascara
inches down my face
my tears tell the story that you
were here
not even all the makeup in
the world can cover up the
look of fear
that lies in my eyes
because nobody looks good
with bleeding mascara
but nobody looks good with
bleeding mascara, tears, or the
look of fear in their eyes combined
yet the only fear I have is
of losing my everything
and you're just that.
My everything.

Carolina G.

"Your love life will be happy and harmonious," the fortune cookie told me.

Will my future live with happy love and me awaiting every day? Will I not want to wake up because that fortune cookie lied to me?
Because I live in sorrow and depression.

What comes for the future?

I know what I dream to have, but yet I'm not sure it might await me.

Yet I fall in love with what that fortune cookie gave me.

On a Walk
Bethany B.

First of thought
out on my walk
I see a tree
flowing so free
it's own sacred dance
I see by chance
The wind it screams
for the one that fleed
stands still for a moment or less
the devious air, stops its caress
watching a flower ripped from it's home
the desolate wind being the guilty one.

Adriana C.

The night life is for you,
starlit darkened skies,
surrounding an ivory shining moon,
stay up listening,
to the secret of the world,
written in the stars,
the Earth cries for help,
though silent in the night,
its sun rises yet again,
slowly but surely the world will go.

Khalid Z.

I was in this weird land far away what I heard was something singing the "Candyman" song and under me was a flying dragon and next to me was a talking dog and monkeys eating bananas, on a huge banana. And in my hands was a cheeseburger and ten more on the side, and I was eating with an alien that looked like a human and on a cloud was the three stooges playing on a huge TV when the stooges were over I had many videos right on top of the cheeseburgers so me and alien played next thing I know I wake up in my room and people are walking through walls and then out of nowhere some fall face first into the floor and die then the person comes and attacks me then I really wake up and its told to me I fell down from my bed.

Horror!
Olivia G.

The scary movie was playing
the dim light shining
upon us each of my friends
in the arms of their
boyfriends and me all alone
suddenly the
movie happens to us.

One by one until its
just me and Stephanie

There's no way out
then out of nowhere comes
a creepy shadow calling
my name I woke up
realizing it was my dad
waking me up for school.

Dream G.H.O.S.T.
Eduardo L.

Ghost in my yard. I once saw one.
        floating around in an eerie way.

How it got there, I don't know.
        Amazing. No. Scary. Yes.

Our yard, my family and me.
        We all saw it. Floating.

Screaming I hear in the distance.
        So into the car we go.

To the store we now are.
        We meet the fleeting ghost.

        When will this dream ever end? Never.

        The floating ghost scared me since I was four.

Bag
Cesar P.

I am a bag caught in an updraft on a cold winter day. I get stuck in trees. People find me a nuisance and hate me. The words on my bag say Pete's and I was once filled with treats. Now I am nothing but a bag in the wind. I once visited the west side and was shot at. I am now back in the southeast flying into Indiana. The wind dies down and I start to skim the water of the lake. I feel like a bag of hate, nobody catches me and I am alone. I am just a bad ripped bag with holes, please recycle me.

Omar G.

Dear Ferdinand,

I was at a place named Moe's Café. It was so disgusting and the food tasted horrible. Outside looked like an empty motel no cars flickering lights. I wouldn't expect much I found it near a deserted town. The workers there talked a foreign language and the waitress looked sad, but who wouldn't be in a place like that also a dirty dog that was blind and had 3 legs was laying in the corner but the odd thing was that George W. Bush was there. Then the lights went out and I heard a scream so I ran into my car and drove. Then someone got into a car behind the place and followed me. They started shooting at me so I slowed down turned around and crashed the driver's door now I'm here in the hospital writing you this.

        from your friend,

        Omar

Jabba the Hutt the big fat mutt
Erik R.

Jabba the Hutt the big fat mutt
evening in tattione
in Jabba's palace
with the roaring of the rancor
under your feet
and Jabba laughing

slimy like a slug
fat as 5 fambas
tricky, greedy, and unforgiving
if you don't cooperate
you may end up in the rancor's belly

Ode to Books
Luis L.

Books are masterpieces,
An open door that leads us to a land abundant,
of imagination and wonder.
Books possess dragons, lore, love, castles, and fairies.
They also express feelings that television has yet to express and
contain information on just about everything, that's what makes them so magical.
Some judge books because of its cover, yet it's not the outside that's
important,
It is important on what is inside, a world of imagination and wonder.

Martin F.

Something it is, no one knows it but nothing,
who knows the something they say but nothing,
nothing is in their way
or is it something
nothing is only half something,
something is full of nothing
because it is so much nothing
it makes it, in a way, something
who knows,
not many people,
know what people mean,
when they say nothing,
it never is something

The brown rocking chair
Marina M.

There is a chair
a brown plain chair
and sitting there
is a grandfather
my grandfather
we watch television
just me and him together
now I'm looking back.
That's how it used to be.
And again, I remember,
when I was little older
maybe 6 or 7.
I would not sit with my dear
grandfather, anymore
I think it would make him sad
it makes me sad now
because now I would give anything,
to sit with him again

A baby boy
Selena R.

My mom is having a baby
I am so excited
I wonder what it would be like to have a brother
my mom is glowing
its really showing
I can't wait until it's born
to see how it's formed.

The O.C.
Oscar C.

The O.C. is gonna be so good today! Marissa Cooper's sister comes back! Katlyn
Cooper. Last season she was like 11 and now she's like 16! Weird. Anyway it is
going to be awesome!

Finally Katlyn comes back. We thought that she was coming back last week but she
didn't come. They had advertised her coming back but she didn't. But Marissa C.
went back to harbor.

Today the O.C. is gonna be cool. I can't believe that Johnny fell off of a cliff! It was
so awesome! Katlyn started crying and Marissa just stared at him. I really don't think
he is dead but just really hurt. Not too long ago he got shot and now he is falling off a
cliff!

Standing Alone
Nicole G.

Standing alone in the fields
there's no one here to guide me
nothing at all to do
I have to leave this forsaken place

There's something holding me back
it's so quiet and peaceful
I wish I could stay here forever

My little place to think
there's not a worry in the world
everything's perfect

Road Trip
Matthew P.

It was a bright early morning we
were going camping in Michigan
we got there in the middle of the day
we spent that day unpacking
in the morning I got up early
it was so cool the sun was just rising
it was about 60 degrees it smelled of moss
it was so relaxing
I didn't want it to end

Washington Irving Elementary

Matthew Nesvet, Poet in Residence
Principal: Mary Ellen-Garcia Humphries
Teachers: Ms. Deacy, 6th; Ms. St. John, 6th; Ms. Ulvila, 5th

Four Kids No Space
LaJae M.

Four kids no space
Please get out of my face.
Four kids no space
I'm all tied up in a shoe lace.
Four kids no space
I need to catch up on the pace.
Four kids no space
I feel like I have no face.
Four kids no space
I have no valentine except my kids
And no space.

This is NBA on NBC
Patrick D.

This is NBA on NBC
We are showing highlights from this week's show.
The clip: 'Here's Carter. He jumps.
Now, from the free throw line.
Bam! He dunks the ball to win the game.
I have never seen a player do that before.
The crowd is going wild.'

I wish I Were a Person
Jacquelia P.

I wish I were a person.
People eat whenever they like.
When I ask for a little bit – strike!
People go to school.
I'm stuck in this house – like a mule.
People have a big bed
When I lay down I'm pushed from the bed.
People talk to their friends about me.
People, please – leave me be!
I try to sleep but when they leave – I weep.
I wish I were a person.

Wind, Rain, Thunder
Josiah A.

For company, paper, pencil, bodies.
Thinking about what lunch he is having:
Chicken mash potatoes, greens, French fries;
Mac and cheese and broccoli casserole;
Pork chops and ham and sweet potatoes.
It smells as nice as flowers.
I feel like a log.

The Sears Tower
Kayla L.

The Sears Tower
Is like a gigantic step stool.
People see over it as high as they need.
Its top is like a garden tool.
It is as pointy as a blade in a lawn mower.
On foggy days you lose the top of the building.
It is like taking a shower – you get lost if you sit down.
The Sears Tower looks like it is dipping a fork into a bowl of Jello.
Its antennas are as pointy as tongs.
They dip into the Jello bowl sky.
The windows seem to never stop.
You will never reach the top.
The Sears Tower is like a crayon.
It is pointy on top and flat as a pancake at the bottom.
The Sears Tower is like an ocean and holds a giant school of fish.

Sunday 1958 on the Basketball Court
William J.

The court has new bare rims, and they just installed new lights.
My friends are playing ball with me and
William is thinking about freedom.
White kids on the court are cheating,
Every time we score they add a point –
To their score!
Every time we win they get mad and say –
They win!

Scuba Diver
Victor H.

Snap, Snap, Snap.
There once was a scuba diver who swam like a fish.
He was very clever – like a silverware dish.
He swam very deep down water very steep,
He was one of a kind… oh to never sleep.

Saturday Night at the Gas Station
Courtney T.

Dark outside,
Raining hard.
My clothes are damp,
Babies crying, people walking.
For company, my mom, my book,
My crybaby sisters.
I sit down and start thinking about my dog at home.
Then, the rain stops raining,
The babies stop crying,
I finally dry off.
We get in the car and drive away.
Away, Away!

Who I Am
Marielle D.

Dancing is like exercise,
I do it everyday.
People ask me why,
I say I express myself this way.
When I mess up on stage I don't cry,
The audience claps anyway
'Cause they know I tried.
Dancing is like a book,
I'm in another place.
As the people look,
I bring a smile on their face.
Dancing is something I really love to do.
I know if I can do it,
You can do it too.

When I Came Home From the Test
Eduardo L.

When I came home from the test
I said I needed a big rest.
I complained, "I'm in trouble."
My brother said – "double."
He took my C test and said
It is best to make people laugh.
Just a silly poem

Kitten
Janiqua C.

He jumped and licked me.
White and Brown
He jumped and licked me.
Big round eyes
He jumped and licked me.
Small pink nose
He jumped and licked me.
Small furry ears
He jumped and licked me.

The Woman is Like a Bus, with Twenty Kids
Jeremia W.

The woman is like a bus, with twenty kids
She can't trust.
A woman is like a bus, with twenty kids
She rushes into the family truck.
This is the woman who is like a bus.

Ugh! That Floor!
Anam S.

I look at the floor and stare at the tiles,
It stretches and stretches for miles and miles.
I look at the floor and stare at the tiles,
I am small,
Tiny like a fish in the Nile.
I look at the floor and stare at the tiles,
It's cluttered with papers and thousands of files.
I look at the floor and stare at the tiles,
My eyes are blinking really wild.
I look at the floor and I stare at the tiles!

The House Smelled like Fart
Miles M.

Sniff, sniff... something just died 'cause of that fart.
It was shaped like a dart.
There were apes in the house and a
Gigantic mouse.
Something just died... it was my heart.

In Bed
Marilyn B.

Saturday morning in the bed
The blinds drawn, the T.V. on
The sound of soup on the stove
In bed soup is hot and good
For company a movie on
Happiness remembers me
The cold snow on my face
The sound of children
Screaming

Inside the Haunted House
Michelle P.

Lights out, phone dead.
Sounds and voices speaking to me.
People running
Up and down the stairs.
Standing on my tiptoes looking outside
I see nothing but darkness.
Almost midnight,
Voices shouting and screaming,
People running
Faster and faster.
I don't know what's happening.
Then I hear the voice of a girl
Telling me to get out of the house,
There's an emergency!
"I can't," I say. "The doors are locked,
So are the windows."
Now I am trapped
Inside the haunted house…
Forever?

I Fell down on the Floor
Ricky R.

I fell down on the floor
I hit my head on the door.
I fell down on the floor
My mom was eating S'mores.
I fell down of the floor
Now I have a sore.

Friday at Midnight
Adrian V.

I'm at my cousin's house.
The TV is on and
I'm playing my X-box and
The phone is ringing.
For company, a mouse
Talks to me.
He says, "let me play."
I say, "never."
Then he runs away.

I am a Tree
Amani C.

I am a tree,
I stand tall and strong,
Never fall or grow weak.
But right now I wish I would fall,
Stop standing tall.
I feel weak, not strong.
Let me feel weak and stop standing tall,
Please I want to leave that is all.
Believe, believe I am planted in the right place.
Please let me leave, let me be,
Let me see where I should be.
Should I be here?
Should I be there?
Then where?
Please – just let me leave.

Big Lemonhead in the Sky
Zoe M.

How is the sun a big lemonhead in the sky?
I put my finger up to my eye to reach the lemonhead
But it's only make believe and
I can't reach it.
I turn around and then look back,
It's still there, my tasty snack.
I don't look at the sun for long because it can hurt my eyes,
Tomorrow I'll be back to look at my lemonhead in the sky.
I will try to think of other ways to bring it down to me,
Today I will just say it was very nice to see.

This is the Sound of Thunder
Cristian G.

Very dark.
For dessert, cocoa and toast.
Remembering last April when it was
Raining.
Remembering the shock of electricity
Moving through my body.
Remembering me – injured on the curb
Listening to rain and thunder.
Me – frightened.

A Cat Barks
William J.

A cat barks
On the back porch
Top of the sky
In the Rocky high
Mountains.
It dares to look at people
Only because it's shy.
It climbs on everything but the sky.
Sometimes I'm strong,
Sometimes I'm weak.
Sometimes I wish I had something to eat.
A rat, a mouse – anything besides old meat.
I love people, I love creatures, I love everything
Besides that nasty old meat.

Widow
Daniela G.

There once was a widow who lived in a willow
Who hated saying "please."
She had a tail like a dog,
A face like a log,
And she had lots of fleas.
Did I tell you she had a disease?
Her eyes lied and after a week
She died.

Zookeeper
Lorena R.

Saturday at the zoo
Monkeys yelling,
Elephants eating,
For company, nothing but animals and trees.
Jungle, nobody here.
Animals screaming,
Lions like the sun.
Polar bears like snow.
Smells like elephant poo,
Garbage on the floor,
Wish I had friends.

Slavery
Anonymous

What the heck is happening?
Who put me in these chains?
That is my brother covered in blood.
Who is this telling me to call him master?
I have to pick cotton, which I hate.

Find a Seat
Amber H.

"Try to find a seat!"
"How long will this be?"
Popcorn and candy on the floor,
Twizzlers and starburst everywhere.
People kicking chairs, theater totally dark,
I'm kind of scared.
But I have company.
Mom, and lots of people everywhere.
The movie was kind of long.

Lost in the Egypt Room
Tiffany R.

Lost in the Egypt room
Tired
Hungry
Stomach rumbling
Wandering in the building
Days and days pass
Cod cataracts
Rocky
Brown and beige
Big
People eating from the gift shop
Big sandwiches
Mustard
Relish
Dripping
Nice
Juicy
Lost in the Egypt room

At Home
Chloe W.

Saturday night at home the
Game on, telephone ringing, talking.
For company my dog, Mom and the T.V.
I think about what I could be
Doing instead of just sitting there.
I am watching a show, rain on
The window pane, ground soggy, leaves
Wet and dog barking.
My mom is
Talking but she is ignored.
Now there is yelling
I finally listen
She is nagging me to put my pajamas on.
I go upstairs
Good night I go
To sleep.

Happiness
Tara P.

Happiness is like the sun on a gloomy day
A pool when you're hot, food when you're starving.
Happiness is like a friend when you're sad,
Cake on your birthday,
Butterflies in summer.
Happiness is when you can't stop smiling,
When you're alone but not sad,
Cheerful, fulfilled, glad.

Poets in Residence Biographies

Danielle Aquiline (Jane A. Neil Elementary School, Louis Pasteur Elementary School) is a recent graduate of Columbia College Chicago's MFA program in poetry where she teaches composition. Her poems have appeared in *Columbia Poetry Review* and are forthcoming in *Pebble Lake Review*. In her free time, she enjoys painting, coming to terms with her Southern heritage, and all things food.

Nannette E. Banks (Edward N. Hurley Elementary School) is a poet and public speaker. She has worked extensively with the Neighborhood Writing Alliance as a group facilitator in Canada, New York, Minnesota, and Chicago. For the past five years she has been commissioned by the Office of the Mayor, City of Chicago to participate in the annual KidStart Book Club Conference, facilitating poetry writing workshops. Nannette holds a Masters Degree in Urban Planning and Policy from the University of Illinois at Chicago (she completed her master's Project *Writing the World: a Link between Community Based Writing and Community Development*) and a Bachelors Degree in Psychology from Aurora University.

Meg Barboza (Joan F. Arai Middle School) is an MFA candidate in Poetry at the School of the Art Institute of Chicago. She was a finalist for the 2005 Ruth Lilly Fellowship from the Poetry Foundation. After graduation, she plans to pursue community arts education full time.

A native of Chicago, **Raymond L. Bianchi** (Robert C.Grimes Elementary) lived and worked in Latin America for most of the 1990s. His poetry has appeared in *26, Bird Dog, Antennae*, and *The Economist*. His first book, *Circular Descent,* came out in 2004 and a Chapbook *American Master* came out in 2006. He has been a poet in residence since 2003.

K. Bradford (Jose De Diego Community Academy) is a poet, performer and teacher. In addition to her Hands on Stanzas residency at De Diego Elementary she teaches poetry, literature and composition at Columbia College and runs The Raw Works, a poetry and performance program for LGBT youth. In her spare cracks of time, K. writes poetry for the page and the stage. Her publications include Web del Sol's *In Posse Review, Columbia Poetry Review* and, forthcoming, *Gulf Coast.*

Garrett J. Brown's (Addams Elementary School) poems have recently appeared in the *American Poetry Journal*, *Urbanite Baltimore*, and the *Ledge*. In 2000, he won a Creative Writing Fellowship from the School of the Art Institute of Chicago, where he graduated with his MFA in Creative Writing. Garrett's chapbook, *Panning the Sky*, was published in 2003 by Pudding House Publications and his book-length manuscript, *Manna Sifting*, was runner-up in the 2003 Maryland Emerging Voices competition. In 2005, Garrett won the Poetry Center of Chicago's 11th Annual Juried Reading, judged by Jorie Graham. He is currently teaching writing at the University of Illinois at Chicago, where he is pursuing his PhD.

Margaret Chapman (George Washington Elementary School) is completing her MFA in Creative Writing at the School of the Art Institute of Chicago. She writes poetry, fiction, and, more often, some hybrid of the two.

Naima Dawson (John F. Eberhart Elementary School, Jacques Marquette Elementary School), playwright and author of *Hotwater Pancakes,* graduated from DePaul University and is a Columbia College Master of Fine Arts candidate. Naima's passion for poetry quickly developed over the years, from performing for audiences to sharing her gift for poetry with children who live in some of Chicago's most stressed neighborhoods. As a teacher, mentor and volunteer, Naima shepards these young people's frustrations and delusions with their current life situations into a positive art form, which allows them to develop constructive outlets through which to communicate both their hardships and joys.

Larry O. Dean (James Shields Elementary) is the author of seven books, the most recent being *I Am Spam* (2004), a series of poems "inspired" by spam email. In addition, Larry is a singer and songwriter, working both solo as well as with several pop bands, currently, The Injured Parties. He has released numerous critically acclaimed CD's, including *Fables in Slang* (2001) with Post Office, and *Gentrification is Theft* (2002) with The Me Decade. Go to larryodean.com for more info.

Eric Elshtain (Galileo Scholastic Academy)is currently a Ph.D. candidate in the University of Chicago's Committee on the History of Culture and a poet in residence at Children's Memorial Hospital in Chicago through the Snow City Arts Foundation. His poetry, reviews and interviews have appeared in or are forthcoming in *GutCult, Ploughshares, Chicago Review,* the *Denver Quarterly, Skanky Possum, Notre Dame Review, New American Writing, McSweeney's, Interim* and other journals. He is also the author of two chapbooks, *The Cheaper the Crook, the Gaudier the Patter* (Transparent Tiger Press) and *Here in Premonition* (RubbaDucky Press). He is the editor of the on-line poetry press, Beard of Bees.

Carina Gia Farrero (Lyman Trumbull Elementary School) received her MFAW from the School of the Art Institute of Chicago. She was a founding member of the theater/dance company The Turnbuckles and toured nationally with both The Turnbuckles and the performance collective, Sister Spit. She was also a founding member of *Poetry for the People*. Her poems have been published in *Ink, The Color of the Longest Day and What Now* and her play was produced as part of the PAC Edge Festival

Besides writing, **Manda Aufochs Gillespie** (George Armstrong International Studies Elementary) spends her days teaching poetry to kids and standing on her head. The day when she can do both simultaneously is timed to coincide with the publication of her first novel. Manda received her BA with honors in Environmental Studies from Oberlin College and her MFA in Writing from the School of the Art Institute of Chicago. Manda has learned a lot teaching poetry to 6th graders at Armstrong Elementary: like jerk can be used in replace of a full stop and dictionaries are obsolete. The best lesson, though, is that poetry is more alive than ever and in good hands with the next generation of poets.

Lee Glidewell (Philip A. Randolph Magnet Elementary School) is a doctoral candidate in the English department at the University of Chicago. This makes him sound far more sophisticated than he actually is. His sense of humor is very closely matched with that of many of the fine young men and women at Randolph Elementary, and for that reason his residence there has been a welcome relief from the stuffiness of academic life.

Daniel Godston (William Howard Taft Academic Magnet Center, Luther Burbank School) teaches poetry through The Poetry Center of Chicago and The Center for Community Arts Partnerships. He also teaches literature and composition classes at Columbia College Chicago. His poetry and fiction have appeared in *Chase Park, Versal, 580 Split, Kyoto Journal, California Quarterly, after hours,* and other magazines, and he has published articles in *Teaching Artist Journal* and other publications. He also composes music and plays the trumpet and other instruments in ensembles in the Chicago area.

Allison Gruber (Theodore Herzl Elementary School) earned her MFA in Writing from The School of the Art Institute of Chicago. As a poet, playwright and essayist, her work has appeared in literary publications, including *The New Zoo Poetry Review* and *Ink*, and on-stage as part of Chicago's PAC/Edge festival. This is her first year with *Hands on Stanzas*.

Poet and teacher, **Erica Kholodovsky** (Ellen Mitchell Elementary, James Shields Elementary) is a first generation American, niece to two Russian poets living here in Chicago. After studying Russian literature and gaining a strong proficiency for the language, she moved to San Francisco, where she edited and wrote for a literary and photography Zine called *Nufoto*. She earned her BA from the University of Wisconsin and will be returning to school next fall for two Master's degrees at Columbia University in New York. She hopes to frequent Poets House, Nuyorican Poets Café and the Teachers and Writers Collaborative once living in the city.

Becca Klaver (Hannah G. Solomon Elementary School) was born and raised in Milwaukee, WI. After studying screenwriting and English at the University of Southern California, she returned to Milwaukee, where she worked in schools as an AmeriCorps*VISTA member and middle school teacher. Currently, Becca is pursuing her MFA in poetry at Columbia College Chicago, where she is a Follett Fellow and serves on the editorial board of the *Columbia Poetry Review*. She is an editor for *Switchback Books*, a new women's poetry press.

Joshua Kotin (Bernhard Moos Elementary School) is from Hamilton, Ontario. He edits *Chicago Review* and lives in Wicker Park.

Toni Asante Lightfoot (Off the Street Club) is a native of Washington, DC who moved to Chicago 3 years ago. This is her second year at Off The Street Club. Lightfoot writes and performs poetry as well as teaches it. She is the co-editor of the 2006 Tia Chucha Press anthology *Dream of a Word*. Her work has been anthologized several times and her voice and poetry can be found on several east coast CD projects.

Felicia Madlock (Amelia Earhart Elementary School) is a graduate of Loyola University where she obtained her Master Degree in Social Work. Felicia is a published author and poet. Her literary work has been featured in the *Journal of Ordinary Thought*, Boston College's *Anthropology Writing Places*, and other media venues.

Richard Meier's (Tarkington Scholastic Academy) second book, *Shelley Gave Jane a Guitar*, is forthcoming from Wave Books (www.wavepoetry.com) in September 2006. His first book, *Terrain Vague,* was selected by Tomaz Salamun for the Verse Prize and published by Verse Press in 2001. He was taught poetry in the public schools in New York City, Pittsburgh, Beloit, and Chicago, and at Beloit Columbia Colleges. His poems have appeared in *Conjunctions, Volt, Boston Review, Lungfull,* and other literary journals and magazines.

Matthew Nesvet (Washington Irving Elementary School) has an M.A. in humanities from the University of Chicago. A Yale University-Kokkalis Foundation research fellow in Greece during the summer of 2005, he has delivered lectures on political philosophy and early modern history of ideas at Brown University, University of Manchester (UK), and several colleges.

Adam Novy (Philip Rogers Elementary School) received his MFA from the School of the Art Institute of Chicago. His work has been published in *The Believer, Verse, and American Letters and Commentary.*

Pam Osbey,(School of Entrepreneurship, South Shore Campus, Charles Kozminski Community Academy Paul Revere Community Academy, Jacob Beidler School) has been published in nine books, including her latest chapbook, *Tears of a Woman: The Light Within,* several anthologies and literary publications. Currently moving from author to publisher, she is working with authors through her literary company, Osbey Books. She is finishing her tenth poetry collection to be released in June 2006.

Cecilia Pinto (Hiram H. Belding School, Jordon Community School, Walter Payton College Prep High School) has been associated with the *Hands on Stanzas* program for seven years. In addition to teaching, she writes and publishes poetry and fiction.

Aaron Plasek (John Hay Community Academy) is currently completing an MFA in Writing at the School of the Art Institute of Chicago, and has received a BA in English Writing and a BS in Physics and Astronomy from Drake University. He is currently working on a book of poetry and a novel and hopes (wistfully) to have one of the two completed in the next year.

Matthias Regan (Henry Clay Elementary School) writes, teaches, and publishes poetry and cheap art. His books include *The Most of It, Utility, Code Book Code,* and *Core Samples.* He is a founding member of the CafF Collective and of Rubbah Ducky Press. He is currently finishing a dissertation on populist poetry at the University of Chicago. He believes, with Ed Dorn, that the art of poetry is the same thing as the art of perception.

Parry Rigney (William T. Prescott Elementary School) received her BA from the University of Notre Dame in 2003. This is her first year with Hands on Stanzas. In addition to being a poet and teaching artist at Prescott Elementary School, she works for a small public relations company.

David Rosenstock (Cesar Chavez Multicultural Academic Center, Smyser Elementary School) received a B.A. from The New School and his M.F.A. from The School of the Art Institute of Chicago. He was the recipient of the Irwin Shaw award and the Ottilie Grebanier award (chosen by Mac Wellman). His work has been published in *The Brooklyn Review, Not For Tourist Guide,* and *Centerstage.*

James Shea (Helen C. Peirce School of International Studies), a graduate of the University of Iowa Writers' Workshop, has published poems in *American Letters and Commentary, Gulf Coast, jubilat* and the anthology *Isn't It Romantic: 100 Love Poems by Younger American Poets.* He currently teaches writing and literature courses at DePaul University and Columbia College Chicago.

Joris Soeding (George Washington Elementary School) holds a B.A. in Poetry from Columbia College Chicago. His second and most recent chapbook, *Trees. Otherness. Instance.*, is based on television show *The X-Files*. A few of his publishing credits include *City Works, Columbia Poetry Review, Red River Review, Romantic Outsider* (England), *Third Coast Press*. He is also a poet in residence at Chicago Children's Museum and Assistant Editor for *Another Chicago Magazine.* He is currently pursuing a Master of Arts in Teaching: Language Arts, Elementary, at Northeastern Illinois University.

Cassie Sparkman (Christian Ebinger School) received her MFA in poetry from the University of Washington. Her work has been nominated for a Pushcart Prize. She has been published in *32 Poems, American Poetry Journal, The Laurel Review, Crab Orchard Review,* and *Story South, Verse Daily* and other journals. She hosts the Literary Gangs of Chicago reading series at the Museum of Contemporary Art.

Dana Vinger (Gale Community Academy) is currently working towards her MFA in writing at The School of the Art Institute of Chicago. As a playwright she has had works produced at the Shotgun Theatre Lab in Berkeley, CA, and the Oakland Playhouse. She was a 2005 finalist for *Risk is This - The Cutting Ball Experimental Plays Festival*, San Francisco, and a selected participant for Clubbed Thumb's 2003 *Springworks Theatre Festival* in New York City. This is her first year with *Hands on Stanzas.*

Alyson Paige Warren (Dewitt Clinton Elementary School, Shields Elementary, Louisa May Alcott Elementary School) received her Masters of Fine Arts in Writing from the School of the Art Institute of Chicago in 2005. She teaches at with High Jump program, the Live and Learn continuing education program (both at the Latin School of Chicago), the Princeton Review and St. Augustine college. Paige is currently working on her socio-anthropomorphic non-fiction memoir. This is her second year with the Poetry Center.

avery r. young (John Hay Community Academy) has been a staple in the spoken word community since 1996. His style of writing and performance is labeled "Sunday Mornin' Juke-Joint." avery edited *Abstractvision* and is a columnist for *Say What* Magazine. He is the author of *lookin fo/words that rhyme: the un-spoken word of avery r. young* (FayeRic 2005) and is currently working on an album of original music and a multi-media performance based on the life and works of James Baldwin.

Tracy Zeman (John C. Burroughs School, John B. Drake Elementary School, Casimir Pulaski Fine Arts Academy) received her MFA from George Mason University and her BA from DePaul Univesity. Her poetry has appeared in *CutBank* and *So to Speak.* In addition to teaching with the *Hands on Stanzas'* program, she also teaches humanities and literature at Benedictine University.

How Hands on Stanzas Works

Schools Receive:

Poets in Residence: Each 20-week residency provides weekly instruction for three classes, or approximately 90-100 students, as well as special projects that have a school-wide impact.

Collaboration: *Hands on Stanzas* is designed to fit seamlessly into school curriculum goals.

Books: Each participating school receives a copy of the Hands on Stanzas Anthology of Poetry, as well as donated poetry books for the school library.

Special projects: Examples of school-wide *Hands on Stanzas* projects include: a wall of similes, a poetry club, poems read over the PA system, a poetry reading and a traveling poetry parade.

Students Receive:

Communication tools: Writing for self-expression motivates students to explore how words can work to convey their own thoughts, visions and emotions. Vocabularies grow, imaginations spark, and books are read.

Spotlight: Students share their work on stage in the Ballroom of the School of the Art Institute. These readings bring together students from around the city.

Access to the arts: "Before Hands on Stanzas, I thought poetry was only for rich people and fancy people. Now I think poetry is for all kinds of people." -6th grade *Hands on Stanzas* student

Recognition: Each year, students have the opportunity to be published in the Hands on Stanzas Anthology of Poetry and receive one free copy of the book.

Inspiration: "Reading poetry makes me feel like what the writer wrote was so great, I want to do it, too." -6th grade *Hands on Stanzas* student

Poets in Residence Receive:

Support: Poetry Center staff regularly visit classrooms and assist with arrangements between schools and poets-in-residence.

Professional development: Two intensive workshops conducted by leaders in the field are provided each year, as well as feedback and brainstorming sessions.

Stipends: Chicago poets obtain employment in their field, while making a positive impact on the city's most important resource—its youth.

Resources: Books about creative writing instruction are provided to each poet in residence.

Recognition: Each year the Gwendolyn Brooks *Hands on Stanzas* Award provides $1,000 in cash awards to poets in residence of distinction.

Acknowledgements

The Poetry Center of Chicago would like to thank the following foundation, corporation and governmental sponsors:

Chase Bank, Children of the American Revolution, Department of Cultural Affairs, CityArts Division, Elizabeth F. Cheney Foundation, Elizabeth Morse Charitable Trust, Gaylord and Dorothy Donnelly Foundation, Illinois Arts Council, Illinois Humanities Council, James S. Kemper Foundation, Kenneth and Harle Montgomery Foundation, Kraft Foods, Inc., Lannan, Louis R. Lurie Foundation, MacArthur Fund for Arts and Culture at the Richard H. Driehaus Foundation, National Endowment for the Arts, Northern Trust, Northern Trust Centennial Fund of the Chicago Community Trust, Polk Bros. Foundation, Prince Charitable Trust, Seabury Foundation, Turow Foundation

The 2006 *Hands on Stanzas* Anthology of Poetry is being partially funded by Miss Jess Vogt, State President 2005 – 2006, of the Illinois Society, Children of the American Revolution (C.A.R.), for her State Project.

Funds for her project were raised by selling a hand-designed *Hands on Stanzas* pin. The C.A.R. is a patriotic organization for girls and boys from birth to age 22, who are lineally descended from a person who gave direct aid in the American Revolutionary War. C.A.R. promotes American History, preservation of historic documents and places, celebrations of patriotic anniversaries, honors and cherishes the American Flag, promotes to uphold and extend the principles of American liberty and patriotism, along with other programs in literacy, conservation, and government. Members gain invaluable leadership experience in conducting meetings, following parliamentary procedure, standard protocol and public speaking at local, state and national meetings. More information visit our website www.nscar.org.

The Poetry Center of Chicago would like to thank these individuals for their dedication to *Hands on Stanzas*:

Alex Jovanovich
Sheila Keeley
Easton Awesome Miller
Anna Shane

Gwendolyn Brooks *Hands on Stanzas* Award Winners:

2004-2005: Matthias Regan and Adam Novy

2005-2006: Eric Elshtain and Richard Meier

Thanks, as always, to The School of the Art Institute of Chicago.